SENTINEL OF THE SOUTHERN PLAINS

Ft. Lyc[o]

COLORADO

■ Ft. Garland

Rio Grande R.

■ Ft. Marcy
● Santa Fe

■ Ft. Union

● Albuquerque

Ft. Bascom ■

Ft. Sumner ■

NEW MEXICO

Pecos R.

■
Ft. Stanton

THE NORTH TEXAS
FRONTIER

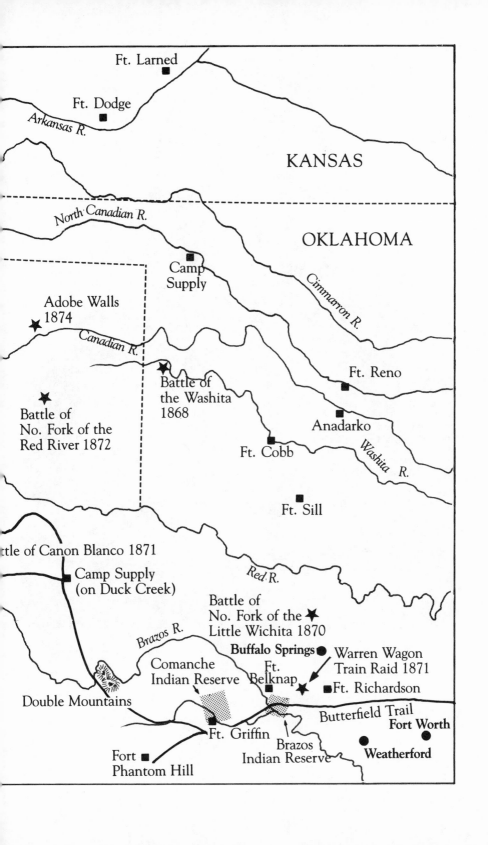

Guipago (Lone Wolf), major chief of the Kiowas (National Archives)

SENTINEL

Fort Richardson and the

OF THE

Northwest Texas Frontier,

SOUTHERN

1866–1878

PLAINS

BY ALLEN LEE HAMILTON

NUMBER FIVE IN THE CHISHOLM TRAIL SERIES

TEXAS CHRISTIAN UNIVERSITY PRESS

FORT WORTH

LIBRARY OF CONGRESS
Library of Congress Cataloging-in-Publication Data

Hamilton, Allen Lee.
    Sentinel of the southern plains : Fort Richardson and the
northwest Texas frontier, 1866–1878 / by Allen Lee Hamilton.
        p.   cm.—(Chisholm Trail series ; no. 5)
    Bibliography: p.
    Includes index.
    ISBN 0-87565-073-2
    1. Fort Richardson (Tex.)—History.   2. Jacksboro Region (Tex.)—
History.   3. Frontier and pioneer life—Texas—Jacksboro
Region   4. Texas—History—1846–1950.   I. Title.
II. Series.
F394.F64H35   1988
976.4'544—dc19   87-17379
                                                                                CIP

Designed by Whitehead & Whitehead
Maps by Barbara Brooks Clubb

For Leona and Nig

The Chisholm Trail Series

CONTENTS

CHAPTER NINE

I reckon you know those people in Texas; they are a mighty hard
people down there.

BUFFALO GOOD, WICHITA CHIEF, ADDRESSING
A CROWD IN NEW YORK CITY IN 1871.

ACKNOWLEDGEMENTS

NO PROJECT SUCH AS THIS can reach completion without much assistance. I am deeply indebted to these persons who gave freely of their time, skills, and knowledge; without them, this book would not exist.
My grateful thanks to Jerry Betts and Oscar Metzger of the San Antonio College Library, for never batting an eye when I would request some century-old out-of-print volume, and for unfailingly and amazingly securing it within days.

My thanks to Jerry Sullivan of the Texas Parks and Wildlife Service, who saved me a fortune in travel expenses by loaning me the microfilm of all of Richardson's records; and to his co-worker Denis Cordes, who helped secure many illustrations.

My thanks also to Russell Jones and W. W. Bill Dennis of Jacksboro, two fine county historians who are living encyclopedias of knowledge about Jacksboro and North Texas, for willingly sharing their knowledge with me. Mr. Jones, an old family friend, was especially generous with his time, and his suggestions and help in securing photographs were indispensible.

My sincere appreciation goes to the entire staff of the Fort Richardson State Park, for always finding time in their busy schedules to cope with my mostly unannounced intrusions; to Suzanne Brosios for typing the manuscript; and to Barbara Stockley, for reading the first rough draft and pointing out many needed changes.

But my most special thanks must be reserved for my family; for my wife Suzanne and her parents, Vivian and Russell Shaw, for their constant support and encouragement; and for my parents, Leona and E. E. Hamilton, for always believing. If Richardson lives in these pages, it is because of them.

Allen L. Hamilton
San Antonio

INTRODUCTION

YOU CAN FIND THE TOWN
of Jacksboro on any Texas road
map. Simply locate the cities of
Fort Worth and Wichita Falls,
trace an imaginary line from one
to the other, and you will discover Jacksboro, sitting rather
isolated midway between the
two. The map symbols will inform you that it is the county
seat of Jack County and has a

population of fewer than 5000. Jacksboro hardly seems out of the
ordinary, and indeed it is truly a typical Texas community in most
all respects save one: it was here in 1868 that the federal government chose to construct what was to become for a time the most
important military installation on the Texas frontier, Fort Richardson. This decision helped change the course of history in North
Texas, had a dramatic influence on the future of Jacksboro and the
surrounding countryside, and over the span of a century affected
the lives of thousands, of which I am one.

I was born in Jacksboro, in a hospital which stood where cavalry troopers once pitched their tents, and I grew up literally within
gunshot of the remains of the old fort. Richardson was one of the
constants of my boyhood world, just like the perpetually dusty concrete highway that bisected the town carrying cars, buses, and
trucks from places unknown to places undreamed of; or the red-tile-
roofed schools that I attended where, curiously enough, all the
teachers knew my name before I could introduce myself; or even
those extraordinary summer nights so full of magic and promise that

anything seemed possible. These were things that were simply there and had been from my first inkling of understanding, parts of my life that were accepted without question and without comment.

Richardson was often the center of community activities, and I attended such affairs at the post as rattlesnake roundups, county fairs, circuses, donkey baseball games, and even political rallies. I recall that one fall a gubernatorial candidate helicoptered onto the grounds to make a speech from the porch of the old hospital building and then, in the true sense of a whirlwind campaign, disappeared back into a star-filled night sky. My friends and I stood watching the craft's blinking lights, mightily impressed, until we lost them on the horizon. If twelve-year-olds could have voted, that man might well have become president.

I would like to say that at that particular moment, or at some other equally dramatic and recognizable instant, I decided that the history of such a place as Fort Richardson needed to be written and that I was going to be the one to do it. Unfortunately, it just is not true. Even though a week hardly passed without my going out to the post for some reason or other, I never truly realized the significance of the place while I was growing up. Cowboys and Indians and frontier forts, all particular passions of mine as a child, seemed to be parts of some far-away West, not of North Texas. Hollywood and television of the 1950s depicted the cavalry and Indians waging war over some arid, desert-like landscape, nothing like the countryside around Jacksboro. And all forts had stockade walls, with great blockhouses at each corner, and huge barred gates. Richardson was simply seven old buildings, surrounded more-or-less by a barbed wire fence with a cattle guard entrance. Hardly the stuff to fire a young imagination.

Even when I entered high school, and Fort Richardson was named a National Historic Landmark, I remained unimpressed. Familiarity, apparently, does breed contempt or, at least in the case of my uninformed youth, indifference.

It was not until I went off to college and decided to pursue an academic career that my research into Richardson's history began. And the more I investigated, the more interested I became. The

Warren Wagon Train Raid, I discovered, was not just some minor occurrence of only local interest (as I had always half-believed) but an event of major significance in the history of the West. And Richardson, far from being an unknown outpost on a faraway and forgotten frontier, was the linchpin of the army's defensive strategy in Texas, a post whose name regularly appeared in the newspapers of New York, Chicago, and Washington and, most amazing of all to me, was at one time the largest military installation in the country. Just as a twelve-year-old had once been impressed by a mere politician, a twenty-four-year-old became more impressed by something of real historical importance and value.

This book started as a graduate term paper, grew into a lengthy Master's thesis, and now, after some twelve years of stops and starts, has metamorphosed into this final form. As my perceptions of history and writing changed through the years, so too did the format of this work. It has become almost without intention two books: one for the general reader, and (with the footnotes) one for the serious student of Texas frontier history. This was not my original plan, but I rather like the result and hope readers of both persuasions agree.

One intention of mine that has not changed from the beginning of this project was the decision to produce a fairly straightforward narrative history. When I first started digging into Richardson's past over a decade ago, I wanted to gather as much information on the place as I could and to produce a useful biography. After all the hours of scanning microfilm, turning dusty pages, poring over government records, and sifting through old photographs, about the only thing of which I am totally certain is that there is still much information left to be uncovered. If this effort helps someone else to produce the final interpretive word on Richardson and the North Texas frontier experience, then my effort will have been worthwhile.

Finally, this book is a way of paying back some old debts. Growing up in the sheltered world of small-town Texas is a unique experience, one for which I am unashamedly grateful. There will always be some part of Jacksboro in me. And just as Fort Richardson was a part of the town's collective consciousness, one of the vital factors that shaped Jacksboro's identity, so too did the fort and the town shape a part of my identity. Thus in many ways this book is about old friends and about home; in many ways it is a family history.

SENTINEL OF THE SOUTHERN PLAINS

The Woods' house, one of the first settlers' homes in Jack County and an example of a typical frontier dwelling, photo ca. 1890 (Russell Jones Collection)

CHAPTER ONE

ON JULY 5, 1866, CAPTAIN
George Clarence Cram and
Company I, Sixth Regiment,
United States Cavalry, rode
into the tiny village of Jacksboro, the northernmost settlement on the West Texas frontier
and the last vestige of the white
man's civilization on the edge of
the vast and forbidding Southern Plains. Captain Cram's ar-

The Frontier
of Northwest
Texas,
1836–1866

rival began a federal military presence in Jack County that would
help to conquer the Southern Plains Indians and permanently open
the stretches of West Texas to Anglo-American cattlemen and
farmers. That undertaking had been in progress for thirty years, but
during the Civil War, the Indians had gained the upper hand. The
tide of settlement had been checked and in most instances reversed.

As the frontier of the United States moved westward, the
Indians had been pushed before it. The sedentary eastern tribes
simply could not cope with the superior weapons and the vast numbers of Anglo-American pioneers. Those who did not bend with
the wind of white settlement were broken and swept away. Some
tribes were moved wholesale off their ancestral lands, and others
were completely exterminated. But once out of the forests of the
East and onto the plains, the pioneer came up against the mounted
Indian, a foe for whom, initially, he was no match. With every full
moon, raiding parties of Comanches, Kiowas, and Kiowa-Apaches
struck with awesome fury, killing, maiming, and stealing.[1]

During the years of the Texas Republic, the government, with little money and few men, could do little to defend the frontier. As a result, settlers were compelled to rely mostly upon themselves for protection. The most famous form of this protection was the Texas Rangers.[2] On December 29, 1845, Texas became part of the United States of America, but war with Mexico quickly followed and the Indian problem was again put off. In 1850, an estimated two hundred Texans were killed, wounded, or carried into captivity by Indians,[3] and the settlers showered Washington with petitions and protests.

In response to their appeals, the federal government decided to launch a campaign against the depredators in Texas. No doubt Washington believed that the army which had so lately mauled the Mexicans certainly could handle a few bands of ragged savages, so it sent out the Second Dragoons led by Lieutenant Colonel William J. Hardee and a company of Texas Rangers under the command of Captain John S. (Rip) Ford and Captain W.A.A. (Big Foot) Wallace. After these units wandered aimlessly and ineffectually through the mostly unexplored territory north and west of San Antonio, the government quickly changed its policy.[4]

At that time the western limit of white settlement in Texas was roughly a line through Sherman, Farmersville, Dallas, Waxahachie, Ennis, and Fredericksburg, all along the eastern edge of Comanche and Kiowa country. To protect the settlements from Indian incursions, the new policy in Texas established a chain of forts: Fort Washita in the Indian Territory, south through Fort Worth, Fort Graham, Fort Gates, Fort Croghan, Fort Martin Scott, Fort Lincoln, to Fort Duncan on the Rio Grande. Unfortunately, from Washita to Duncan the frontier line was over thirteen hundred miles long, far too great a distance for the soldiers to defend adequately. The forts hampered but never halted the Indians' movements into and out of the settlements.

There were other defects in this defensive system as well, particularly in the numbers and kinds of soldiers used to garrison many of the posts. In 1850 the army's frontier force in Texas consisted of ninety-three officers and 1,462 enlisted men,[5] far too small a number. Some forts were so severely undermanned that one company of fifty or sixty men formed the entire complement. Often, after sick call and assignment of camp details, fewer than a dozen soldiers were left for scouting duties,[6] and not all of these were mounted. Furthermore, while facing some of the most mobile antagonists in the world, many posts had no mounted troops whatsoever. In 1850, only 20 percent of the defensive force had horses, and by 1860 this number had risen to a mere 25 percent.[7] The San Antonio *Daily Express* aptly summed up the situation when it declared that: "The idea of repelling mounted Indians . . . with a force of foot soldiers, is ridiculous."[8] In addition, the troopers were mostly inexperienced in the methods of plains warfare, had little knowledge of the geography of the area, and rode, those few who did, horses of poor quality. With all these handicaps, they stood little chance of matching the swift-striking guerrilla tactics of the Indians.[9]

Nevertheless, within two years after the line of forts was established, settlers began pressuring Washington to let them move farther west, to the Cross Timbers area of Texas. Therefore, the federal government decided to build new military posts in more strategic sites, generally one hundred miles westward.[10]

By 1852 seven new forts had been established: Forts Belknap, Phantom Hill, Chadbourne, McKavett, Terrett, Mason, and Clark. These bastions formed a fairly regular line from the Brazos River to the Rio Grande and, together with the interior line of forts, proved moderately successful at stopping the Indian raids.[11] The area between the two lines of forts rapidly filled with settlers, and during the years from 1852 until 1860 several villages sprang into being. Jacksboro was one of them, being settled in 1856,[12] approximately the same year that Weatherford, Archer City, Palo Pinto, Comanche, and Hamilton were established. Initially Jack County had fewer than two hundred inhabitants, but by 1860 the population had increased to 946, of whom fifty were black slaves.[13]

These new settlers, upon realizing the limitations of regular army protection, fitted out their own ranger and minutemen companies and started a savage, unrelenting assault against the Indians. Through perseverance and often ruthlessness, the frontiersmen became the equal of the red man at plains warfare and began to drive the hostiles back.

3

Until 1854, Texans had been rushing into the newly opened lands and immediately surveying them for counties. No provisions were made for the Indians in this process. Finally, in February 1854, federal pressure forced the Texas Legislature to provide land for Indian reservations. However, of the hundred million acres at its disposal, the legislature granted to the Indians a meager 55,728 acres to create two reservations. The Brazos Agency was set up on the Brazos River, and the Comanche Reserve was organized forty miles away on the Clear Fork of the Brazos. By 1858, some 1,100 Caddos, Kichais, Wacos, Anadarkos, and Delawares had settled on the 38,152 acres of the Brazos Agency, but fewer than 400 Comanches had come to their 17,576-acre reserve.[14]

Friction between these reservation Indians and the settlers developed immediately. Any livestock losses the whites suffered were blamed upon the first Indians at hand—usually those on the two reservations. On two different occasions, only the intervention of the military prevented large citizen forces, enflamed and led by that famous Indian-hater John R. Baylor, from attacking the reserves. A Jack County citizen wrote, "Our troubles constantly grow worse. It has been unanimously resolved by [Jack County] citizens that the country must be immediately abandoned, or the lower Reserve Indians be speedily removed."[15] The Indian agents realized that only trouble would attend maintaining the reservations in Texas. Consequently, on July 31, 1859, all Indians from the Brazos Agency and the Comanche Reserve were removed under military escort to the Indian Territory, an accomplishment which met with Texas-wide acclaim.[16] Thus, the only remaining Indians in Texas were either scouts for the army or hostiles, and the hostiles were steadily being driven by white pressure into the northern and western reaches of the state. It seemed imminent that the Comanches and Kiowas would either accept the will of the white man or perish.

But the Civil War halted the drive to subdue the Plains Indians in Texas. The federal army was gone, and only then did the settlers realize what an aid it had been. As Governor Sam Houston informed the state legislature on January 21, 1861: "The Federal army had been the constant factor in the defense arrangements;

4

the state forces were the varying element, and, therefore, the more spectacular."[17]

In 1860, one-fifth of the regular federal army, a total of 121 officers and 2,727 enlisted men, had been stationed in Texas.[18] When these troops withdrew, they were replaced by local militia.[19] The new Confederate government attempted to provide for frontier defense by negotiating peace treaties with the Comanches. Reverting to an old federal policy called "peace purchasing,"[20] the Confederate government gave blankets, food, and trinkets to the Indians when they signed peace treaties in the fall and winter, although the Indians had a history of voiding these treaties during the good raiding weather of spring and summer. But to take as few risks as possible, the government also organized the Frontier Regiment,[21] ten companies of Rangers under the command of Colonel James M. Norris, to patrol the frontier in conjunction with the militia and to prevent Indians from entering the settlements. Despite the Rangers' efforts, by the end of 1863 raiding parties had driven off more than ten thousand head of cattle from Cooke, Denton, Montague, Wise, and Parker counties.[22] As the Civil War dragged on, the Frontier Regiment was depleted by Confederate demands for men, leaving the frontier with almost no defense. The Kiowas and Comanches had joined the Arapahoes and Cheyennes in Colorado in a war against the United States,[23] but they returned to Texas by late 1864. Indian raids stepped up in intensity almost immediately. In October, two hundred Kiowas and Comanches attacked a Confederate outpost near Murray, Texas, and killed five troopers. The Indians moved on to assault the Elm Creek settlement, sixteen miles northwest of Fort Belknap, where they killed eleven people and carried off seven women and children.[24]

The end of the Civil War also ended any pretensions at frontier defense. The line of settlement, which had remained about the same during the war, retreated more than a hundred miles in most instances.[25] Those settlements not abandoned fortified themselves against attack by drawing outlying families together to form a nucleus of defense. Most families remaining in northwestern Texas were concentrated in and around Jacksboro.[26]

In 1865, four thousand Union troops returned to Texas, but instead of being sent to the embattled frontier, they were stationed at interior posts where they became instruments of martial law for the new Reconstruction government.[27] The legislature in 1866 responded to the settlers' appeals for help and authorized one thousand state troopers to protect the frontier. But from his headquarters in New Orleans, General Philip Henry Sheridan, the commander of the Division of the Gulf, of which Texas was then a part, vetoed the use of state troops, even under federal officers. In his annual report to the Secretary of War, Sheridan explained his reasons: "During the last six months Indian depredations have taken place on the remote frontier. Their extent is not defined as yet, but they are not very alarming, and I think the [state] government has to some extent been influenced by exaggerated reports, gotten up . . . by frontier people to get a market for their produce, and . . . by army contractors to make money. It is strange that over a white man killed by Indians on an extensive frontier the greatest excitement will take place, but over the killing of many freedmen in the settlements nothing is done."[28]

To frontiersmen, it appeared that the new government was not anxious to do anything about the Indian problem and would not allow the citizens to act either. Sheridan did allow an inspector to investigate conditions on the frontier, however, and on the basis of his report decided to send federal troops to protect the settlers. Governor James W. Throckmorton had recommended that a new post be established at Jacksboro, so Captain Cram and Company I, the vanguard for the Sixth Cavalry, were sent there in 1866.[29]

Unfortunately, Cram and his men represented an army that, in many ways, was as ill-prepared for the task of defending the Texas frontier as the one that had departed the plains five years earlier. The new regular army faced such serious problems as declining quantity and quality of enlisted men, demoralization of the officer corps, and shortcomings in arms and equipment.

At the close of the Civil War, 1,034,064 men were serving in the nation's armed forces. By mid-1866, this total had been reduced to 54,641 officers and men, and by the end of the year not more than 25,000 soldiers were available for field service. In the years to

6

come Congress would continue to reduce the strength of the army until, by 1874, it would be set at 27,000, of which fewer than 19,000 actually were present for duty.[30]

Also in 1866, Congress fixed the size of the regular army at ten regiments of cavalry, forty-five of infantry (reduced to twenty-five in 1869), and five regiments of artillery.[31] Only three cavalry regiments, the Fourth, Sixth and Ninth, initially were assigned to the Texas frontier. Their combined strength of 45 officers and 1,453 enlisted men was some 1,400 fewer soldiers than the frontier force of 1860.[32]

With such limited manpower, the army could not hope to reestablish the defensive posture of the 1850s. The frontier was too vast and the forces stretched too thin. Many military men felt that, handicapped as they were by Congress, the task at hand might prove impossible. Years later General Philip Sheridan would write: "No other nation in the world would have attempted the reduction of (the) wild tribes and occupation of their country without less than 60,000 or 70,000 men, while the whole force employed and scattered over the enormous region never numbered 14,000 men . . . No other body of men [had to] overcome so many embarrassing obstacles in their unequal contest with wily savages, and none ever lost so heavily in officers and men."[33] Major General Nelson A. Miles spoke for many fellow officers when he dryly noted that, "Congress had fixed the limit of the enlisted men. Congress, however, had not limited Indian wars."[34]

Those men who served in the ranks of the dwindling regular army were a mixture of raw recruits and Civil War veterans, many of whom had tried to adjust to civilian life, failed, and returned to the army. About half of all the enlisted men were foreign born, the majority being Irish and German, the rest French, British, Scandinavian, Italian, even Russian. And, for the first time in the West, a new element was added: the negro. Black soldiers with white officers made up the Ninth and Tenth Cavalry and the Twenty-fourth and Twenty-fifth Infantry.[35]

Many of these recruits were illiterate, and most were unskilled. The wave of patriotism engendered by the Civil War had passed, and the federal government found that attracting men of the same quality as those who had fought against the Confederacy was almost impossible. Soldiering was not a glamorous profession, especially on the frontier. Troopers endured long hours in the saddle in searing heat and numbing cold, as well as back-breaking labor and stupefying boredom, poor food and execrable living conditions, harsh discipline, disease, disability, and death. For all this suffering they were rewarded with the indifference of Congress, the contempt of the civilian population, and the niggardly pay of thirteen dollars a month. It is small wonder that the quality of the enlisted men rarely rose above mediocrity and that desertion and alcoholism decimated the ranks.[36]

Officers, too, had their problems. The end of the Civil War brought the release of thousands of volunteer army officers, and those who wanted to make the regular army a career saw their rank reduced: generals became colonels, majors, sometimes even captains.[37] Equally demoralizing was the pay scale, which ranged from $3,600 yearly for a cavalry colonel to $1,400 yearly for an infantry second lieutenant, amounts significantly below what men could earn in comparable positions in civilian life.[38]

But even more damaging to officer morale was the promotions system, which was based on seniority in the regiment through captain, seniority in the army (cavalry, infantry, artillery) from major through colonel, and by presidential appointment through major general. According to a government survey, a newly commissioned second lieutenant might require as long as thirty-seven years to rise to the grade of colonel.[39] Officers of talent and energy were frustrated by the knowledge that men with less ability but more seniority would be promoted over them. Unhealthy rivalries, petty jealousies, and even bitter hatreds developed as initiative, enterprise, and the desire for self-improvement diminished. The unfortunate truth was that "the parade ground of a two- or three-company post in the West defined the intellectual and professional horizons of most line officers in the postwar decade."[40]

In arms and equipment, the postwar frontier army was somewhat better off than its predecessor, having the benefit of thousands of tons of supplies stored in government arsenals and warehouses. The infantry carried a modified version of the ubiquitous Civil War

8

Springfield rifle-musket until it was replaced with the model 1873 Springfield rifle, a .45-caliber breech-loading single-shot weapon that became standard issue for the next twenty years. The cavalry, however, had no standard carbine at first. Some regiments used the .50-caliber single-shot Sharps, while others preferred the .50-caliber seven-shot repeating Spencer. In 1873 cavalry regiments were issued the .45-caliber single-shot Springfield carbine which they carried for the remainder of the Indian wars. Although not as rapid-firing as the Spencer, its greater range and durability made it more desirable for frontier service.[41]

For sidearms, the troopers carried Colt and Remington cap and ball six-shooters until 1872, when the Colt .45-caliber six-shooter known as the "Peacemaker" became the standard.[42] And, of course, each cavalryman was issued that classic weapon of the mounted army, a sabre. During the Civil War the sabre had occasionally proven useful, even effective, but on the frontier, where most engagements were long-range rifle duels, it was a cumbersome, noisy, and unnecessary piece of equipment. It was polished for inspection and worn on parade but almost never carried into the field.[43]

Cavalry posts often possessed artillery pieces but seldom fired them except to signal daily retreat. Only the Hotchkiss 1.65-inch 2-pounder "mountain gun" proved to be light and compact enough to be carried with fast-moving columns.[44] Even when deployed, the artillery would never enjoy Civil War-style targets, such as close-packed regiments of men. Only in surprise attacks on sleeping Indian villages, such as Sand Creek or Wounded Knee, would artillery prove worth the effort of dragging it across the countryside.

The cavalryman went to the frontier wearing the standard uniform of the Union armies, a dark blue woolen or flannel waist-length jacket, a loose thigh-length coat, and sky blue jersey trousers with riding breeches. These articles were manufactured in only a few standard sizes, and the soldier had to bear the cost of individual tailoring to make them fit acceptably. The trooper was also issued a shirt, drawers, belt and suspenders, high boots, hat and cap, and a greatcoat made of heavy blue cloth, double-breasted, with two rows of eagle buttons in front and a wide semicircular yellow-lined cape.[45]

The uniforms proved to be hot in summer and cold in winter and made of cheap materials that quickly wore out in hard service. Regulations often gave way to expedience, experience, and personal taste. Kepi caps were replaced with straw hats and sombreros, blue flannel shirts gave way to gray and even checkered cotton ones, and wool jackets were discarded for buckskin and buffalo robe coats. As a result, the typical cavalry column on the Texas frontier often bore a greater resemblance to a band of Comancheros than to a military unit. One reporter noted that the troopers had "a wild, bushwhacker appearance, which was in amusing contrast with their polished and gentlemanly manners."[46]

The final accoutrement which the government provided for the cavalry was, in many ways, the most important: the horse. For it was the horse, or more precisely the mobility which the horse provided, that set the cavalry apart from the infantry and in theory made it the more effective arm in frontier warfare. In practice, the cavalry's vaunted mobility usually proved to be more illusion than reality, for at least three reasons.

First, the army preferred large, heavy horses for the cavalry, animals that could more easily carry the 160–200-pound load of a trooper and his gear. But this "American" stock was accustomed to grain feed and could not remain in good condition on prairie grass alone, as many veteran soldiers well knew. One testified that "accustomed as our cavalry horses are to a regular and liberal allowance of grain, they very soon weaken and break down when pushed rapidly upon an Indian trail, with no other forage but grass." Thus, when the troopers moved, they were forced to carry with them, on mules or in wagons, not only their own rations but their horses' grain as well, depending upon the land for nothing but water. A large force could never stray too far from a line of supply, and long periods in the field demanded a steady flow of supplies. Thus, a cavalry column was somewhat like a powerful dog on a short chain—within its reach it was a force to be reckoned with, but beyond the length of its tether, it was helpless.[47]

Second, although government officials and even the cavalrymen themselves were often reluctant to admit it, the animals obtained for the service were frequently of less than outstanding quality. In part this was due to the contractors' practice of purchasing from the local ranchers. For years the Kiowas and Comanches had raided the ranches in Texas, driving off the finest stock. The ranchers naturally kept the best of what was left for themselves, and the government contractors were forced to choose the cavalry's mounts from the remainder.[48]

Finally, each cavalryman was provided with only one horse, and its strength had to be carefully nursed lest a trooper find himself in a fight or ambush riding an exhausted mount. But despite the soldiers' best efforts, the poor quality of their animals and the rigors of service frequently combined to produce disastrous results. During Lieutenant Colonel George Custer's winter campaign on the plains of Oklahoma and Kansas in 1868–1869, four months of hard riding almost totally unhorsed his command of over eight hundred men. In one three-day period alone, Custer lost 276 horses to exposure, exhaustion, and malnutrition.[49]

Arrayed against the troopers on the frontier of Texas were the "Overlords of the Southern Plains,"[50] the Comanches, Kiowas, and Kiowa-Apaches. These tribes were nomadic buffalo hunters who ranged over hundreds of miles and practiced little or no agriculture. They had acquired and mastered the horse sometime prior to 1750[51] and had become some of the finest horsemen in history, with the Comanches generally regarded by frontiersmen as the best. The artist George Catlin, who observed their superb horsemanship, wrote that the Comanche was awkward and unattractive on foot, "but the moment he lays his hand upon his horse, his *face,* even, becomes handsome, and he gracefully flies away like a different being."[52] On foot, the Plains Indians presented no greater obstacle to the white settler than had the earlier Indians of the East; mounted, however, they became fearsome antagonists and formidable opponents even for trained cavalry.[53]

Armed with lance, short bow, shield, and, after 1870, the newest model breech-loading rifle,[54] the Southern Plains Indian was, according to one observer, "as magnificent a soldier as the world can show,"[55] easily a match in fighting abilities for the federal cavalryman or Texas Ranger. Trained as a warrior from early youth, the Indian male lived in a culture that was as militaristic as any on earth.[56] Bravery in combat and wealth, usually measured by the number of horses acquired through raiding, were the only means for men to rise in rank within the tribe. Raiding parties could vary in size from a half-dozen warriors to the entire tribe, and although the Indians were merciless toward their foes and recognized no non-combatants, they frequently raided for the sole purpose of stealing horses and cattle.[57] Warfare was conducted as a sort of deadly game in which each individual warrior sought to gain personal glory through the practice of counting coup. A coup was a great or brave deed, such as being the first to kill an enemy, scalp him, or even touch him. The reputation for being a brave warrior with many scalps could raise a man to a chieftainship, the highest position of prestige among the Indians.[58]

In order to have sufficient space for hunting and grazing, the Comanches and Kiowas divided into loosely organized bands or groups, each of which roamed an area of from five hundred to eight hundred square miles.[59] Their supply source was the very land on which they lived. The great herds of buffalo furnished the Indians with all the necessities of life—food, clothing, tools, shelter, even fuel—and the ocean of grasslands fed and nurtured their wiry ponies.[60]

Colonel Randolph B. Marcy, an early explorer of the West and keen observer of the Indian, aptly summarized the problems of waging war on a people such as the Plains Indians when he wrote:

> To act against an enemy who is here to-day and there to-morrow; who at one time stampedes a herd of mules upon the head waters of the Arkansas, and when next heard from is in the very heart of the populated districts of Mexico, laying waste haciendas, and carrying devastation, rapine, and murder in his steps; who is every where without being any where; who assembles at the moment of combat, and vanishes whenever fortune turns against him; who leaves his women and children far distant from the theatre of hostilities, and has neither towns nor magazine to defend, nor lines of retreat to cover; who derives his commissariat [sic]

from the country he operates in, and is not encumbered with baggage-wagons or pack-trains; who comes into action only when it suits his purpose, and never without the advantage of numbers or position—with such an enemy the strategic science of civilized nations loses much of its importance.[61]

Despite the warnings of men such as Colonel Marcy, the War Department in 1867 was about to commit itself to a war that most military men believed would be won in five years or less. No one could guess that the last battle of the Indian wars would not take place until 1898. Between 1866 and 1891, the regular army and the Indians would fight over a thousand actions. The cost in lives, time, and money would prove incalculable.[62]

Out on the plains of Texas, it would be a guerilla-type, fast-moving, light-marching war, pitting a savage and brave enemy against men who could scarcely comprehend the enormity of the undertaking. The United States Cavalry went forth with pennants and guidons streaming. On the plains waited some of the finest light cavalry the world has ever known. Their epic struggle would be the stuff of which legends are made.

CHAPTER TWO

IT HAD BEEN A TIRESOME
and dusty march through the
July heat and the "unbroken
wilderness" northwest from
Weatherford, the nearest civilized point. Captain Cram and
Company I of the Sixth Cavalry
had marched almost the length
of the state to reach Jacksboro.
In 1866 the town consisted of a
central square bordered on the

The Federal Army Returns to Northwest Texas, 1866–1867

south side by a two-story stone structure, on the west side by a dilapidated rawhide-covered courthouse, and on the north side by
two tumble-down buildings, one a grocery store. A concrete building stood on the southeast corner, an old frame structure on the
northwest corner of the square. A dozen or more log houses formed
the "suburbs."[1]

Jacksboro represented the last sizable white settlement on the
northern Texas frontier. To the west solitary chimney-stacks and
devastated ranches marked the high tide of settlement before it had
ebbed eastward during the Civil War. Except for a few hardy souls,
the settlers had either returned to the interior or had gathered in
and around Jacksboro.[2]

The men of Company I pitched their tents on the town
square, bathed themselves and watered their horses in nearby Lost
Creek. On the first post return Captain Cram reported he had occupied the "Post of Jacksboro" with twenty-nine men and thirty-
nine horses. The arrival of a second detachment in August in-

15

creased the ranks to two officers, sixty men, and seventy-four horses.[3]

There are no recorded instances, initially, of trouble between the troopers and the townspeople. In time, frustration with the performance of the Sixth Cavalry would lead to scattered incidents involving the soldiers, but these were common to all frontier towns. There was no general resentment of the Union cavalry. Indeed, Jack County had been one of the ten Texas counties that voted against secession in 1861.[4] Although the officers and men of the regiment would never feel they were appreciated by the local citizenry they had come to protect, at least these people would be less likely to resent the presence of Union troopers than would most Texans. The townspeople would have preferred a Ranger company to Yankee soldiers, but General Sheridan had forbidden the use of state militia; the Union cavalry would have to do. Jacksboro's inhabitants hoped that these vanquishers of the Confederacy would prove better Indian fighters than their predecessors, the ineffective dragoons[5] of the 1850s. The settlers would be disappointed.

That the troops had no immediate effect upon the security of the county probably came as no surprise to any citizens with appreciable frontier experience. The soldiers, poorly equipped and ill-mounted, claimed they would be unable to launch offensive actions until September.[6] In truth, all Cram and his men represented was a beginning, and not a particularly auspicious one at that. To the Indians, they apparently represented even less. The raiding continued unabated.

On July 18, 1866, the residents of Wise, Jack, Cooke, Montague, Clay, and Young counties petitioned Governor Throckmorton to provide immediate relief from the Indian attacks, claiming that "Indian Depredations are constantly being made upon our Western Frontier . . . with a boldness never known before, Committing Murders and Stealing horses and driving off cattle in large numbers and herds."[7] On August 3, 1866, T. W. Thomas of Sister Grove, Texas, also wrote the governor describing the situation in Jack and Wise counties:

Govr-
    Herewith I enclose to you memorial from the frontier

16

people . . . that you can see the conditions of our frontier and give such publicity to the letter as you think proper in the premises.

I visited the commandant of the Post of Jacksboro (Capt Cram) last week—and made application to him to recommend to the commanding Genl of the department as well as to the Govr to call out a volunteer force of Rangers of at least 500 men to protect the frontier and it met with his hearty approval and has sent up the recommendation[.] he is aware of the condition of the country and knows the necessity of the aid of rangers—that is well acquainted with the Indian character and country[.] he Capt Cram has not exceeding 50 available Troops and them badly mounted hence he can do nothing in the way of protection[.] while I was at Jacksboro the Indians shot Calves in the Edge of Town and attacked his wagons on the Road from Veals Station but done no damage as he had an escort that held them off[.]

Col Pickett Et al of Wise County visited Jacksboro with me and they say there never has been as many Indians in the west part of Wise and Jack County before since they lived in the country . . . the best information we can get from the cowmen is that some 5 or 6,000 head of cattle is drove off[,] Cattle that was gathered in Jack[,] Wise and Young and herded at our Wichita Ranch. . . .

T. W. Thomas[8]

The situation on the Texas frontier was desperate. The Indians were raiding more because there was little danger of resistance or retaliation. Never before had the warriors found the Texans as defenseless as they now were with the Yankee troops for protection. The bluecoated soldiers presented no problem to the Indians, because they generally stayed in their forts. When they did emerge, they were so foolish as to ride only one horse. The average Comanche or Kiowa warrior always went raiding with more than one pony in his "caviard"[9] or personal herd, and he could mount a fresh pony every twenty miles in a hard chase. The soldier could be easily

17

outdistanced. Besides, the troopers' horses were generally poor, while the Indians rode only the best horseflesh in the country. The settlers' cattle and horses were so easily stolen that the powerful Kwahadi Comanches had some 15,000 horses, almost 400 mules, and innumerable cattle in their camps on the headwaters of the Colorado, Brazos, and Red rivers.[10] Since an Indian man had no honorable profession except that of a warrior, and a great many horses could buy a fine wife, the nearness of a rich and oftentimes vulnerable enemy encouraged raiding. Settlers in the area of Jack County desperately needed effective military protection, but what they were to receive for the next few years would fall short.

In mid-September 1866, Ernest Jones, his son, and two ne-groes traveled some twelve miles from Jacksboro to cut hay; they were attacked and murdered by marauding Indians. Captain Cram detailed Lieutenant William A. Rafferty and twenty-five men of Company I and newly arrived Company A to pursue the Indians and punish them. Rafferty marched to the Little Wichita River, but finding no traces of the marauders, he returned to camp. Mean-while the Indians entered Wise County, where they attacked sev-eral ranches, killed a woman, carried off another and two children, and stole several horses.[11] The first military action in Jack County was a dismal failure.

By December, seven companies (A, D, E, F, I, K, and L) of the Sixth Cavalry were stationed at the post of Jacksboro: a unit total of 9 officers, 322 men, and 280 horses and mules.[12] The men continued to be quartered in tents around the town square, but the canvas shelters were quickly wearing out. Companies A and I had constructed enough picket stables along Lost Creek to house their own mounts, but the horses of the five newly arrived companies were without protection and were suffering and dying from ex-posure. The sutler's store was located in a stone building behind a run-down structure on the north side of the square, while the com-manding officer's headquarters were in a tent at the southwest cor-ner, surrounded by a picket stockade. There were no medical facili-ties or personnel available save for a hospital steward, and the

18

command was without quartermaster's stores, camp supplies, garrison equipage, or even spare clothing. Many of the troops were in rags and nearly barefoot.[13] The enlisted men responded to this grim life by evading their duties, drinking Pine-Top or White Mule whiskey,[14] playing cards, and deserting. From July to December 1866, thirty-eight men, 12 percent of the garrison, had tired of military life and deserted, most of them making their way back to Weatherford. The garrison lacked interest and serviceable mounts for desertion details, so only two of the fugitives were apprehended.[15]

On January 14, 1867, with the arrival of 125 recruits, the total strength of the post rose to 465 officers and men and 325 horses. By the end of the month, two men of the expanded garrison had died of disease, twenty-four had deserted, and seventy-eight of the horses had been judged "unserviceable."[16]

Shortly after the arrival of the recruits, the erection of a permanent post of picket construction began on the town square. Thousand of pickets were cut and dragged to the site to build quarters, fences, and corrals. Construction of each building involved digging a trench one foot wide and one foot deep in the shape of a rectangle, fourteen by twenty feet. Logs were set on end in the ditch and driven into place, with four extra-sized logs forming the corners of the structure. A piece of lumber ran from one corner log to the next, and all the pickets were nailed to it to keep them in place. One row of logs was left slightly higher than its opposite so that the timber poles laid on top for a roof would have a slight incline; the finished huts were roughly seven feet high. The soldiers used boxes from the quartermaster's department to make doors, and rock and clay to construct chimneys and fireplaces. Twigs and dirt covered the roof. Because this type of roof habitually absorbed rain, for as long as two days after the rainfall had ceased outside, water seeped through the dirt roof and the rain continued inside the hut.[17] Gaps in the walls were chinked with chips and plastered with twigs and mud, but the pecan trees used as pickets warped badly when they dried, allowing all the laboriously placed chinking to fall out.[18] Six huts accommodated a company, and five sets of huts were eventually finished, facing south on the town square.[19]

In late January 1867, Major Samuel H. Starr arrived at Jacksboro to assume command of the post. Referred to by his troops as "Old Paddy," Starr was a long-service veteran now nearing retirement who had fought in the Creek and Seminole wars in Alabama and Florida, the Mexican War, and the Civil War. On April 25, 1863, he became a major in the Sixth Cavalry and at the end of hostilities was ordered to Texas. Sergeant H. H. McConnell described Starr as "every inch a soldier, and a just and honest man"; he also called him "captious, querulous and cranky."[20] Perhaps Starr was too old for the rigors of frontier service, or perhaps his many old wounds (including the loss of an arm) had sapped his vitality, or perhaps he found the problems of manpower and mounts simply too pronounced to be overcome. Whatever the reasons, and despite his long record of capable service, the Sixth Cavalry did not prove to be an efficient frontier fighting unit under Major Starr's command.

In February, an epidemic broke out among the horses at the post. It was blamed on the poor quality feed—prairie grass hay and musty corn hauled from Grayson County, for which the army paid $3.20 a bushel. The exact number of horses to die is not known, but the post return for the month lists eighty-eight animals as unserviceable.[21] The loss of so many mounts further reduced the effectiveness of the Sixth.

Details were sent out in February to Camp Colorado on the Colorado River and to Rock Creek in western Jack County to investigate reports of Indian depredations and murders.[22] Little else of importance was accomplished, except that work continued on the buildings necessary to house the troops. Many of the men discovered the joys of hunting in Texas. Deer, antelope, rabbit, wild turkey, raccoon, duck, quail, squirrel, and opossum abounded in the vicinity, and fresh meat was always a welcome change from the regular army fare.[23]

Five inches of snow fell on March 4 and again on March 15 and 29. The Record of Events section of the post return, for lack of anything of greater interest, is taken up with the comment, "The weather has been cold. Part of the time the thermometer [dropped] to ten below zero. Good sleighing."[24]

The army at this time employed Tonkawa Indians as scouts. The tribe was transferred from Austin in March, arriving in Jacksboro on April 18, 1867, with 103 men, women, and children. They had been given a letter from the Indian Commissioner in Washington, D.C., Louis V. Bogy, stating that they were to be issued any food supplies they needed for their journey. The state government was to be responsible for the debts the Indians incurred. During the forty-six-day trek from Austin to Jacksboro, the Indians consumed thirty-one head of cattle and cost the state $598.55.[25] A disgusted Major Starr reported upon their arrival that, "These Indians [Tonkawas] are a very lazy, vagabond race, and will not hunt or do anything else as long as they get enough to eat without."[26] Altogether they were a sorry spectacle, what one soldier called "the disgusting remnant of a once powerful tribe."[27] But despite appearances the Tonkawas proved to be first-class scouts and through the years became invaluable as the far-ranging "eyes" of the cavalry columns. Also, the Tonkawas' four stock phrases which seemed to encompass their entire grasp of English—"Mebbe so, yes!" "Mebbe so, no!" "Mebbe so, now catch 'em!," and "Mebbe so, no catch 'em!"—were soon adopted as favorite quotations by the cavalry troopers and officers alike.[28]

In late March, orders came from Washington to abandon Jacksboro. Accordingly, on April 16, 1867, Companies A and E marched to Buffalo Springs, a point in Clay County some twenty miles due north of Jacksboro, to establish a new post nearer to the Red River, the boundary of Indian Territory. The army concluded that the site offered more timber for construction and a better water supply than Jacksboro. Major Starr, with the remainder of the Jacksboro garrison, was ordered to reoccupy Fort Belknap, an abandoned post in Young County some thirty miles southwest of Jacksboro. Belknap was first established in 1852 when its main purpose was to guard the Butterfield Stage Road.[29] Apparently the army wished to reopen regular traffic on the stage road, which ran through Jacksboro and on east to Weatherford. Starr left Jacksboro on April 27, 1867, with companies G, I, K, and L of the Sixth and, despite his misgivings, with the newly arrived Tonkawa scouts as well.[30]

The choice of Buffalo Springs as the site for a new permanent fort was questionable. While it was twenty miles closer to Indian Territory than Jacksboro, it was also twenty miles farther from the supply depots at Austin, 350 miles away. Supply trains moving from Weatherford to Jacksboro to Buffalo Springs needed escorts of soldiers to prevent Indian attacks. Also, Buffalo Springs was isolated and lonely, with supply trains and the weekly mail the only contact with the outside world. To the soldiers, even the pathetic pleasures of Jacksboro seemed luxuriant when compared to the nonexistent ones of Buffalo Springs. Movement across the country was difficult; there were not enough horses to mount all the men of the garrison, a problem which also had existed at Jacksboro.[31]

Despite these obvious problems, the army planned to establish a permanent four-company post at Buffalo Springs, and by July 1867, a hundred civilian workers had arrived to start construction.[32] They erected a guardhouse, stables, stockade corral, officers' houses, headquarters offices, quarters, and hospital, most being built in the picket style. Camp life assumed a regular monotonous pattern of escort duty, construction duty, and occasionally scouting duty. This routine was broken rather harshly on July 19, 1867, by a series of events which illustrated all too well the effectiveness of the Sixth Cavalry in northwestern Texas.[33]

A timber detail consisting of a sergeant named Hall, a corporal and twelve men, and four government mule teams driven by civilians had finished their day's work along the West Fork of the Trinity, about eighteen miles south of the post and eight miles north of Jacksboro. The soldiers returned to their bivouac and busied themselves preparing supper, washing in the stream, and attending to general camp duties. One of the teamsters was with the mule herd in an open grassy area one hundred yards from the camp. Suddenly a party of about three hundred Indians swept through the herd, stampeding the mules before them. They lanced the teamster from his horse and killed him. The soldiers, momentarily transfixed by the spectacle, dashed for their weapons but managed only one ragged volley before the wildly whooping Indians and the twenty-four mules disappeared to the south. The troopers quickly buried the dead teamster and rode for the post, arriving early the next afternoon, Saturday, July 20. Within an hour of hearing their report, Captain Benjamin T. Hutchins mounted thirty men (using all the serviceable horses he had) and started in pursuit. Forty-five soldiers and sixty civilian employees remained behind under the command of Lieutenant Francis Matheny. Among them they possessed a grand total of twenty-seven rifles.

Retreat had just been sounded at the post on Sunday when the troopers spied the Indian raiders coming down the Jacksboro road, driving a large herd of horses and mules before them. Instantly the trumpeter sounded "To Arms." Shouts of "Indians! Indians!" followed. The warriors approached the post on the west and south sides and calmly surveyed the situation with the cool and reserved arrogance of experienced conquerors pondering a new conquest.

The garrison was in a state of bedlam. The officers' families and the laundresses hurried to the security of the log forage houses. The corral, in the midst of the camp, was barricaded with wagons, driven or pushed hurriedly into place, end to end. Companies A and E took positions on the south side of the corral with the men stationed three paces apart. The twenty-seven men with rifles checked their weapons and slammed shells into the chambers. The men without firearms stood with sabres drawn and prepared to retrieve any fallen comrade's rifle. At a distance of about four hundred yards, the Indians formed an unbroken semicircle around the post. The soldiers were ordered not to fire until the Indians charged and were in close range. To many, the situation undoubtedly appeared hopeless.

Meanwhile, acting on their own, two men crept out of the post through a ravine and approached to within rifle range of the Indians. They rose in unison, fired two shots, and toppled a warrior from his pony. The Indians responded with a great war whoop and a volley of shots which fell short of the barricaded corral. When the war party moved forward to attack, the troopers raised their weapons to pick out potential targets among the mass of red men.

At this crucial moment, the sixty or so construction workers, forgotten in the general alarm, came running down to the corral from their camp a half-mile north of the post. The Indians, supposing these sudden reinforcements to be armed, halted and held a quick council. A bugle sounded from among the warriors,[34] but instead of attacking, they fell back and proceeded to encamp one-half mile from the post. The timely arrival of the workers, almost none of whom were armed, saved the garrison from almost certain annihilation.

Sabres were issued to the construction workers, and the post settled down to an uneasy night, fully expecting to be attacked during the dark. The rising moon revealed, however, that the Indians remained in their camp.

The Indians camped by the post for almost two days but made no effort to attack. Apparently they were waiting for the soldiers pinned inside to exhaust their forage. Once this happened, the troopers would be forced to turn out their horses and mules which the Indians could then add to their growing collection. At Tuesday noon, however, the Indians suddenly abandoned their camp and started northward. The reason for this move was soon apparent. Captain Hutchins and his command were sighted approaching from the south. The two-day siege of Buffalo Springs was over.[35]

One of the defenders of Buffalo Springs later wrote that Captain Hutchins had campaigned at a leisurely pace and, finding no Indian trails, had turned west to Fort Belknap and played poker for two days.[36] This allegation cannot be verified in other records, but the evident failure of Captain Hutchins to find such a large war party and the tragicomedy of the Buffalo Springs siege both highlight the ineptitude of the federal defenders of North Texas. It appeared that the settlers would have to provide their own protection.

In September, Buffalo Springs was reinforced by Companies C and D of the Sixth Cavalry. But a drought left the post without adequate water for four companies of cavalry. Captain Hutchins informed Washington of the problem on October 11, 1867, and recommended a return to Jacksboro, which had "splendid grass, firewood, great quantities of stone, and a delicious and inexhaustable stream of water." On October 24, he reported that he had "discovered a spring [which] yields at least one hundred gallons an hour of pure and sweet water, this making the supply for men, animals, and building purposes an adequate amount."[37] However, the captain's first report had stirred the governmental wheels into motion, and their momentum could not be checked by his subsequent letter.

A four-man board of inspection arrived at Buffalo Springs on November 18, 1867, and after a half-day's observation and evaluation, duly condemned the post.[38]

Around $42,000 had been spent on Buffalo Springs, but it had not all been wasted. The mere presence of federal soldiers had given a certain sense of security to many civilians who had earlier left the area, and they began to filter back into the countryside joined by new settlers. The money spent on payrolls, contracts for supplies, feed, and transportation had helped spur the local economy. And, finally, the Indian siege of the fort itself alerted Washington to the Indian danger and that fall prompted the establishment of a camp on Cache Creek in Indian Territory—a camp which eventually became Fort Sill.[39]

Two days after Buffalo Springs was condemned, Captain Daniel Madden's Company E and the construction crews left for Jacksboro. The other three companies remained at the post until April to protect the valuable stores of supplies and government property accumulated there.[40]

When Captain Madden arrived in Jacksboro, he discovered that the townspeople had torn down the barracks and stables and appropriated the materials. The weary troopers unpacked their canvas tents and prepared for more construction work. The soldiers brought with them the plans that had been drawn up for Fort Buffalo Springs. A high rolling prairie a half-mile southwest of the Jacksboro town square was chosen as the site for a new post.[41] The Fort Buffalo Springs plans were unrolled and transformed with the quick mark of a foreman's pen into the plans for the newest frontier bastion, Fort Richardson.

General Israel Bush Richardson (National Archives)

CHAPTER THREE

SPECIAL ORDER NO. 27 stipulated that Fort Richardson was established "for the more complete and efficient protection of the north-western frontier of Texas."[1] Along with two new sister forts, Concho and Griffin, that the board of inspectors recommended, Richardson was destined to become one of the keys to federal protection of the frontier against the hostile Comanche and Kiowa Indians.[2]

The Construction of Fort Richardson, 1868

Fort Richardson was named for General Israel Bush ("Fighting Dick") Richardson, who was mortally wounded at the Battle of Antietam in 1862. Born in Fairfax, Vermont, in 1815, he had attended the United States Military Academy, fought in the Seminole War in Florida, the Mexican War, and the Civil War.[3]

The site chosen for the fort was an area of almost three hundred acres one-half mile from Jacksboro, on the south and east side of Lost Creek, a tributary of the Trinity River. Fort Richardson was located some forty-two miles northwest of Weatherford, forty miles west of Decatur, and forty miles southwest of Montague. The new post sat astride the Overland Mail route to its equally new sister post of Fort Griffin, seventy-five miles to the southwest. The next post, Fort Concho, was another 155 miles beyond Griffin. The nearest railroad terminus was that of the Texas Central Railroad in Calvert, 202 miles to the southeast.[4]

The majority of military buildings at Fort Richardson were completed by January 1870, at which time the last civilian work crews were dismissed. Thereafter, the infantry units at Richardson, assisted at times by the cavalry troopers, assumed the task of keeping the post in a state of good repair, a job that continued until the day Richardson was ordered abandoned. Construction and repair work so dominated the troopers' daily routines that cavalry Sergeant H. H. McConnell was prompted in his memoirs to refer to himself and his men as "armed laborers, nothing less, nothing more."[5]

Had the original plans been followed faithfully, Fort Richardson might have been one of the most handsome posts in the United States.[6] But the whims of individual post commanders, wide variation in the workmen's skills, and problems of supply and scarcity of materials combined to destroy whatever symmetry the original blueprint contained. Buildings were erected with little regard for order or arrangement. The result was a collection of stone, picket, and lumber buildings, scattered over a rectangular area almost a mile long and one-quarter mile wide, that more resembled a small village than a fort.

The fort complex was dominated by a large parade ground which ran 415 feet north to south and 1100 feet east to west. North-south pedestrian crosswalks divided the area into four equal parts, and an "Avenue Road" for riding and driving outlined its perimeter. A parade ground was a must for any cavalry post, and despite orders by the commandant that horsemen and pedestrians should use the avenues and footpaths, the ground was probably soon devoid of any grass due to daily trampling by the horses.[7]

Facing the south side of the parade ground were the officers' quarters. In all, ten buildings were erected by 1872. Five were story-and-a-half frame structures built of cottonwood lumber, while the others were the old faithful standby, the "picket" house.[8]

Married officers of field and staff grade and their families generally quartered in the frame houses, which were ceiled and plastered, with attics, fireplaces, and painted woodwork. These four-room frame cottages included a kitchen set off to the side in the rear and contained approximately 1050 square feet. A veranda ran the entire length of the front, and there was a porch in the rear. During those times when Richardson's garrison was increased, it was common for two families to share one house. . In 1870, Dr. Joseph

H. H. McConnell, sergeant in the Sixth Cavalry, mayor of Jacksboro, and author (Russell Jones Collection)

View of Fort Richardson, circa 1872, looking south from the edge of the reservation. Possibly taken by the photographer with the Kellogg expedition. (National Archives)

Officers' quarters around 1900 (National Archives)

Patzki, one of the post surgeons, described the buildings as "neat in appearance" and "as comfortable as could be expected, considering the green lumber used in their construction."[9] Later that same year an acting inspector general reported that the cottonwood lumber had warped badly, causing "large cracks in the floor through which the wind and dust have full course."[10] In 1875, the quarters were described as being "in bad condition and very crowded. Many of the roofs leak . . . and floors [are] warped and open. Many of the quarters [are] without privies and many more with privies terribly [run] down and unfit for use."[11]

The four picket quarters ranged from forty-seven feet long by sixteen feet wide by nine feet tall, to seventy-three feet long by eighteen feet wide. The former were divided into three rooms by picket walls, and the latter into four. These structures were much inferior to the frame houses, having no ceilings, rough board flooring laid on the bare ground, no porches, and large stone fireplaces at which, according to Robert B. Carter, a young lieutenant in the Fourth Cavalry, "one might freeze his back and roast his face during

Officers' picket quarters and tents at Fort Richardson, ca. 1871 (National Archives)

a 'Norther.'" He went on to note that "when the dried chinking dropped from the picket partitions . . . an arm could be readily thrust through into the neighboring officer's room, and any noise above a whisper was easily heard in the adjoining quarters." Also, during a strong wind, so much dust sifted from the ceiling that it was necessary to sweep the dinner table before dining. Supposedly, the officers of the Sixth had used the buildings for dog kennels, and they were forever after infested with fleas. Certainly centipedes, tarantulas, and scorpions roamed at will, while mice and rats gambolled around the legs of the army cots at night. [12]

It is small wonder that in times of overcrowding at the post many junior officers preferred to live in tents pitched along the flanks of the picket quarters. Lieutenant Carter, for example, had spacious tent quarters, which he called "Carter's Village": a large framed and floored hospital tent formed the center of his five-tent abode. With canvas on the floor and a red-and-black-figured wool rug over that, a small vented wood stove to provide ample heat and several windows for ventilation, his tent quarters were probably more comfortable than any picket building. [13]

The adjutant's office, the post library and reading room, and the commissary and quartermaster's storehouses were located on the

31

eastern side of the parade ground. The adjutant's office, a picket building forty-seven by sixteen feet, was occupied on December 10, 1869. It had a shingle roof, used wood stoves for heat, and was divided into three rooms used by the commanding officer, the adjutant, and the clerical staff.[14]

The post library and reading room was first housed in a tent on the north side of Lost Creek. In 1870, it was moved into the post commissary and in 1872 found a final home in a picket structure just north of the adjutant's office. The library offered literary works by Sir Walter Scott and Charles Dickens, as well as the *Army and Navy Journal*, *Harper's Weekly*, the daily and weekly *New York Tribune* and weekly *Herald*, the Boston *Morning Journal*, the Chicago *Daily Tribune*, and the Washington *Weekly Chronicle*. It is said that by the time the post closed, the library contained over eighteen hundred volumes which the adjutant had purchased with monies from the post fund.[15]

The quartermaster's storeroom and the commissary building were two separate sandstone structures, each sixty by twenty-four feet, which stood end to end with a twenty-foot space between them. At the time they were completed, in February 1868, it was intended that this space be arched to form an entrance to the post. Instead, by the next year, the space had been filled with a frame structure which was built flush with the two storehouses, making them one continuous building. The commissary sergeant used the lower part of this addition as a storeroom and the upper story as his office and sleeping quarters. The quartermaster's office was divided into four rooms, three for the quartermaster and one for the veterinary surgeon and post quartermaster sergeant. An additional picket commissary storehouse, a sutler's store, and three auxiliary picket quartermaster's buildings were later added, extending in a northerly line past the parade ground.[16]

Bordering the northern side of the parade ground were the ten enlisted men's barracks, all of the picket variety, with shingle roofs and wooden floors. Most of the buildings were eighty-five by twenty feet, although two were somewhat larger. Wings as large as seventy-three feet by twenty-seven were added to the rear of five of these barracks, and the enlisted men's kitchens and mess halls were located twenty-five feet behind each building.[17]

The barracks were designed to house from thirty-four to eighty men, but at various times one hundred or more soldiers were crowded into them. Small rooms were partitioned off at each end for the sergeants' quarters. In the winter two large wood stoves supplied heat, and in the summer six windows, three in front and three in back, and two doors provided the only ventilation. The enlisted men slept on wooden bunks, 4 by 6½ feet, with two men sleeping below and two above. Mattresses were double bedsacks filled with hay which was supposed to be changed monthly. Privies with zinc-lined troughs were located 150 feet to the rear of each set of barracks; these were replaced in 1873 by two picket buildings twenty-two by sixty feet, set 300 feet behind the barracks line.[18]

Five hundred feet behind the barracks were the stables. By 1870, two had been constructed, each two hundred feet long, made of pickets with shingle roofs. As the garrison of the post expanded, additional stables were required and by 1872 four more had been erected. The buildings had double doors at each end and in the middle, and 4½-foot stalls along the sides. The capacity of each structure was about sixty horses. There was also a picket quartermaster's corral, 170 by 200 feet, located in the northeastern corner of the fort. It had roofed stalls capable of accommodating one hundred horses. Like the other picket structures at Richardson, the corral and stables deteriorated rapidly. In 1875, an inspector reported that he feared "their falling down under the influence of any bad storm." Although repairs were attempted, by 1877 all the structures were roofless and unserviceable.[19]

The western side of the parade ground was occupied by the post hospital, the finest structure at Fort Richardson and one of the finest military hospitals of its time in the Southwest. Many post hospitals of this period were collections of tents or rude picket structures that promised an enlisted man no more comfort than his barracks. But the hospital at Fort Richardson proved to be such an excellent facility that the shirkers and malingerers among the enlisted men would seize upon any opportunity to gain admittance to its wards.[20]

The hospital was built according to an 1867 plan furnished by the Surgeon General's Office.[21] It was first occupied on September 4, 1868, but major construction continued for another two

Post Hospital, Fort Richardson, ca. 1872. This photo was glued into the Medical History of Fort Richardson maintained by the post surgeon. (National Archives)

Sketch and diagram of post hospital (from Medical History of Fort Richardson, National Archives)

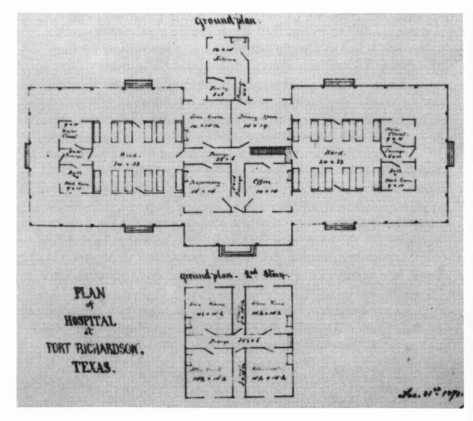

years. The building was made of native stone and has been described by latter-day artists as an example of "impeccable rock work."[22] Cottonwood lumber was used throughout, except for the doors, window sashes, and ceiling boards, which were sent from the San Antonio quartermaster's depot. Facing east, the hospital consisted of a two-story main building, thirty-three by thirty-five feet, with two wings, forty-four by twenty-four feet, on either side. A veranda twelve feet wide ran around the entire structure.[23]

The lower part of the main building was intended to be used as the medical officer's office, a dispensary, a room for the hospital steward, and a dining room, all fourteen by fourteen feet, with a twelve-by-fourteen-foot kitchen and six-by-eight pantry. Each room had a fireplace and one or more windows for ventilation. The office also housed the medical library, which consisted of about two hundred volumes of medical texts, government circulars, and issues of the *London Lancet*. The upper story was intended as a dead room and more storerooms, but the narrow and steep stairs (2 feet 8 inches wide and built at a 45-degree angle) and the hot climate made it necessary to move the morgue to a picket and canvas structure in the rear of the hospital. In the summer of 1875, this was replaced with a stone morgue, fifteen by eighteen feet, located some forty feet behind the main building.[24]

The two wings contained the patient wards, each thirty-three by twenty-four feet and furnished with twelve iron bedsteads, twelve side tables and chairs, and one large table. Each ward was heated by one wood-burning stove and ventilated by two windows and a door front and back and had a washroom and a privy located at one end. The washroom contained a bathtub and wash basins, while the privy had airtight closet stools. Two "sinks" were located one hundred feet in the rear of the hospital, one for the medical officers, the other for the ambulatory patients.[25]

The wood used in the hospital's construction began to deteriorate almost immediately. The roof was reported leaking as early as 1870 and required extensive repairs in October of that year. In 1872, the new post surgeon reported that the hospital was in very bad condition, with warped floors and door facings, and needed immediate attention. Again, in 1873 and in 1875, repairs to the roof,

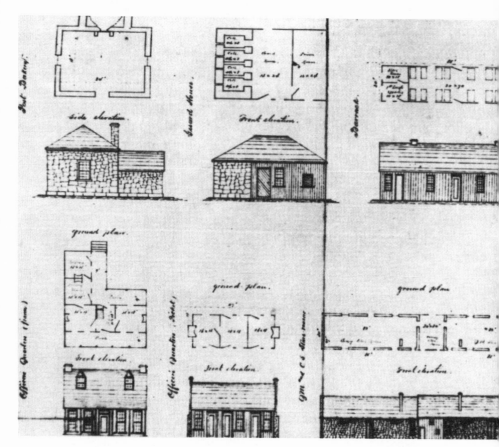

Sketches and diagrams of post bakery, guard house, barracks, officers' quarters, and quartermaster's commissary, ca. 1870 (from Medical History of Fort Richardson, National Archives)

floors, windows, and doors were necessary. In 1877, the post surgeon reported that the roof leaked so badly that the wards could not be used during rainy weather, but, as the garrison had shrunk considerably by then and the post was soon to be abandoned, no further repairs were undertaken.[26]

Extending in a northerly line from the hospital were the post bakery, guardhouse, and magazine. The bakery was a stone structure, twenty-six by twenty-six feet, with a stone floor, shingle roof, and two windows. Built into the back wall was a fourteen-by-fourteen-foot brick oven which was capable of turning out four hundred

36

loaves of bread every twelve hours. The guardhouse consisted of a central picket guard room, thirteen by twenty-four feet, with a twelve-by-twenty-four-foot picket prison room on the right, and four 4½-by-8-foot stone cells on the left. Heat for the entire structure was furnished by one wood-burning stove in the center of the guard room. Ventilation for the cells was provided by a twelve-by-eighteen-inch grated opening in the outside wall, while the prison room was unventilated. Sanitary facilities consisted of an open tub in the prison room and a bucket for each cell. Finally, in the northwestern corner of the fort, two hundred feet beyond the guardhouse, was the magazine, a stone structure eighteen by sixteen feet with double walls each eighteen inches thick. Small offset windows provided ventilation. The magazine's stone vault roof was covered with cement, tar, and gravel which effectively rendered it fireproof. Another temporary picket magazine, used when Richardson's garrison occasionally expanded, was located between the guardhouse and bakery.[27]

Located behind the magazine, scattered along the banks of Lost Creek, were the quarters of the married soldiers and the laundresses. These consisted of log huts, picket and frame shanties, and tents, collectively called "Sudsville" in army parlance, over which a general aura of squalor prevailed. The size of Sudsville expanded and decreased along with the garrison. For example, in 1870, with an average of about 275 officers and men present at Fort Richardson, there were nineteen soldiers' wives, twenty-one children, and twenty-five hired servants living in Sudsville. Near Sudsville there was a segregated colony of negro women, many of whom were prostitutes working out of nearby brothels or out of their shanties.[28]

Lost Creek, the main source of water for Fort Richardson, ran along the fort's western edge behind the post hospital. An early problem of the post arose because water used for cooking was taken from the creek downstream from Sudsville and was often polluted. Due to the extreme slope of the land to the creek (which created excellent drainage for the fort) the relatively level area of Sudsville was the only place a team could be easily maneuvered to the water's edge to draw off water for hauling to the fort. A board of officers investigated the problem, and Sudsville was ordered removed to a point downstream.[29]

Drinking water came from several area springs, two of which were located on the east bank of Lost Creek, behind the hospital. The spring water was described as being "remarkably sweet and free from organic impurities" and in constant supply. A 500-gallon wagon carried drinking water to the post from these springs, and each cavalry company had a small water cart to fetch water for its animals.[30]

The army had abandoned Buffalo Springs because the local water supply failed. The troops had returned to Jacksboro, more than for any other single reason, because of Lost Creek. It was generally shallow and fast-running, and although the flow of water diminished in the dry season, there was always enough available in the numerous deep holes for culinary purposes. These pools, some of which were said to be "bottomless," supposedly gave the creek its name. They also furnished the only bathing facilities at Fort Richardson, aside from the tubs in the hospital, and it was not uncommon, at the end of a hot summer day, for officers and men to doff their clothing and dive into one of the inviting pools. The nineteenth-century artist M. K. Kellogg, during a visit to Fort Richardson, wrote: "The deep water of the creek gives good bathing places under the dense shade of its bushy banks. Soldiers from the fort are now amusing themselves in it and our men will soon replace them. Turtles float about in quiet pools."[31]

A two-acre area along the creek just below the original location of Sudsville was cultivated as the post garden. Here two enlisted men, using seed and tools purchased from the commissary officer with money from the post fund, cultivated sweet potatoes, lima beans, beets, tomatoes, and lettuce. Army rations generally consisted of beef, hardtack, baked beans, bacon, and, very infrequently, vegetables. This garden provided most of the vegetables which the army rations did not furnish. But lack of rainfall made the country around Richardson unfavorable for agriculture, and the garden often failed. At these times details were sent to Weatherford, which had the nearest open market, for the express purpose of buying vegetables.[32]

38

	BREAKFAST	DINNER	SUPPER
Sun.	beef & pork, coffee, bread	roast beef, gravy, baked potatoes	coffee, bread
Mon.	beef, bread, coffee	roast beef, turnips, bread	coffee, bread
Tues.	roast beef, coffee, bread	roast beef, baked potatoes, bean soup	roast beef, served cold, bread, coffee
Wed.	beef, bread, coffee	roast beef, baked potatoes, bread	roast beef, served cold, bread, coffee
Thur.	beef, bread, coffee	roast beef, baked potatoes, bread, bean soup	coffee, bread
Fri.	beef, bread, coffee	roast beef, baked potatoes, bread	coffee, bread, potatoes
Sat.	beef, bread, coffee	roast beef, bean soup, bread	bread, coffee

From Post Medical History, October 1877, A. A. Yeomans, post surgeon. "Beef," means *boiled beef*, as opposed to roast beef. "Bread" usually means hardtack in the morning (which can be soaked in one's coffee), and baked bread from the post bakery at dinner and supper.

The construction work at Richardson was accomplished by civilian laborers and fatigue details of soldiers. For their labor, the soldiers received forty cents a day in addition to their salary. The various civilian masons, carpenters, plasterers, and laborers were contracted by the post quartermaster beginning in June 1868 and were dismissed in September 1869. During this time, the government spent approximately $83,000 for their services. A typical list

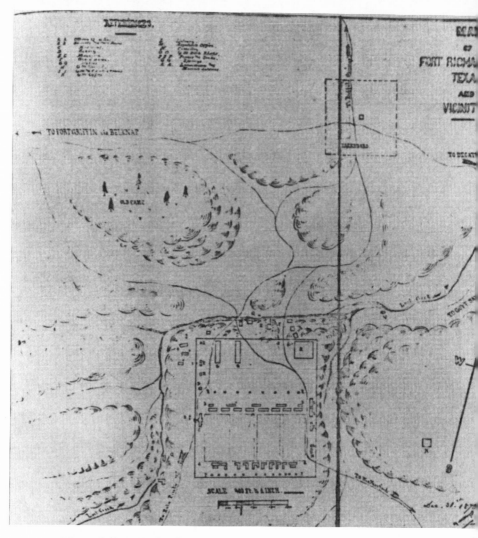

Map of Fort Richardson in 1870, from "Circular No. 4" (National Archives)

of civilians employed at the post and their salaries is this one of September 1868:

2	Clerks	@ $150 & $125	$ 275
1	Agent	@ $150	$ 150
46	Mechanics	@ (2–$150) $75	$3,600
1	Wagon Master	@ $75	$ 75
3	Asst. Wagon Masters	@ $45	$ 135
58	Laborers	@ $40	$2,320
40	Teamsters	@ $40	$1,600
151	Employed		$8,155[33]

The total cost of building Fort Richardson—including the cost of cutting the timber, hauling it to and from the government-operated sawmill on Big Sandy Creek in Wise County, some thirty-eight miles away, quarrying stone, bringing these materials together to construct the various buildings, and paying the salaries of the workmen—is not known, but it may have run as high as $800,000.[34]

Construction of the new fort had a marked effect on nearby Jacksboro. Almost overnight, the sleepy little hamlet was transformed into a bustling frontier town, with an estimated population of 650 in 1871.[35] Settlers flocked back to Jack County, their hopes of making a life on the frontier renewed by the presence of the soldiers and their fort. The soldiers also drew another group to Jacksboro: the to-be-expected gamblers, saloonkeepers, and prostitutes.

For a few years, times in Jacksboro were truly red-hot. Twenty-seven saloons ministered to the needs of the soldiers and townspeople, and "drunken men used to shoot up the town about every night, and sometimes during the day." All along the half-mile from the town square to the fort, tents, picket shanties, and log houses sprang up sporting such names as Union Headquarters, Gem, Little Shamrock, Emerald, Sunflower, Island Home, First National, Last Chance, Coffee House, and Mollie McCabe's Palace of Beautiful Sin.[36]

Business was brisk almost every night, but on those evenings following the visits of the army paymaster, Jacksboro truly boomed. Keno and roulette tables offered their slim chances of instant wealth, and numerous "damsels of spotted virtue" offered their particular charms. Even such legendary gamblers as Doc Holliday and Lottie Deno made regular visits to Jacksboro to help lighten the pockets of the suddenly affluent soldiers. Sergeant McConnell estimated that after the paymaster disbursed from four thousand to six thousand dollars to each company at the post, the leading saloons in town would take in as much as a thousand dollars a night.[37] Henry Strong, a civilian scout for the army, wrote that the owners of the Wichita Saloon, which was located on the town square, told him that just before the Sixth Cavalry departed for Kansas, their establishment took in over ten thousand dollars in a single night. Strong reported, "Drinks were twenty-five cents straight and it took three men to wait on the bar and then the customers could not be served as fast as they came."[38] The results of such dissipations were all too predictable. According to McConnell, "At early dawn the road to the post would be strewn with the forms of belated soldiers who 'fell where they fought,' and who perchance had opportunity afforded them to spend a few days in the solitude of the guard-house, reflecting on the uncertainties and vicissitudes of human affairs." Long-time Jacksboro resident Thomas F. Horton, who was a youngster during this period, left his own graphic description of what he called the "payday orgy": "I am not exaggerating when I say I have seen the time when I could have walked on soldier[s] lying drunk along the road from the south side of the Square to the creek and not touch the ground."[39]

It would be a mistake to think of the contributions of Richardson to Jacksboro and North Texas only in military terms. Because of the fort, Jacksboro became, for a time, one of the major centers of trade in North Texas. Two or three times a year contractors from all across the state would gather in town to bid on lucrative government contracts to supply the post with commodities such as hay, corn, flour, and beef. Periodically the army would sell off surplus materials such as clothing, horses, weapons, and wagons at public

Wichita Hotel, ca. 1870, where once $10,000 was spent on entertainment in a single night (Russell Jones Collection)

auctions which would attract hundreds of settlers from all over the Texas frontier. Many of these people stayed in the local hotels, and most drank down some of the local whiskey, and all left at least some of their money with the local inhabitants. Sergeant McConnell, who later returned to Jacksboro to live and become its second mayor, perhaps put the presence of the fort best in perspective when he noted that from 1868 to 1873 Richardson brought five hundred thousand dollars per annum into the pockets of the people. If for no other reason than this, it must be said that Fort Richardson and her troopers were a potent factor in the settlement of Northwest Texas.[40]

Colonel James Oakes, Sixth Cavalry. Courtesy Special Collections of the
University of Texas at Arlington Libraries, Arlington, Texas.

FROM JANUARY 21, 1868, to April 20, 1871, Fort Richardson served as headquarters for the Sixth Regiment, United States Cavalry. Being mostly a mixture of raw Irish, German, and Anglo-American recruits, inexperienced in Indian warfare and, on the whole, indifferently led, the Sixth proved to be an inefficient frontier fighting

The Sixth Cavalry at Fort Richardson, 1868–1870

force.[1] During thirty-nine months that the Sixth Cavalry called Richardson home, twenty-six full-scale Indian scouts were dispatched from the post, in parties ranging in size from one officer and ten enlisted men to two full companies. Of these twenty-six scouts, only five actually encountered hostile Indians, resulting in the deaths of three troopers and an estimated seventeen Indians[2]— a less than impressive record in a period when Indian raiders were active even around Jacksboro itself.

Rather than fighting Indians, the men of the Sixth spent the majority of their time aiding the local civil authorities in their various peacekeeping and Reconstruction duties, pursuing criminals, escorting wagon trains and cattle herds, constructing and maintaining the buildings at Fort Richardson, and, in ever-greater numbers, deserting. In 1868, fifty-one men deserted, and only seven were apprehended. The next year, thirty-three men deserted; only nine were caught. Finally, in 1870, a grand total of eighty-four men left the ranks without permission, and only twenty-one were apprehended, despite the army's offer of a thirty dollar reward for the arrest of each deserter.[3]

Fort Richardson's location afforded an almost infinite number of directions in which fugitives could flee. One hard day's ride to the southeast lay the settlements, where deserters could not be trailed. To the north lay Indian Territory, to the west empty frontier, and far away to the east Arkansas and Louisiana. In no direction was there a great chance of being arrested. In addition, the lack of adequate mounts and the incessant demands on the cavalry usually precluded genuine efforts to capture deserters. And, of course, once they deserted, desperation spurred the fugitives on, for they knew that if apprehended, they would most likely be incarcerated in the federal military prison at Baton Rouge, Louisiana.

Behind they left a hard life that promised few rewards and delivered a great deal of work. For instance, in 1869 the average daily schedule for a trooper at Richardson was:

Reveille	5:15
Assembly	5:30
Stable Call	Immediately after
Surgeon's Call	6:30
Breakfast	7:00
General Fatigue Call	8:30
General Mount	9:00
Battery Drill	9:30
Recall	10:30
First Serg. & Water Call	12:00
Dinner Call	1:00
Fatigue Call	1:30
Stable	4:00
Recall	4:30
First Call for Dress Parade	5:30
To Arms	6:00
Tattoo	8:00
Taps	8:15[4]

46

The commander of the Department of Texas, Major General J. J. Reynolds, recognized the growing problem and reported that "desertions are caused by varied calls made upon soldiers for labor in getting out lumber, quarrying stone, making adobe, running saw mills, burning brick and lime, driving wagons, which are not within their enlistments when they sign-up."[5] In other words, the troops had joined the army to fight but instead were spending their time in manual labor which could be accomplished just as well by civil contract. It is probably closer to the truth to say that the low pay, the tedious work, the hard, long hours on scout, the occasional dangers from Indian attacks, and the less-than-enthusiastic acceptance of the army's presence by some unreconstructed ex-Confederates in the community all combined to produce such a state of frustration and low morale that, to many soldiers, desertion seemed the only recourse.

In April 1869, Colonel (Brevet Brigadier General) James Oakes replaced Major Starr as commanding officer of Fort Richardson and as regimental commander of the Sixth Cavalry. Major Starr retired the next year, after almost thirty years of service.[6] Colonel Oakes, an 1842 graduate of the United States Military Academy, had fought with distinction in the Mexican War and had served on the pre-1860s Texas frontier. Although he saw action in the battles of Shiloh and Corinth, he spent most of the Civil War recruiting soldiers for the Union Army.[7] This change in command did not improve the efficiency or effectiveness of the Sixth Cavalry. Indeed, when Colonel Oakes took charge of the regiment, he found only three companies at Richardson and the remainder spread over the interior of the state. The next month the garrison totaled two companies of only sixty-nine men. Oakes complained to General Reynolds that "after the ordinary details for civil and detached service are made, the morning report shows six privates for duty."[8]

On May 24, 1869, a party of Indians stole several horses from a house only two miles outside of Jacksboro. The only response Oakes could make was to send a scout made up of one second lieutenant and a citizen company of one captain and thirteen enrolled men.[9] The people of North Texas were astounded and appalled that only two companies of cavalry should be deemed sufficient to guard their tormented frontier during the Indians' main raiding season, and they lost no time in expressing their outrage. In a memorial to Congress they protested that "the small amount of soldiers sent upon the frontier of Texas is wholly insufficient to afford protection to the country." And in a petition to the Secretary of War, the settlers charged that the commander at Fort Richardson was "indifferent to the suffering of the people." While defending himself against the citizens' accusations, Colonel Oakes had to admit that "up to this time the duties of the Cavalry have been almost entirely of a civil nature." It appeared to most observers that, for the present time anyway, the radical state government was more concerned with "reconstructing" ex-Rebels and enrolling freedmen than with protecting the frontier. And, indeed, in his annual report for 1868, General Reynolds wrote that "the bold, wholesale murdering in the interior of the State seems at present to present a more urgent demand for troops than Indian depredations."[10]

In spite of General Reynolds's opinion (expressed from the relative safety of his offices in San Antonio), Indian raids *were* growing worse, in both frequency and ferocity. Relations between the United States and the Southern Plains Indians had deteriorated steadily since the early 1850s, when the Kiowas, Comanches, and Kiowa-Apaches were forced northward and westward into the Texas Panhandle and western Indian Territory by the ever-increasing pressure of white civilization. The Civil War had eased that pressure somewhat, but the wholesale massacre of an entire Cheyenne village at Sand Creek, Colorado, by Colonel John Chivington and a thousand state militia on November 29, 1864, had enraged the Indians and horrified the collective conscience of eastern America.[11]

Easterners, far removed from the frontier, had a tendency to view the Plains Indian as the much maligned and wronged "Noble Red Man" of James Fenimore Cooper's novels. After the Sand Creek atrocity, a wave of public sentiment swept the East, spearheaded by the Quakers who had taken it upon themselves to civilize the savages. Accordingly, the politicians in Washington deemed it advisable to extend the olive branch rather than the sword to the tribes.

The Treaty of the Little Arkansas was signed in October 1865 by the Kiowas, Comanches, and Kiowa-Apaches. The Indians agreed, although with much grumbling and many misgivings, to accept a reservation composed of the Panhandle of Texas and all of Indian Territory west of ninety-eight degrees of west longitude, plus regular ration issues and peaceful arbitration of disputes. Signing for the Kiowas were Dohason, Lone Wolf, Satank, and Kicking Bird.[12] To make certain the Indians stayed on their new reservation, General William Tecumseh Sherman, commanding general of the Military Division of the Missouri, hit upon the idea of ringing the great reservation with forts. In the white man's eye, the reservation became a reserve. In the Indian's eye, it became a prison, and the newly established Fort Richardson became one of the prime guardposts.

After the Treaty of the Little Arkansas, several events boded ill for the future. In the summer of 1867, Dohason (Little Mountain), the great chief of the Kiowas and a true seeker of peace, died. Although he had favored peace, he deeply resented his people's being forced onto a reservation. Another chief, Little Wolf, tried to fill the void left by Dohason's death, but he could never command the respect that the old leader had. Consequently, subchiefs such as Satanta, Quitan, and Stumbling Bear tended to go their own way, which meant back to raiding.

Besides the untimely death of Dohason, other factors combined to wreck the Little Arkansas Treaty. Texas refused to relinquish dominion over her lands so the great reservation could be created. As the railroads continued to push toward the Pacific, bringing more and more white men, the game began to disappear and the Indians could see their way of life fading. Finally, the quality of the rations issued to the Indians proved unsatisfactory. The Southern Plains Indians resumed their war upon the Texans. When called to account for their renewed hostilities, the chiefs blandly stated that the military officials of the United States had told them to go on raiding because Texas was at war with the Union. Thus the Kiowas were keeping their treaty with the United States by only warring on their neighbors to the south. The concept of secession and reunification apparently escaped the tribes, although some contemporaries believed that the Indians knew perfectly well the Civil War was over and were pleading ignorance as an excuse for their raids.[13]

The dissatisfaction of the Southern Plains Indians resulted in the Treaty of Medicine Lodge. On October 21, 1867, the Kiowas, Comanches, and Kiowa-Apaches agreed to refrain from attacks on the whites and to cease opposition to the building of railroads and military posts in the Southwest. The Indians accepted a far smaller reservation than the one offered in the Treaty of the Little Arkansas. It embraced the area from the ninety-eighth meridian west to the North Fork of the Red River, north to the Washita and south to the Red River, some 4,800 square miles. To obtain this land, the Indians had to give up their claims to 60,000 square miles of territory that had been theirs, but they were promised that no white settlers would be allowed on their reservation and that they would receive rations and presents in the amount of $25,000 a year for thirty years. Schools to educate the Indian children were to be established. Finally, the Indians could range off the reservation in pursuit of the buffalo herds, but they could not take up permanent residence outside its borders.[14]

The flaws of this treaty, like those of the Treaty of the Little Arkansas, readily became apparent. The off-reservation hunting clause proved objectionable to many whites who believed Indian war parties would use it as an excuse to leave their territory unhampered. White incursions into Indian Territory also continued. The railroads kept advancing over the plains and game grew scarcer. Congress dealt the treaty its greatest blow by not ratifying it immediately, thereby blocking the necessary money for removing the Indians to the reservation. Finally, not all the Comanches had attended Medicine Lodge. The implacable Kwahadis spurned the offers of peace and remained in their camps on the Staked Plains, still at war with the whites, and their taunts caused many Kiowas to join them.

On November 27, 1868, Lieutenant Colonel George A. Custer and the Seventh Cavalry, in an effort to force the Indians onto the reservation, attacked the Cheyenne camp of Black Kettle on the

Washita River and killed 103 men, women, and children. The camps of the Arapahoes, Kiowas, Comanches, and Apaches were located a few miles just below Black Kettle's camp, and these tribes quickly fled. When Custer seized Satanta and Lone Wolf and threatened to hang them if the tribes did not report to Fort Cobb, the tribes surrendered as directed. Though set free, the chiefs and their people never forgot their treatment at the hands of white soldiers.[15]

Thus it was that the Kiowas, ridiculed by the Kwahadis, insulted by the soldiers, made prisoners on a small reservation, and seemingly in danger of losing their manhood by being reduced to farming, resumed their raiding in Texas on a full scale, prompting Major General John Pope, the military commander of the Department of the Missouri, to write, "The Kiowas have been altogether the worst Indians we have had to deal with. They are . . . the most faithless, cruel, and unreliable of all the Indians of the Plains."[16] The Kwahadis, bent chiefly on taking horses and cattle, were also seemingly unstoppable. The Kiowa and Comanche bands that had remained off the reservation struck over a wide area, penetrating far into the settlements. In July 1869, a band of Indians ravaged the country around Mary's Creek, near Weatherford, killing and scalping four persons and running off cattle. A posse of citizens finally forced them to retire. In September, a band of Comanches rounded up more than one hundred horses near Jacksboro. When surprised by the ranchers, the Indians chased them to within a mile of the town and then executed a leisurely escape unmolested by the troopers of Fort Richardson.[17]

One of the men most distressed by these raids was Lawrie Tatum, the new Quaker Indian Agent for the Kiowas, Comanches, and Kiowa-Apaches. This gentle, peace-loving man had arrived in July 1869 with high hopes of "civilizing" the Indians with kindness and understanding, buoyed by his predecessor's report that the "Kiowas, Comanches, and Apaches are now upon their reservation . . . and have . . . conducted themselves quite peacefully." These hopes were quickly dashed. In Tatum's first meeting with his charges, a prominent chief calmly informed him that if "Washington did not want his young men to raid in Texas, then Washington must move Texas far away, where his young men could not find it." In the years to come, Tatum tried everything in his power to stop his charges from raiding, but eventually he was forced to admit that the Indians he had been sent to supervise were beyond his control and that military action was the only solution. This departure from the established Quaker policy of nonviolence repeatedly brought Tatum into conflict with the Executive Committee of the Society of Friends and eventually caused him to resign.[18]

Another man who was distressed by these raids was Major General Reynolds. In his annual report for 1869 he conceded that "Indian raids during the year have been unusually bold, [with] heavy losses in livestock and property."[19] It was apparent to Reynolds that as the number of settlers in North Central Texas grew and the frequency of Indian raids in the area increased, the demands upon the soldiers of Richardson could only multiply. At his recommendation, the army responded during the winter of 1869–1870 by increasing the size of the garrison. By the summer of 1870, Richardson was the largest post in Texas, staffed with eleven companies totalling over five hundred officers and men.[20]

Since Richardson was designed as a cavalry post and only mounted soldiers were thought to be effective against the highly mobile Kiowas and Comanches, most of the companies stationed at the post belonged to the Sixth Cavalry. However, at this time and for most of Richardson's history, some infantry units were also present. From May to September 1868 Company D of the Seventeenth Infantry played a major role in the construction of the fort. It was replaced by Company I, Twenty-fourth Infantry (a black regiment), which was relieved by Company K, Eleventh Infantry in August 1870. Eventually Richardson became the headquarters of the Eleventh Infantry until that regiment departed Texas in November 1876 for service with General Alfred Terry against the Sioux in the Dakota Territory.[21] Prevailing army doctrine preached that infantry detachments in the West were most useful in support roles, taking over the daily chores of the post and freeing the cavalry units for scouts and mounted escort duties. But, as is so often the case, a

Lawrie Tatum, Fort Sill Indian Agent, with Mexican captives ransomed from the Kiowas and Comanches. His charges called him "Bald-head" Tatum, for obvious reasons. (Fort Sill Museum)

wide gap existed between official doctrine and reality. In truth, at least one-quarter and often one-half of the cavalry stationed at Richardson might just as well have been called infantry, for the same problem that had existed at "the post of Jacksboro" and at Buffalo Springs continued at Richardson: there were not enough horses to mount the entire regiment, and those available were described by the commanding officer as "miserable."[22] This glaring inadequacy in the army's supply system continued long after the Sixth left Texas for the plains of Kansas. More often than not, the cavalry troopers who should have been scouring the countryside for hostile Indians or galloping off in hot pursuit of depredators found themselves taking places alongside the infantry digging latrines or repairing stables, bearing out Sergeant McConnell's incisive appraisal of them as "armed laborers, nothing less, nothing more."

Despite these problems, the soldiers of Richardson were charged with the protection of hundreds of square miles of North Central Texas, and they soon got the chance to prove their mettle. In early 1870 many of the agency Indians left the reservation to hunt buffalo. In June the great Kiowa Sun Dance on the North Fork of the Red River was well attended by the Comanches and Kiowa-Apaches, many of whom decided to remain out on the plains, never to return to the hated reservation. They pledged war upon the whites, and the results in Jack County alone were disastrous.

Late in May a force of twenty enlisted men under Lieutenant Sumner H. Bodfish departed Richardson for scouting purposes. They were accompanied by a Professor Roessler from the Geological Survey of the Department of the Interior and five other citizens who were to explore the country. On May 30, the expedition was attacked near Holliday Creek in Archer County by about forty Kiowas who killed two of the citizens, Ben Dawdrick and Joseph Taylor, and one soldier, Private Harry Kennare. The Indians were thwarted in what appeared to be their main objective, the capture of the patrol's wagons and mules. The attackers were finally beaten off, and the exhausted troopers and the stunned civilians staggered back to Fort Richardson.[23]

In all, as many as fifteen Jack County residents died at the hands of Indian raiders in June, despite the efforts of seven full-scale scouts from Richardson.[24] The post adjutant reported that "these scouts have been rendered necessary by the increasing boldness manifested by the Indians in their late depredations and acts of violence near this post."[25]

Early the next month, a war party of over one hundred warriors crossed the Red River into Texas. This was the largest such party to enter the state since the great raid of 1867 which had laid siege to Fort Buffalo Springs. Leading them was the Kiowa chief Tene-angopte, or Kicking Bird. A signee of both the Treaty of the

Little Arkansas and the Treaty of Medicine Lodge, Kicking Bird had long been distinguished by his eloquence, bravery, military ability, and good sense, and by his friendship for the white man. But this amity forced him into leading a war party after members of his tribe accused him of consorting far too much with the whites and of talking too much of peace with them. They implied that the whites had made him a coward. Some called him a woman, and his councils were ignored. Determined to restore his influence and prestige, Kicking Bird organized this raid,[26] with his cousin Stumbling Bear and two of his severest critics, Lone Wolf and Satank, among the more significant members. In their councils the warriors decided to move against the nearest white soldiers, and on July 5, Kicking Bird hurled the gauntlet at Fort Richardson.

No warrior was supposed to leave the war party to steal, but shortly after entering Texas several braves robbed a mail stage at Rock Station on the Salt Creek Prairie, sixteen miles from Richardson.[27] This, in effect, delivered the challenge. Smarting from the defeat Lieutenant Bodfish had suffered the previous month, the Sixth Cavalry responded quickly. Ordered to "pursue and severely chastise the Indians"[28] responsible, Lieutenants C. H. Campbell and H. P. Perrine, acting army surgeon G. W. Hatch, post guide James Doshier, and fifty-three men of Companies A, B, D, H, K, and L moved out on July 6 under command of Captain Curwin B. McClellan.[29] McClellan, born in Scotland, was a career soldier who had enlisted as a private in 1849. He had been with the Sixth Cavalry since 1859, had won commendations for his bravery in action at Williamsburg and Gettysburg, and had been promoted to major, only to be reduced in rank as so many fellow officers were after the end of the war. He was, in every respect, an admirable opponent for Kicking Bird.[30]

McClellan marched to Rock Station and picked up the trail of eight to ten braves. He followed northward, slowed considerably by a severe rainstorm which washed away all vestiges of the trail. Giving up hope of overtaking so small a party of depredators, McClellan could not know that this was one group of Indians who had no intention of fleeing across the Red River. The captain proceeded to Flint Creek, about twenty-two miles from Richardson, where he found Lieutenant James H. Sands and Company F patrolling in the area. On July 8 McClellan discovered Indian signs at the water holes on Mesquite Prairie, sixteen miles north of Salt Creek. The next day he crossed the headwaters of the North Fork of the Trinity and discovered the trail of five or six Indians. At the South Fork of the Little Wichita, McClellan found the mail driver's stolen whip. These scattered signs lured the column farther north over the Middle Fork of the Little Wichita and into camp on the banks of the North Fork, where storms forced them to remain encamped until the morning of July 12.[31]

Around 10:00 A.M., McClellan's advance guard located what they thought to be Kicking Bird's main war party after traveling only five miles from their camp. The troopers formed ranks, unfurled the flag and regimental guidons, drew sabres, and moved forward at a trot. After covering about one-half mile, McClellan sighted the Indian band one thousand yards ahead. The Indians were arrayed in their finery, both horses and riders lavishly painted and decorated. McClellan had advanced five hundred yards toward them when two other bands of equal strength appeared on his flanks. The group on his left threatened to cut off his pack train and rear guard which had fallen some four hundred yards behind. McClellan halted and opened fire.

Kicking Bird watched McClellan's deployment coolly, his braves excited and nervous. The word was given, and away they flashed, racing over the prairie with bells tinkling and feathers streaming, each of the warriors delighted to engage in the one act that gave their lives meaning and purpose. Years later, Indian informants would claim that Kicking Bird personally led the first charge and claimed first coup by sweeping past the front ranks of the troopers and impaling a soldier on his war lance. Such a dramatic incident surely would have been reported by McClellan, but he did not mention it in his report. Instead, he spoke of being subjected to such a galling fire from all sides that he became convinced the only way to save his command from total annihilation was to retreat. He dismounted his men and, with every fourth trooper holding the reins

56

Tene-angopte (Kicking Bird), Kiowa chief and leading advocate among his people of peace with the whites (National Archives)

of the mounts while the rest of the men fired from between the horses, began trying to effect an orderly withdrawal.[32]

For six hours under the broiling July sun, Kicking Bird drove the soldiers before him across the prairie. He directed a masterful action which struck at McClellan's men continuously from almost all sides. Kicking Bird kept three-fourths of his warriors engaged, maintaining the others in reserve, resting until they too would race across the prairie to hit the soldiers. Several times McClellan had to dislodge the Indians from commanding positions in his line of retreat.[33]

The prairie gave way to marshy and broken ground as the troopers neared the Middle Fork of the Little Wichita River. McClellan and his harried command forded the river at 3:00 P.M. under a heavy fire from the Indians. At 4:00 P.M. the cavalry crossed the South Fork of the Little Wichita, again under a galling fire. Toward nightfall, Kicking Bird broke off the action, his honor and prestige amply restored. A small group of braves, not wishing to lose such sport, continued to follow McClellan's command, which had crossed the West Fork of the Trinity and gone into camp at midnight about ten miles northwest of Flat Top Mountain. The die-hard warriors discovered the camp around eight the next morning and promptly drove in McClellan's pickets. The captain, thinking these braves to be the advance guard of the entire war party, promptly burned all his supplies which were not readily transportable and hastily began another forced retreat.[34] The Indians allowed McClellan and his mauled unit to return to Fort Richardson without further disturbance.

McClellan's losses were two men dead and twelve wounded, with eight horses killed and twenty-one wounded.[35] In his report of the action, McClellan claimed he was opposed by "not less than two hundred and fifty warriors, . . . all well mounted and armed with Spencer carbines, rifles and revolvers." He estimated Indian losses at "fifteen killed and a large number wounded." Considering the course of events of July 12 and 13, the closing remarks of the captain's report display an incredible amount of braggadocio. "I regard the expedition as a perfect success. I . . . fought them with my small command . . . and taught them a lesson they will not soon forget."[36]

"The Battle of the Little Washita River" by Nola Montgomery. Courtesy Texas Parks and Wildlife Department.

Dr. Julius Patzki, the post surgeon, interviewed several members of the command and afterwards paid the unknown leader of the Indians the compliment that McClellan could not: "The systematic strategy displayed by the savages, exhibiting an almost *civilized* mode of skirmish fighting, struck the officers and men engaged." [37] Fortunately for the army, Kicking Bird never led another war party. Expressing regret that he had been forced to fight the soldiers, he dedicated the rest of his life to the establishment of peaceful relations between his people and the whites. [38]

As for McClellan, he was praised for leadership which prevented his entire command from being wiped out. Thirteen of his men were awarded Medals of Honor for "Gallantry in Action at the North Fork of the Little Wichita." [39] When the Sixth Cavalry moved to Kansas in the spring of the next year, the Indians at Fort Sill recognized McClellan as the leader of the soldiers they had fought. They admitted that he had "killed *heap* many Indians" that day.[40]

In September, Colonel Oakes ordered Companies A, D, and G of the Sixth and Company K, Eleventh Infantry, under the command of Major R. M. Morris, to establish a temporary camp on the East Fork of the Little Wichita River, some ten miles northeast of Buffalo Springs. Named Camp Wichita, it was intended as a forward base of operations against those Indian raiders coming from the reservation who, Oakes believed, made up the major percentage of the depredators. Camp Wichita was also intended to silence some of the criticism being voiced by settlers about the inability of the soldiers of Richardson to protect the frontier. As Oakes wrote to the assistant adjutant general of the Department of Texas: "This is the best I can do for the country between the Red & Brazos Rivers during the grass season."[41]

The next month Captain William A. Rafferty and twenty men of Company M, with the post guide and five Tonkawa scouts, intercepted a raiding party near the North Fork of the Little Wichita, not far from where McClellan's fight had taken place. The Indians were returning from the settlements with a large herd of stolen horses. In a running fight over eight miles of open prairie, Rafferty and his men managed to kill two Indians, wound another, and recover eighteen of the stolen horses while suffering no casualties themselves. One of the dead Indians was Keech-quash, chief of the Kichais. A hunting pass from the reservation was found on his body, reinforcing the contention that most of the depredating Indians were coming from the reserve. For this engagement, five Medals of Honor were conferred upon the men of Rafferty's command.[42]

In November 1870, Captain Adna R. Chaffee and Lieutenant Henry M. Kendall, with twenty-five men of Company I, the post guide, and two Tonkawas, intercepted an Indian party about twenty miles north of Richardson. In a long chase over fifteen miles, the soldiers managed to recapture seven ponies.[43] These limited accomplishments were overshadowed, however, by other serious setbacks.

On January 24, 1871, four black men—Brit Johnson, Jack

Crawford, Tom Dockery, and Dennis Jordan—were hauling supplies from Weatherford across the Salt Creek Prairie to Johnson's ranch, fifteen miles south of Fort Griffin. Johnson was something of a local hero because of his efforts to recover captives from the Indians. Following the Elm Creek raid in 1864, he had trailed the raiders back to their camps and managed to recover his wife and two of his children, as well as three white prisoners. His courage and determination won him the respect of the frontier settlers. In an 1869 letter of introduction addressed to the commanding officer of Fort Cobb, Major Starr said of Johnson: "He is vouched for by some of the best citizens of this and adjoining counties. They say he can do more than any white man in this section of the country with the Indians."[44] While at Fort Cobb, Johnson met Special Indian Commissioner Vincent Calya, who was on an inspection tour of the reservations. Calya described the encounter in his official report: "A stout, vigorous, intelligent-looking negro came to headquarters one morning to see if he could get an interview with the Kiowas. Five years ago they had made a raid upon the settlement in Texas where this man and his family lived. The Kiowas carried off his wife, and a white woman and her two daughters. The white woman and one child, and the colored woman, were recovered; but one white child remained in captivity, and [Johnson] was now, five years after the raid, in search for her. He remained around the camp for a week or more without finding any trace of her. I gave him quarters in my tent, and tried in every way to prosper him on his errand; but . . . without success."[45]

Unfortunately, Johnson's exploits had earned him the enmity of several powerful chiefs, among them Maman-ti (Walking Above or Sky Walker), the Kiowa medicine man known as the Owl Prophet. At the same time Johnson was buying his supplies in Weatherford, Maman-ti was leading a large raiding party across the Red River, heading into the settlements by way of the Salt Creek Prairie. The next day when his scouts reported four black men traveling in a heavily laden wagon, Maman-ti gave the order to attack. Johnson and his companions must have realized they stood no chance of escape, so they killed their horses and used their bodies as barricades. The negroes put up such a hard fight that the ground around them was covered with empty shell casings, but all were killed and their bodies mutilated. Maman-ti rode north with Johnson's scalp dangling from his war lance.[46]

A scout from Richardson under the command of Lieutenant William A. Borthwick discovered the grisly scene and buried the bodies. The troopers then pursued the Indians northward, caught up with them, and were soundly defeated. Lieutenant Borthwick was wounded and the entire command was driven back to Richardson.[47]

The Salt Creek Prairie, between Forts Richardson and Griffin, had long been a favorite spot for the Indians to waylay travelers. The old Butterfield Stage trail, fairly well used, ran across the area. Indians striking due south from Fort Sill used the prairie as a passageway into and out of the settlements. The land was dotted with the graves of seventeen people killed by marauding Indians, to which four more had just been added. Oakes ordered a picket post to be erected on Salt Creek, about two miles west of the spot where Johnson and his companions were murdered. A 167-square-foot enclosure with a zigzag stake and rail fence surrounding it and a lookout post on top, it was manned by a sergeant and ten enlisted men.[48] The picket post, unfortunately, was inadequate to the problem.

Altogether, the spring of 1871 saw twelve persons killed by Indians in the vicinity of Fort Richardson.[49] The settlers' demands for more protection poured into Washington in an ever-increasing volume. William T. Sherman, who had recently been promoted to General of the Army, realized that something had to be done. The Sixth Cavalry, due to the ineptness of its officers or the inferiority of its troops or perhaps just to a lackadaisical attitude, was not protecting the frontier. It had received few accolades for its service, and most settlers would not be sorry to see it replaced. And, according to its historian, W. H. Carter, the regiment would not be sorry to go. He described the difficulties of the previous five years of service thus:

> Ordered direct from the scenes of the great civil conflict to the distant frontier to combat a savage foe unexcelled in ability, cunning and cruelty by any other tribes . . . the offi-

cers and men found themselves confronted with all the hatred and bitterness left by the Civil War. It was enough to
contend against the Indians, but when, by ill-treatment . . .
the men were finally made to recognize the contempt in
which the community held them, . . . there was not much
regret in the regiment when the headquarters and troops . . .
moved out . . . for the north.[50]

Sherman directed that the Sixth should be transferred to Kansas and superseded by a more vigorous unit. Furthermore, Sherman
had a very definite idea of just who should command the Sixth Cavalry's replacement: Ranald Slidell Mackenzie.

Consequently, on March 20, 1871, Colonel Oakes, his headquarters, and Companies E, G, H, I, K, and M of the Sixth Cavalry
moved out for Fort Harker, Kansas. The remaining four companies,
A, C, D, and L, two having joined the post from Fort Griffin,
marched for Kansas on April 20,[51] amid the good-byes of citizens
who had come to see them off. The regiment had been in or near
Jacksboro for five years, since the fort's inception, and some townspeople regretted the unit's departure because they had friends among
the troopers. Many shopkeepers also regretted the unit's departure
because the soldiers owed them a great deal of money.[52]

Time would validate General Sherman's decision to replace
the Sixth Cavalry. Its record up to 1871 casts doubt that this regiment could have subdued the hostile Indians in Northwest Texas.
Fort Richardson's days of glory would belong to another regiment
and its vigorous commander.

Colonel Ranald S. Mackenzie, Fourth Cavalry, ca. 1872 (National Archives)

ON APRIL 8, 1871, TWO companies of United States cavalry and their baggage train moved among the post oak and mesquite that encircled Fort Richardson far out on its western side. Their approach heralded a wind of change that would eventually bring defeat to the Indians and peace to the settlements.

The Fourth Cavalry and the Warren Wagon Train Raid, 1871

If a Kiowa or Comanche warrior, perhaps returning from a raid or scouting for a war party, had chanced to observe from hiding the troopers' movements, he probably would not have been impressed, for the Indians had learned not to fear the men of nearby Richardson. Nor would the slim erect officer riding near the head of the column have elicited any special notice from the warrior. Of course, it would have been impossible for the Kiowa to know that this particular man was soon to play a major role in destroying the Indians' way of life. The Indians would call him Mangomhente, meaning "no index finger" or "bad hand,"[1] because two of his fingers had been shot off during the Civil War. The whites knew him as Ranald Slidell Mackenzie.

Colonel Mackenzie has become a legend on the Texas frontier. Civil War hero and Indian fighter, he appears to have few equals in the annals of his day. His biographers have called him chivalrous, gallant, fair, loyal, and bold; and also impatient, impulsive, imperious, and impetuous.[2] But above all else, Mackenzie was competent. He would not allow himself to become a martyr nor a glory-seeking adventurer.

Mackenzie's meteoric rise in rank during the Civil War has few parallels in American military history. From his entrance into the army from the United States Military Academy in June 1862 until he was mustered out of the volunteer army in January 1866, Mackenzie suffered six wounds, was awarded seven brevets for gallantry, and rose to the rank of brigadier general, United States Volunteers.[3] During the war Mackenzie earned the respect and acclaim of Generals Grant, Meade, Sheridan, and Sherman. Grant personally requested that Mackenzie come to Appomattox to take charge of surrendered Confederate property and later wrote in his memoirs that Mackenzie was "the most promising young officer in the army."[4]

For three years after the war Mackenzie commanded a negro infantry regiment, the Forty-first (later to become the Twenty-fourth), along the Rio Grande. He turned the ex-slaves into a first-class fighting unit but was quick to recognize the handicaps of infantry in plains warfare.

On December 15, 1870, he was given command of the Fourth Cavalry, stationed at Fort Concho. When Mackenzie arrived at that post on February 25, 1871, he found the officers and men engaged in a life of hunting, fishing, and heavy drinking. All officers above lieutenant were Civil War veterans and had become discouraged over the unsuccessful policy of defensive reaction to Indian raids—intercepting war parties *after* they had committed some depredation—and this disgust and frustration was reflected in their attention to duties. They spent more time organizing expeditions to hunt buffalo, antelope, and turkey than on Indian scouts. Mackenzie had no patience with this. He intended that never again would the Fourth fall below any other regiment in efficiency. The hunting rifles were ordered cased and put away. From that moment the troopers would be hunting a far more dangerous quarry.

For the next month the Fourth worked from sunup to sundown on the basics of military drill. Under Mackenzie's watchful eye, the officers and men practiced, hardening themselves to long hours in the saddle. What Mackenzie wanted—indeed, demanded—was "results—things accomplished," and soon the troopers began to work together as a finely meshed unit.[5]

Then, on March 25, Mackenzie led companies A and E and

66

the regimental band out of Concho for the journey to Fort Richardson, a base of operations 230 miles nearer the reservation. The march took them through old Fort Chadbourne, Fort Phantom Hill, and Fort Griffin. On April 6, the column moved past old Fort Belknap and out onto the Salt Creek Prairie, where, as Second Lieutenant Robert G. Carter wrote, they "passed 'Dead Man's Cross' where four men had but recently been killed by Indians"[6]— the common grave of Brit Johnson and his companions. In all there were now twenty-one graves on the lonely stretches of Salt Creek Prairie, a fact which no doubt deeply impressed Mackenzie and his men.

Early on April 8, Colonel Mackenzie and his column rode into Fort Richardson, where they were welcomed by Major Abraham K. Arnold, the temporary post commander, Colonel Oakes having departed for Kansas some three weeks earlier. The enlisted men of the Fourth camped in tents outside the post, along Lost Creek. The bachelor officers gallantly offered their quarters to the ladies of the Fourth who spread mattresses upon "flea infested gunny sacks, or burlaps upon the warped floors of the pecan log huts."[7] Mackenzie was angered to find that the quarters and stables in the fort were not finished, although the deputy quartermaster had dismissed most of the workmen.[8]

On April 20, Major Arnold and the last four companies of the Sixth Cavalry left the post for Kansas, escorted by Company K, Eleventh Infantry, and fifty-five men of Company F, Fourth Cavalry.[9] The post was now home to the Fourth Cavalry and Company C, Eleventh Infantry.

The Indians quickly offered the new Richardson garrison an opportunity to prove themselves. On April 19, a man named John W. Weburn was killed and scalped on Salt Creek Prairie. The next evening a party of citizens was attacked within sight of the fort. The very next day another party of citizens was attacked and robbed of their horses just three miles from the post. First Lieutenant George A. Thurston in command of Company E set out after the Indians who had attacked the party of citizens on April 20, while Captain Wirt Davis with Company F pursued the Indians who had taken the horses on the twenty-first. Although both parties proved unsuccessful, each remained out for nine days and marched over two hundred miles searching for Indian trails.[10] Local citizens may not have been happy with the scouts' results, but no one could complain that vigorous action was not being taken. Conditions at Richardson had changed.

On May 2, 1871, General William T. Sherman, general-in-chief of the army, left San Antonio for a three-week inspection tour of the Texas frontier.[11] Four years earlier, Sherman had developed the idea of ringing the Indian Territory with forts from which the army could operate to intercept whatever raiding parties might be moving into or out of the settlements.[12] However, the pleas and petitions from Texans demanding help and protection from the reservation Indians had increased rather than decreased. Earlier, in 1868, the Society of Friends and other religious philanthropists had persuaded President Ulysses S. Grant to give them management of several Indian agencies, the Fort Sill Agency among them. Their idea, known as the Quaker peace policy, was to win the Indians by Christian acts rather than by force.[13] But Washington was deluged with cries for help from the Texans, who claimed that raiders from the Fort Sill Reservation had killed hundreds of settlers, stolen thousands of head of livestock, depopulated entire counties, and forced the line of settlement back over a hundred miles in places. If the Texans' reports were true then both Sherman's defensive plan and the Quaker peace policy were failures—prospects that Sherman and Grant and supporters of the Quakers did not wish to accept. Many well-meaning individuals, seeking other explanations for the continuing attacks, put the blame elsewhere. Quaker Indian agent J. N. Leavenworth wrote: "That wrongs of great magnitude have been committed on the people of Texas there is no doubt; but I do know other Indians, besides the Kiowas and Comanches, have been doing much of this wrong." And Professor N. B. Martin of Cooper Institute in New York told an audience of visiting Indian chiefs and eastern dignitaries that "Indian wars and disturbances come not out of the brutal savagery of the Indian, but out of the frauds and crimes of the depraved frontier population." Finally,

General of the Army William T. Sherman (National Archives)

however, in spite of the opinions of Agent Leavenworth and Professor Martin and many others like them, the volume of letters and protests could no longer be ignored. Sherman decided to visit the Texas frontier himself.[14]

Traveling with Sherman were Major General Randolph Barnes Marcy, the inspector-general of the army, Colonels John E. Tourtellotte and James C. McCoy of Sherman's staff, and seventeen black troopers of the Tenth Cavalry. Their itinerary was to take them to Forts Concho, Griffin, Belknap, Richardson, and finally Fort Sill. Most of the time they were to follow the Butterfield Stage trail, a route that General Marcy had laid out many years before. Sherman had come to Texas convinced that the settlers' entreaties were exaggerated, and by the midpoint of his trip, he had not changed his mind. He wrote to General J. J. Reynolds, commander of the Department of Texas:

> I have seen not a trace of an Indian thus far and only hear stories of people which indicate that whatever Indians there be, only come to Texas to steal horses . . . and the people within a hundred miles of the frontier ought to take precautions such as all people do against all sort of thieves . . . but up to this point the people manifest no fears or apprehensions, for they expose women and children singly on the road and in cabins far off from others, as though they were in Illinois.[15]

But Marcy, who had traveled and surveyed the country extensively, disagreed with Sherman. He confided to his journal that

> this rich and beautiful section does not contain today so many white people as it did when I visited it eighteen years ago, and if the Indian marauders are not punished, the whole country seems to be in a fair way of becoming depopulated.[16]

On May 14 the party reached Fort Griffin, overlooking the Clear Fork of the Brazos. Two days later, they reached the ruins of Fort Belknap, some thirty-five miles northeast and, around noon on May 17, moved out of the post oak and mesquite trees onto Salt

Creek Prairie. If Sherman knew about the twenty-one graves of Indian victims said to be located there, he apparently remained unconcerned, for he had refused an offer by the Fort Griffin post commandant to reinforce his small escort for the journey to Fort Richardson. There is a story, probably apocryphal, that halfway across the prairie, one of the negro soldiers jokingly called out "I see an Indian!" and everyone, including both Sherman and Marcy, laughed.[17]

Their amusement would have been short-lived had they known that two days earlier, on May 15, a large war party from the Fort Sill Reservation had crossed the Red River into Texas. They headed for that remote area halfway between Forts Griffin and Richardson, the place the whites called the Salt Creek Prairie.[18]

The Indians came to Texas partly in reaction to events in Washington. Just before Sherman's tour, the Commissioner of Indian Affairs had invited delegations from the Arapaho, Cheyenne, Comanche, and Kiowa tribes to visit Washington, D.C. The government hoped that the might and wealth of the United States would awe the tribesmen into peace, but the Kiowas and Comanches refused to make the trip. Rather, in order to show their contempt for Washington's gesture and to steal horses and mules which could be traded for guns, they launched a raid into Texas.[19] Over a hundred Kiowas, Comanches, Kiowa-Apaches, Arapahoes, and Cheyennes participated, but the four most prominent members of the war party were Kiowas: Satank, Satanta, Addo-etta, and Maman-ti, the Owl Prophet.[20]

Of these Indians, seventy-year-old Satank (Sitting Bear) was held in most awe by all Plains Indians. For decades he had been the leader of the Koitsenko military society,[21] the ten bravest warriors of the tribe, each pledged to death before dishonor. To most whites he was a paradox. Some portrayed him as an archvillain, a bloodthirsty savage. Lawrie Tatum, the Quaker Indian agent at Fort Sill, called him the worst Indian on the reservation.[22] Yet, of all the Indians at the Medicine Lodge Treaty negotiations in 1868, Satank was the

71

one who most impressed the commissioners.[23] He was described as:

> tall, only slightly stooped with age. . . . His face had a defi-
> nite mongolian cast, with almond eyes and high, sharp
> cheekbones. His nose was long and thin except where it
> flared at the nostrils, and he was wearing ornaments in his
> right ear. . . . streaks of gray marked his long, straight-
> hanging hair. His mustache was a dirty white.[24]

On October 24, after the Kiowas had signed their part of the treaty,
Satank rode to the peace commissioners' camp with a body of
horsemen to say good-byes. Leaving his retinue behind, the old
Kiowa dismounted and walked to meet the waiting commissioners,
leading his well-groomed pony. He gazed at each of the white men,
and then, in his only formal address of the conference, said in
Kiowa:

> You have heard much talk by our chiefs and no doubt
> are tired of it. Many of them have put themselves forward
> and filled you with sayings. I have kept back and said
> nothing.
>
> The white man grows jealous of his red brother. The
> white man once came to trade; he now comes as a soldier.
> He once put his trust in our friendship and wanted no shield
> but our fidelity. But now he builds forts and plants big guns
> on their walls. He once gave us arms and powder and bade
> us hunt the game. We then loved him for his confidence . . .
> he now covers his face with the cloud of jealousy and anger
> and tells us to be gone, as an offended master speaks to
> his dog.

Here Satank lowered his eyes and touched the silver medal which
hung from his neck and bore the likeness of President James
Buchanan. Continuing to hold the medal, Satank told the
commissioners:

> Look at this medal I wear. By wearing this, I have been
> made poor. Before, I was rich in horses and lodges. Today I
> am the poorest of all. When you gave me this silver medal
> on my neck, you made me poor.

We thank the Great Spirit that all these wrongs are now to cease. You have not tried, as many have done, to make a new bargain merely to get the advantage.

Do for us what is best. Teach us the road to travel. We know you will not forsake us; and tell your people also to act as you have done, to be as you have been.

I am old . . . I shall soon have to go the way of my fathers. But those who come after me will remember this day. . . . And now the time has come that I must go. You may never see me more, but remember Satank as the white man's friend.[25]

All the commissioners were deeply moved, and one reporter wrote that he had never known true eloquence before. Satank's, he reported, was the voice of nature and God.[26]

But Satank, "the white man's friend," had traveled an arduous road from Medicine Lodge. Neither whites nor Indians had faithfully maintained the treaty, and each blamed the other for its failure. The old Koitsenko saw the railroads come and the game grow scarce. But worst of all, his eldest son had been killed on a raid in Texas in 1870. Satank was inconsolable. He recovered his son's bones, wrapped them in a new blanket, and placed them on a raised platform inside a special teepee. From then on he thought only of vengeance and seized every opportunity to strike at the Texans.[27]

If Satank was the most respected of all Kiowas, Satanta (White Bear) was the most renowned. More has been written about him than any other member of his tribe, both during his life and in more recent times.[28] Very large for an Indian, Satanta possessed a huge leonine head, long flowing black hair, and a powerful body. On his war pony, his presence was commanding and impressive. Twenty years younger than Satank, he was said to be fond of whiskey, laughter and raiding, and of being the center of attention.[29] He had acquired an army bugle that became a permanent part of his dress, and he announced his arrivals and departures by playing his bugle.[30]

But the frontier settlers knew that Satanta was a great deal more than merely a court jester. They recognized him as a cunning, competent, physically powerful war chief who could be as savage and cruel as any Indian who ever sat on a horse. More than any-

Satank (Sitting Bear), Kiowa chief whom Lawrie Tatum called "the worst Indian on the reservation." Note the white sash, symbol of the leader of the Koitsenko military society. (National Archives)

Satanta (White Bear), "The Orator of the Plains" and most famous of all the Kiowas. Note the peace medal, probably from Medicine Lodge, and the ever-present bugle. (National Archives)

thing, Satanta was fond of power. His ambition had long been to become the principal chief of the Kiowas. Toward that end he had put himself forward on the warpath and around the council fires, and he quickly rose to the chieftainship of his band. He also became the civil chief of the Elks Division of the Kiowas and a senior war chief.[31] When the old prinicipal chief, Dohason, or Little Mountain, died in the summer of 1867, and the various factions among the Kiowas began debating over his successor,[32] Satanta was a leading candidate. In the fall of the next year, at Medicine Lodge, he was the first and most frequent speaker for the Indians. He stunned the commissioners with his insight, once closing a speech with the remark: "I have no little lies hid about me, but I do not know how it is with the commissioners."[33] The reporters covering the negotiations wrote that he was "very grand" and "a powerful speaker. . . . Even the commissioners could not help expressing their admiration at his magnificent figure. There is a . . . nobleness in him."[34] For his eloquence, the reporters dubbed him the "Orator of the Plains," although later writers would claim this was a tongue-in-cheek reference earned by his long, often boring, speeches.[35] When, in 1869, the Kiowas compromised and chose another man, Guipago (Lone Wolf) to lead them, Satanta seemed to take the disappointment well. But more and more, he began to follow his own inclinations, which meant more raiding in Texas.[36]

Addo-etta (Big Tree) was a young warrior, perhaps twenty-two years of age,[37] but already he showed great skill and promise. Slight of build by comparison with his cousin, Satanta, he nonetheless had a reputation for daring horsemanship and reckless bravery which had earned him the civil chieftainship of one subgroup of the Elks Division.[38] He would later be described as "the mighty warrior athlete, with the speed of the deer and the eye of the eagle," and as a "tiger-demon who is swift at every species of ferocity."[39] Probably neither description was entirely correct. More likely, Big Tree was simply a young man who, like all young men, was eager to gain the respect and approval of his elders.

The Do-ha-te, or medicine man, Maman-ti has been described as "sinister" and as "one of the strongest personalities the tribe produced."[40] He was both a popular medicine man and a successful

76

Addo-etta (Big Tree), Kiowa subchief (National Archives)

war chief, and it is said that he was the instigator of every major Kiowa raid of the early 1870s.[41] Yet he avoided contact with the whites so completely that he remains at best a shadowy historical figure of whom no photographs are known to exist. He had already been to Texas once in 1871, leading the raiding party that ambushed and killed Brit Johnson and his companions on the Salt Creek Prairie. In May he returned with a much larger raiding party to that area where the hunting had always proved so successful.

On May 16, this party of warriors reached the Salt Creek Prairie. Half a century later Indian informants would testify that Maman-ti made magic that evening. After consulting his oracle, the owl, he predicted the passage of two groups of whites. He insisted that the first group should not be molested, but the second party to pass could be attacked and easily overcome.[42]

The following day the Indians waited for their prey, watching intently from a hill which afforded them an excellent view. Salt Creek Prairie stretched out before them for three miles to a large hill called Cox Mountain. The Butterfield Stage trail ran near their position and across the open prairie. It would be an easy thing for the Indians to allow a slow-moving wagon train to reach the middle of the open ground and then cut it off, far from the timbered areas which stood at both ends of the stage road.

Around noon, a party of whites emerged from the woods and moved east across the open ground, passing less than a half-mile from the Indians' position. The impatient warriors wanted to attack, but Maman-ti reminded them that his medicine allowed for a successful attack only on the second group of whites to pass. The signal to attack was not given, and the column moved across the prairie and disappeared into the woods to the east. Historians would later speculate that, trusting experience rather than Maman-ti's medicine, the older warriors recognized the formation of the party, wagons with horsemen in front, as the way soldiers traveled and decided to wait for a less well-armed prey. Whatever the reasons—magic, caution, or luck[43]—two of the highest-ranking officers in the United States Army escaped probable annihilation that day at

78

Cox Mountain and the site of the attack on Henry Warren's wagons, ca. 1900 (Texas State Library)

the hands of over a hundred Plains Indian warriors, for it was Generals Sherman and Marcy and their small party that the Indians spared. Sherman's party journeyed on to Richardson unaware of their peril. Upon arriving late that afternoon Sherman wrote: "The road is across rather rough country and water is very scarce. Of course we saw no Indians. . . ."[44]

About 3:00 P.M. the next day, May 18, the Indians' patience was rewarded when they sighted a wagon train moving west along the stage road. They counted ten wagons; a rich prize surely awaited them. The mule train belonged to the freighting firm of Warren and Dubose and was engaged in hauling corn from Weatherford to Fort Griffin. Twelve teamsters manned this particular train, all armed against the possibility of attack.[45] But twelve stood little chance against one hundred.

Satanta signaled the attack by blowing the bugle he always carried, and the Indians swarmed down the hill toward the wagons. The startled drivers tried desperately to circle their wagons, but Big Tree and another Kiowa, Yellow Wolf, cut off the lead mules. Big Tree made the first coup and Yellow Wolf made the second. The

79

teamsters opened fire, killing a Comanche named Or-dlee and wounding Red Warbonnet, a Kiowa subchief. Big Tree responded by shooting one of the drivers out of his seat. Tson-to-goodle (Light-Haired Young Man), a Kiowa-Apache, was hit and knocked off his horse. Two of his companions carried him from the fight. The warriors wheeled westward and began circling the train, whooping and shooting, their bullets tearing through the wagons. Quickly, three more drivers were killed, and another was wounded and down in the back of a wagon.

The seven surviving teamsters realized the hopelessness of defending the wagons. Their only chance lay in escape. The Indians were circling the train in an uneven manner, with a gap in their ranks. The drivers suddenly bolted from the wagons, broke through the Indians, and scattered in flight across the prairie, all sprinting for the timber around Cox Mountain. Several warriors pursued, shooting down two of them. One driver, Thomas Brazeal, was hit in the foot, but he ignored the wound and, along with four of his fellows,[46] reached the sanctuary of the trees and brush. With a last ragged volley of shots, the Indians let them go and turned back.

Most of the braves stayed with the train, convinced there were more whites still inside the corral and probably afraid they would lose their part of the booty if they chased after the fleeing teamsters. The shooting had stopped, but the experienced warriors were still cautious about approaching the vehicles. Hau-tau (Gunshot), a young Kiowa in his first fight, recklessly rushed up to one of the wagons, touched it, and shouted, "A-he! I claim this wagon, and all in it is mine!" Unfortunately for Hau-tau, the wounded teamster, Samuel Elliott, happened to be in that wagon. He raised the canvas cover with the barrel of his rifle and shot Hau-tau in the face. The other warriors were first stunned, then enraged. They swarmed over the wagon and dragged Elliott out. He was chained face down to a wagon tongue pole and roasted over a slow fire. The contents of the train were scattered over the prairie, the dead white men were mutilated, and some of the wagons were set aflame.

Just before the fight a spring rainstorm had begun to blacken the sky, and now it was quite dark and ominous. Anxious to be gone, the Indians buried Or-dlee, gathered their prizes, including

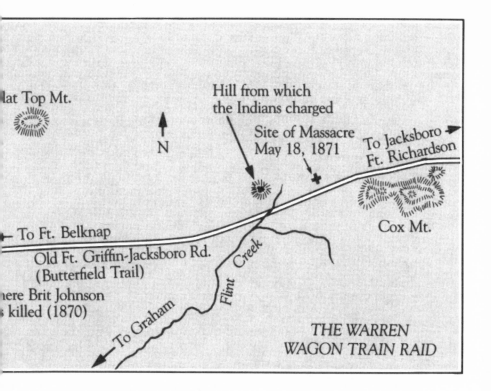

lat Top Mt.

N

Hill from which
the Indians charged

Site of Massacre
May 18, 1871

To Jacksboro
Ft. Richardson

Cox Mt.

To Ft. Belknap

Old Ft. Griffin-Jacksboro Rd.
(Butterfield Trail)

Flint Creek

ere Brit Johnson
killed (1870)

To Graham

THE WARREN
WAGON TRAIN RAID

forty-one mules and six scalps (one of the teamsters had been bald),
and started north on a circuitous route back to the reservation. As
the last of the rear guard turned to look back at the debris-strewn
scene, the heaviest rainstorm of the season broke over the reaches
of North Texas, extinguishing the last smoldering embers in the
wreckage of the corn wagons and washing away the trail of perhaps
the most fateful war party ever to enter the state.[47]

Earlier that morning, at Fort Richardson, Sherman had conferred with Mackenzie on the subject of Indian raids in North
Texas.[48] Mackenzie confirmed the Texans' complaints about Indian
crimes. Later, Sherman received a delegation of citizens from Jacksboro. They presented notarized affidavits and testimonies as to the
depredations that had been committed locally by Indians. Included
was a tabular "Statement of Murders and Outrages Committed

upon the citizens of Jack County by Hostile Indians," which listed the dates of attacks beginning in 1859, the names and numbers of victims, and the locations relative to Fort Richardson. The melancholy total was 129 killed "beside the many taken into captivity."[49] The general listened thoughtfully to the citizens' reports but remained skeptical.

That night Sherman's mind was changed in a dramatic fashion. Just after midnight the post sentries challenged a lone figure. Drenched and bleeding, Thomas Brazeal, one of the surviving teamsters, stumbled into the fort after walking twenty miles in the rain and darkness on a badly injured foot. The sentries carried him to the post hospital and then roused Mackenzie from his quarters and Sherman from his tent which was pitched nearby. Both officers went immediately to hear Brazeal's story.[50]

Sherman realized that the previous day he had passed over the very spot where the teamsters had been attacked. Instead of seven drivers it could well have been the general and his party lying dead in the rain on the Salt Creek Prairie. Sherman quickly dictated orders to Mackenzie, directing him to go to the scene of the attack, to pursue the raiders even onto the reservation, and attack them if possible. He was to recover the stolen stock and arrest the Indians responsible.[51]

Mackenzie took Companies A, B, D, and E, a total of 193 enlisted men, sixteen Tonkawa Indian scouts, and the two post guides, Henry Strong and James Doshier,[52] and set out in the driving rain for the Salt Creek Prairie. There, a sickening sight awaited the troopers. Julius Patzki, the assistant army surgeon who accompanied the column, reported:

> I examined on May 19, 1871, the bodies of five citizens killed near Salt Creek by Indians on the previous day. All the bodies were riddled with bullets, covered with gashes, and the skulls crushed . . . with an axe. . . . Some of the bodies exhibited signs of having been stabbed with arrows, one of the bodies . . . [was] found fastened with a chain to the pole of a wagon lying over a fire with the face to the ground, the tongue being cut out. . . . It was impossible to

82

determine whether the man was burned before or after his death. The scalps of all but one were taken.[53]

Mackenzie sent a rider to Sherman to report that Brazeal's account was true.[54] He then buried the corpses in a wagon bed[55] and turned his troopers north toward the Red River. The rain had wiped out the raiders' trail, and the scouts groped futilely for some sign of the Indians. Grimly, Mackenzie and the soldiers of the Fourth pushed on into Oklahoma.

The storm that had covered the war party's tracks had also hindered its escape by causing all the rivers to flood. The Indians had to build boats out of willow branches covered with canvas to float their loot and wounded across. The warriors swam alongside the boats, pushing them. This rigorous journey proved to be too much for the injured Hau-tau, who died shortly after crossing the Red River. The rest of the Indians were safely back in their villages by May 21.[56]

The raiders, however, did not all retreat from Texas totally un-punished. Four Kiowas lingered behind to hunt buffalo and on May 20 were surprised by Lieutenant Peter M. Boehm and a twenty-five man patrol from Fort Richardson. In a quick, sharp fight, a warrior named Tomasi was killed; one of Boehm's men was wounded.[57]

Meanwhile, General Sherman traveled to Fort Sill. On May 24, he wrote to John Pope, commander of the Department of Missouri, that he no longer doubted that the western border of Texas was suffering greatly from Indian raiders. Further Sherman told Pope that he was now satisfied that the majority of these raiders were coming from the Fort Sill Reservation, and he intended to see what could be done about it.[58] Sherman visited Lawrie Tatum, the Quaker Indian agent, to tell him of the attack on the corn train. Tatum was horrified. He knew that Satank and Satanta were away from the reservation, and he promised Sherman that he would question the chiefs when they came in for their rations.[59]

Four days later, on Saturday, May 27, Satank, Satanta, Big

Panoramic view of Fort Sill, 1873 (Fort Sill Museum)

Tree, and several other chiefs arrived at the agency to draw their rations. When Tatum asked about the raid, Satanta stood up and said, "Yes, I led in that raid." He then launched into a series of complaints about arms and ammunition that had not been delivered and a railroad that was rumored soon to be built through Indian Territory. "More recently," he said, "I was arrested by the soldiers and kept in confinement several days.[60] But that is played out now. There is never to be any more Kiowa Indians arrested. On account of these grievances, a short time ago I took about a hundred of my warriors to Texas, whom I wished to teach how to fight." Satanta then went on to say that several chiefs accompanied him, including Satank, Eagle Heart, Big Bow, and Fast Bear. He might have named more but Satank angrily interrupted him, saying in Kiowa not to reveal any more names of the war party participants. Apparently unconcerned, Satanta admitted that the raiders attacked a mule train and killed seven white men. Although three of the raiders had been killed,[61] the Indians were "willing to call it even." Satanta concluded by saying, "If any other Indian claims the

84

Kiowa-Comanche Indian Agency, Fort Sill, Indian Territory, 1871 (Fort Sill Museum)

honor of leading that party he will be lying to you. I led it myself."[62]
The Kiowas present were greatly disturbed at Satanta's open admission. They vigorously agreed with his boast that he had led the raid, no doubt more than willing to allow the naive warrior to claim full public credit.

Tatum told the chiefs that a great warrior chief from Washington was at Fort Sill and that if they spoke with him he might authorize the agent to issue guns and powder to them. Tatum then sent a note to Colonel Benjamin Grierson, the post commander, telling him of Satanta's boastful confession and requesting the arrest of the chiefs.[63]

When Sherman and Grierson read Tatum's note, they quickly notified the agent to send the chiefs to the post for a council, for the army could not make arrests on agency grounds. Then they laid plans to trap the Indians inside the fort.

Meanwhile, Lone Wolf informed Tatum that Big Tree had also participated in the raid. Tatum wrote another note to Sherman telling him of this new information and requesting the arrest of Big Tree as well as the other chiefs. Tatum decided to deliver this himself, but before leaving the agency he told Lone Wolf to summon all the chiefs to Sherman's council.[64]

Satanta, in the company of Horace Jones, the post interpreter, arrived first. He found Sherman, Grierson, Marcy, and two aides casually sitting on the front porch of Grierson's house. After the introductions, Satanta sat down and Sherman questioned him about the raid on the wagon train. The chief repeated the speech he had made earlier to Tatum. Sherman listened, growing more and more angry, until Satanta had finished his matter-of-fact version of the events. Then the general's temper flared. He denounced the attack as cowardly since the Indians had so greatly outnumbered the drivers. He told the chief that if his braves wanted a fight the army would be happy to oblige them.

As Jones translated, Satanta realized that all was not well. He replied: "I was merely trying to show the young men how to fight. If you don't like what I have done, I will go; I am not going to stay here." Satanta started to rise, but one of Grierson's aides, a tall black sergeant, stuck a drawn pistol in his face and forced him to sit

Horace P. Jones, Fort Sill interpreter (Fort Sill Museum)

Colonel Benjamin Grierson, Tenth Cavalry, Fort Sill post commander (Fort Sill Museum)

back down. Then Satank and ten other Kiowas arrived, and with several army officers who had gathered, they all crowded onto the porch. A detachment of soldiers found Big Tree in the trader's store and attempted to arrest him. He tried to escape by leaping through a window, but the soldiers rode him down and dragged him dusty and bleeding to Sherman's council. At the sight of Big Tree being manhandled the assembled chiefs grew excited and angry.[65]

Sherman then sprang his trap. He told the chiefs that Satank, Satanta, and Big Tree were under arrest and would be taken to Texas to stand trial for the murders of the seven teamsters. The scene instantly became turmoil. Satanta stood and threw back his

87

blanket, exposing a revolver in his belt, shouting that he would rather die than be taken as a prisoner to Texas. Others drew pistols and knives. Sherman snapped a command. A column of the Tenth Cavalry double-timed around the corner of Grierson's house and formed in two ranks facing the porch. The front rank knelt and both brought their weapons to the ready. Kicking Bird, long an advocate of peace with the whites, calmly rose and said to Sherman, "You have asked for these men to kill them. But they are my people, and I am not going to let you have them. You and I are going to die right here."[66]

At this moment Lone Wolf, the major chief of the Kiowas, came galloping up to the porch. He dismounted, laid two carbines and a bow and quiver on the ground, and with a great show of bravado, rearranged his blanket. He then picked up the weapons and strode to the porch, tossing one carbine to an unarmed Indian and the bow and arrows to another. He seated himself before Sherman and, gazing intently at him, deliberately cocked his carbine. The black soldiers instantly brought up their weapons to firing positions. A bloody fight seemed imminent. But after a few incredibly tense moments Satanta threw up his hands and cried, "No, no, no!" The chiefs sullenly submitted. Sherman ordered Satank, Satanta, and Big Tree jailed and, after securing promises for the return of the stolen mules, allowed the others to go free.[67]

Many Indians cleared out of the fort while the chiefs were still on Grierson's porch. When Big Tree was arrested, Indians began slipping out as unobtrusively as possible. The sentries tried to stop one young warrior who shot two arrows at them; he died when they returned fire. The sounds of gunfire alarmed the Kiowas and Comanches camped near the commissary, and fearing the worst for their chiefs, they stampeded. Lone Wolf, Kicking Bird, and the other participants in Sherman's council emerged from the fort to find their encampments deserted.

Sherman waited for Mackenzie, but when he had not arrived by May 30 the general continued his tour of inspection, leaving orders for the colonel to escort the Indians to Texas for trial. In the meantime Mackenzie had been scouring the stretches of western Indian Territory for some sign of the raiders, but the heavy rains had

Sherman House, or quarters of the post commander, ca. 1890, Fort Sill, where Satank, Satanta, and Big Tree were arrested (Fort Sill Museum)

wiped out all vestiges of a trail. On June 4, tired and dejected, Mackenzie rode into Fort Sill to find, to his great pleasure and surprise, that his quarry was there and waiting for him in chains.[68]

On June 8, Mackenzie was ready to return to Texas with his prisoners. The chiefs, in leg and hand irons, were led, blinking, into the sunlight where several officers had gathered to watch their departure. Satank lurched forward as if to shake hands with Grierson, who was standing nearby, but Satanta and Big Tree restrained him. Actually, unknown to the soldiers, the old Kiowa had managed to conceal a knife from his jailers and had hidden it under his blanket. No doubt he intended to kill Grierson. Satanta and Big Tree, realizing his intention and probably figuring they were already in enough trouble, probably saved the colonel's life.[69]

The troopers rolled up two wagons. Satanta and Big Tree quietly entered the second wagon with two guards, Corporal John Charlton and a private. Satank refused to move, so the soldiers picked him up bodily and threw him into the bed of the lead wagon. Corporal George Robinson and a private were assigned to watch him. Lieutenant George A. Thurston, the officer of the day, rode near the rear of the wagons with the mounted guard. Before the train moved out, the post interpreter, Horace Jones, warned Corporal Charlton, "You had better watch that old Indian, he means trouble."[70]

In all likelihood, the time spent in jail had allowed Satank to reflect upon his situation. For the leader of the Koitsenko Society, honor was far more important than life, and Satank could find little honor in being dragged to Texas in chains. As the train began to move he called out to George Washington, a Caddo chief who had come to watch the departure: "Take this message to my people: tell them I died beside the road. My bones will be found there. Tell my people to gather them up and carry them away. See that tree? When I reach that tree I shall be dead." To one of Mackenzie's Tonkawa scouts Satank said: "You may have my scalp. The hair is poor. It isn't worth much but you may have it."[71]

He then drew his blanket over his head and began to chant the death song of the Koitsenko:

Oh sun, you remain forever, but we Koitsenko must die.
Oh earth, you remain forever, but we Koitsenko must die.[72]

Caddo George Washington dropped out of the way. Satanta and Big Tree sat very still. Only the soldiers, who did not realize what was happening, were unconcerned. Interpreter Jones, who was watching this scene with the officer of the day, Lieutenant Richard H. Pratt of the Tenth Cavalry, told Pratt, "He is singing his death song, and means to die, and if he has a chance will do anything possible to bring about his death, or he may kill himself."[73]

Under his blanket, Satank succeeded in slipping the handcuffs off his wrists by stripping his flesh to the bone. Then, with a great war whoop, he threw off his blanket and attacked his guards, stabbing Corporal Robinson in the leg. Both soldiers vaulted backwards out of the wagon, leaving their carbines behind. Satank grabbed one of these weapons and worked the lever. However, the gun already had a shell in the chamber and jammed. Lieutenant Thurston reined out from the rear of the column and, taking in the situation in a flash, "concluded that the Indian had better die, and die right speedily." Thurston gave the order to fire. Corporal Charlton shot quickly, knocking Satank down in the wagon bed. Valiantly, with the "vitality of a grizzly bear," the old Koitsenko rose ᴛᴏ a sitting position and pointed the carbine at the troopers. A volley from the mounted guards cut him down, and he died a few minutes later. As Satank had predicted, the soldiers threw his body beside the road. The Tonkawa scouts immediately scalped it.[74]

Mackenzie feared that the Kiowas and their allies might try to free Satanta and Big Tree during the trip to Jacksboro. Nightly, to prevent this, he ringed the camp with pickets and sleeping parties, small groups of men who slept at strategic locations with their weapons at hand. At every stop he ordered the two prisoners chained hand and foot to stakes in the ground. Reportedly, Satanta and Big Tree suffered a great deal from voracious swarms of mosquitoes in the Wichita River bottoms. But despite the colonel's apprehensions, no rescue party appeared, and the trip proved uneventful. At 6:00 P.M. on June 15, the detail rode into Richardson, greeted by the cheering garrison and townspeople and by music from the regimental band. Soldiers and citizens alike crowded around to gawk at the prisoners who rode on mules, their feet lashed together under their mounts' bellies with rawhide lariats. Satanta was described as "proud and defiant," Big Tree as "frightened and tremulous." They were put under a strong guard and marched off to the guardhouse. The post adjutant, Captain John K. Mizner, wrote to General Sherman, "I feel assured a Civil Court in Texas will do them full justice and that on Texas soil they will find an early grave."[75]

The townspeople, perhaps somewhat less certain of events than the post adjutant, organized a home guard unit of sixty-seven men and applied to Mackenzie for weapons and ammunition with which to defend themselves in case of Indian attack. Mackenzie authorized one hundred carbines to be placed at their disposal.[76]

On June 22, members of the bar of Weatherford delivered a petition to Judge Charles Soward of the Thirteenth Judicial District, which encompassed Jack and Parker counties, requesting him not to hold the next term of District Court at Jacksboro because of the "well known and indisputable fact" that the entire countryside around Jacksboro was "infested with large bands of hostile Indians."[77] The petition was denied. One of the most famous and important cases Judge Soward would ever hear or the Weatherford lawyers try was to take place in the tiny village of Jacksboro.

On Saturday, July 1, the grand jury of the Jack County District Court returned a true bill of indictment against Satanta and Big Tree. The spokesman intoned that "with force and malice not having the fear of God before their eyes, but being moved by and seduced by the instigation of the devil" they committed the crime of murder upon N. S. Long, James Elliott, M. J. Baxter, James Williams, Samuel Elliott, John Mullins, and Jesse Bowman.[78]

On Wednesday, July 5, at 8:00 A.M., the prisoners were moved in a wagon from the guardhouse at Richardson to the courthouse on the town square, a distance of about a half-mile. In order to dissuade angry citizens from attempting to shoot the Indians, Mackenzie ordered them placed in the middle of the wagon and surrounded by armed guards. Three soldiers sat in the front of the vehicle, three in the back, and six on either side. Four mounted soldiers rode before the wagon and four more close behind it.[79]

At 8:30 A.M., Mackenzie turned the prisoners over to civil authorities, who escorted them to the second floor of the courthouse where their trial was to be held. Thomas Ball and J. A. Woolfolk were appointed counselors for the defendants, and District Attorney S. W. T. Lanham, who would later use the notoriety of the trial to vault him into the governorship of Texas, represented the state. The attorneys for the defense entered a plea of not guilty and decided that Big Tree would be tried first.[80] A jury was selected, impaneled, and sworn in,[81] and one of the most famous trials in nineteenth-century Texas history got under way.

Big Tree's trial was completed that day and Satanta's the next. In both cases Colonel Mackenzie, Horace Jones, and the teamster Thomas Brazeal were the principal witnesses. In light of the evidence presented, there was little the defense counselors could do. The testimony revealed that Satanta and Big Tree, along with Satank and around fifty warriors, had been absent from the reserva-

Jack County Courthouse in which Satanta and Big Tree were tried for murder. This photo was taken in 1882 just before the building was torn down to make way for a larger courthouse. (Russell Jones Collection)

tion for thirty days, during which time the wagon train attack had taken place; that the chiefs had returned to the reservation with stolen property belonging to the wagon train; that Satanta had boasted of the crime before Tatum, Grierson, and General Sherman; and finally, that Brazeal witnessed the two defendants at what the prosecutor called "the massacre."[82] The fate of the two Kiowas was sealed.

During the course of his arguments, Prosecutor Lanham denounced the government's peace policy and praised Mackenzie and Sherman for taking decisive action. He then described the character of the defendants:

Satanta, the veteran council chief of the Kiowas—the orator, the diplomat, the counselor of his tribe—the pulse of
his race; Big Tree, the young war chief, who leads in the
thickest of the fight, and follows no one in the chase—
the mighty warrior athlete, with the speed of the deer and
the eye of the eagle. . . . So they would be described by Indian admirers, who live in more secure and favored lands,
remote from the frontier—where 'distance lends enchant-
ment' to the imagination . . . and the dread sound of the
war whoop is not heard. We who see them to-day . . . be-
hold them through far different lenses! We recognize in Satanta the arch fiend of treachery and blood—the cunning
Cataline— . . . the inciter of his fellows to rapine and murder—the . . . most canting and double-tongued hypocrite
when detected and overcome! In Big Tree we perceive the
tiger-demon, who has tasted blood and loves it as his food—
who stops at no crime, how black soever—who is swift at
every species of ferocity, and pities not at any sight of agony
or death—he can scalp, burn, torture, mangle and deface
his victims . . . and have no feeling of sympathy or remorse.
They are both hideous and loathesome in appearance, and
we look in vain to see . . . anything to be admired, or
endured.[83]

The jury required only a short time to return a verdict of guilty of
murder in the first degree for both Indians. After Satanta's trial on
July 6, Judge Soward called the prisoners before him for sentencing.
Before doing so, he allowed them the traditional opportunity to address the court. Big Tree declined, but Satanta, never one to be
reticent, responded with a speech delivered "in broken Spanish and
Comanche," which was interpreted by Horace Jones:

I cannot speak with these things upon my wrists [holding up
his arms to show the iron manacles], I am a squaw. Has anything been heard from the Great Father? I have never been
so near the Tehannas [Texans] before. I look around me and
see your braves, squaws, and papooses, and I have said in my
heart, if I ever get back to my people I will never make war

upon you. I have always been the friend of the white man ever since I was so high [indicating by sign the height of a boy]. My tribe has taunted me and called me a squaw because I have been the friend of the Tehannas. I am suffering now for the crimes of bad Indians—of Satank and Lone Wolf and Kicking Bird and Fast Bear and Eagle Heart, and if you will let me go I will kill the three latter with my own hand. I did not kill the Tehannas. I came down Pease River as a big medicine man to doctor the wounds of the braves. I am a big chief among my people . . . they know my voice and will hear my word. If you will let me go back to my people, I will withdraw my warriors from Tehanna. I will take them all across Red River, and that shall be the line between us and the pale faces. I will wash out the spots of blood and make it a white land and there shall be peace, and the Tehannas may plow and drive their oxen to the banks of the river, but if you kill me it will be like a spark in the prairie—make big fire! burn heap![84]

Unimpressed, Judge Soward sentenced Satanta and Big Tree to be taken to some "convenient place near the courthouse at the town of Jacksboro" on the first day of September, and there to be hanged by the neck until "dead, dead, dead!"[85]

The executions, however, were never carried out. Supporters of the Quaker peace policy across America launched a storm of protest upon Washington. Even agent Tatum, who had urged the arrest of the troublemakers, recommended that the death sentence be changed to life imprisonment. He argued that the Kiowas would surely seek revenge if the chiefs were killed, but if held in prison, they could insure peace on the frontier. Tatum also pointed out that Indians feared confinement more than death; thus a life sentence would be a far worse punishment for the Kiowas than execution.[86]

President Grant eventually succumbed to the pressure and ordered Texas Governor Edmund J. Davis to commute the Indians' sentences to life imprisonment. On August 2, 1871, Davis signed a document of commutation which stated, in part, that what Satanta and Big Tree had done was not "the technical crime of murder under the Statute of the State" but rather "an act of Savage war-fare."[87] On October 16, Captain Henry L. Chipman, with Company D, Eleventh Infantry, escorted Satanta and Big Tree from Fort Richardson to the state penitentiary at Huntsville.[88]

The significances of the Warren Wagon Train raid are many and profound.[89] For the first time in Texas history, Indian criminals had been brought to justice in the courts. Civilians hoped there was a lesson there for the Indians, and indeed during the time that Satanta and Big Tree were held in prison, the frequency and ferocity of the Indian raids into Texas decreased markedly. An embattled frontier population was heartened by the results. But more importantly, the involvement of the general-in-chief of the army gave the citizens of Texas hope that soon there would be a new outlook in Washington on the Indian problem. It was not long in coming. The Secretary of the Interior reluctantly concluded that "Lenient measures and forbearance toward these restless and war-loving spirits appear to have no effect in restraining their passion for plunder and war, and a severe treatment would seem to be the only wise and proper course to compel right conduct on their part."[90] On July 6, 1871, Sherman wrote to Assistant Adjutant General W. W. Wood, saying, "The Indian bureau now have instructed the Indian agents that troops may enter the reservation in pursuit of criminals, and that on being captured they shall be surrendered for trial to the civil authorities. I doubt if you could have done this had I not been happily present at Richardson and Sill as I was."[91]

Because Sherman was "happily present," the death knell sounded for both the Quaker peace policy and the army's quarter-century-old defensive policy. The forces were gathering that soon would break the power of the Southern Plains tribes and drive them forever from their beloved prairie onto the reservation. Many raids were far more destructive in terms of lives lost and property destroyed than the one that struck Henry Warren's wagons on May 18, 1871, but few if any have had more far-reaching effects.

Satanta and Big Tree in prison (Texas State Library)

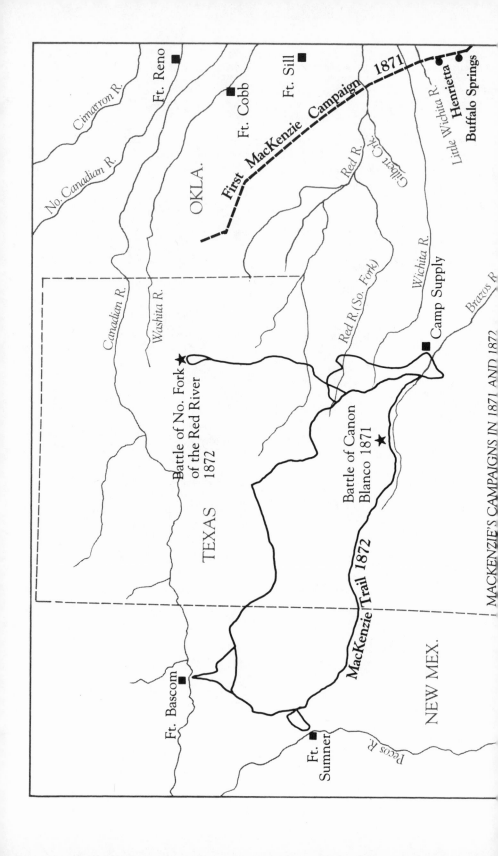

Cimarron R.

No. Canadian R.

Ft. Reno

Ft. Cobb

Ft. Sill

First MacKenzie Campaign 1871

OKLA.

Red R.

Gilbert Creek

Little Wichita R.

Henrietta

Buffalo Springs

Canadian R.

Washita R.

Red R. (So. Fork)

Wichita R.

Camp Supply

Brazos R.

Battle of No. Fork
of the Red River
1872

Battle of Canon
Blanco 1871

TEXAS

MacKenzie Trail 1872

NEW MEX.

Ft. Bascom

Ft. Sumner

Pecos R.

MACKENZIE'S CAMPAIGNS IN 1871 AND 1872

CHAPTER SIX

BEFORE THE TRIAL OF THE
two chiefs, Mackenzie wrote
Sherman suggesting that the
frontier garrisons be concentrated for a campaign against
the marauders, who were all
coming from either the edge of
the Staked Plains or the Fort
Sill Reservation. Mackenzie
also wrote:

The
Campaigns
of 1871

To obtain a permanent
peace . . . the Kiowas and Comanches should be dismounted
and disarmed and made to raise corn. This can only be accomplished by the army. The matter is now within a very small
compass, either these Indians must be punished, or they must
be allowed to murder and rob at their own discretion.[1]

Most of the Kiowas who had fled Fort Sill following the arrest
of Satank, Satanta, and Big Tree had not returned and, indeed,
were busy preparing for war. Their pleas for aid from their Cheyenne
and Comanche allies failed to gain much support, however, and
their enthusiasm waned. Still, they refused to return the stolen
mules, and Tatum, Mackenzie, and Grierson all urged prompt punishment if the stock was not forthcoming. Accordingly, General
Joseph J. Reynolds, commander of the Department of Texas, approved Mackenzie's plan for an immediate summer campaign against
the recalcitrant Kiowas and recommended that the War Department approve a late fall expedition which Mackenzie wished to
lead. Mackenzie received Reynolds's permission for his first foray

from Richardson on July 6, while the trial of Satanta and Big Tree was still in progress.[2]

Meanwhile, Sherman suggested to Secretary of War William Belknap that the military in Texas be given a free hand to enter Indian Territory at any time to overtake and arrest raiders, as well as to recover stolen stock.[3] This was a radical departure from established military policy[4] and against the terms of the Medicine Lodge Treaty, but Sherman's suggestion was approved. The army could always justify the action by pointing out that the Indians violated Medicine Lodge with their raids into Texas.

From all over Texas, Mackenzie gathered additional companies of the Fourth Cavalry. Company C arrived from Laredo, L from Brownsville, and K from McKavett on July 16 and 17. Companies G and I marched into Fort Richardson from Fort Concho on July 28, and Companies D and H reported in from Griffin the next day. Fort Richardson overflowed with 513 officers and men, making it the largest garrison in Texas and the fourth largest in the entire country.[5]

Reporting with Company C was Lieutenant Henry Lawton, an officer Mackenzie respected enough to request his transfer from the Twenty-fourth Infantry to the Fourth Cavalry. Lawton stood six feet four inches tall and had proved himself to be a masterful quartermaster. He was innovative, just as Mackenzie was, and shared his commander's profound dislike of red tape.[6]

As preparations proceeded, Mackenzie sent Captain Clarence Mauck out with a party consisting of Companies B, E, and F, Fourth Cavalry, and Company C, Eleventh Infantry. Mauck had orders to march to Gilbert's Creek, a small tributary of the Red River, where he was to establish a base of supply for scouting operations up and down the river.[7]

Then, on July 31, Mackenzie dispatched Captain Napoleon Bonaparte McLaughlen with companies A, D, G, H, and I of the Fourth Cavalry and Company A of the Eleventh Infantry to build a bridge across the Little Wichita River. On the morning of August 2, Company C, part of Company L, and Lieutenant Lawton and his supply train left the post under the command of Captain John Wilcox. That evening, Mackenzie, Lieutenant Peter Boehm and his Tonkawa scouts, and the remainder of Company L followed under a bright moon and soon arrived at Captain Wilcox's camp on the West Fork of the Trinity River. The first Indian campaign launched from Fort Richardson was under way.[8]

From the West Fork, the command marched through stark country burned over by prairie fire. There had been no appreciable rain since May 18, the day of the wagon train massacre, and the area was parched. The envy of all the officers at this time was Lieutenant Boehm, who affected a white sombrero hat with low crown and very wide brim. Since Boehm commanded the Indian scouts, Mackenzie allowed him this privilege but insisted that the other officers wear the regulation black hats. They all sighed with envy whenever they spied Boehm with his wide, soft hat.[9]

Mackenzie and his men moved through the ruins of Buffalo Springs, past the desolation of Henrietta,[10] and on August 4 joined McLaughlen on the Little Wichita, where he was busy finishing the bridge Mackenzie wanted. Early the next morning the entire command crossed the river; the wagons were run over by hand, while the mules swam across the forty-yard-wide stream.[11]

The country beyond proved broken and difficult to cross. Arriving at the Big Wichita, Mackenzie discovered that the wagons could not cross the river unless the steepness of the banks was reduced. A large detail set about this work, and the next morning the twenty-five wagons crossed the river. The command marched through high grass to Gilbert's Creek where Companies B, E, and F awaited them.

There were now ten companies of cavalry and two of infantry concentrated at Gilbert's Creek. On August 7, Mackenzie organized the ten cavalry companies into five squadrons, loaded the ninety pack mules and a few wagons with provisions, and struck out for the Red River, leaving the infantry to guard the remainder of the wagons and equipment.[12]

The initial going was difficult, for no "packers" (professional mule loaders) had been brought along. The soldiers did their best to load the mules correctly, but the animals panicked at the sound of loose pans banging together. The mules pitched, ran into one another, and scattered their loads over the prairie. After correcting

Captain Clarence Mauck, Fourth
Cavalry (National Archives)

this problem, the expedition managed a long hot march to the
south bank of the Red River and there made camp.[13]

Near midnight, someone spotted a fire in the south. The
troopers were roused from their slumber to see a perfect wall of
flame covering the horizon. The awesome beauty of the scene was
captivating, but all too soon they began to hear the roar of the massive conflagration and realized that the southern breeze was driving the flames toward them. Quickly, orders were issued to pack
up and mount. The cavalry easily moved into the river bottom,
but the few wagons still with the command had to be pushed and
pulled by hand across the dry riverbed and over the sand dunes beyond. The troopers assumed that Indians had set the fire and expected to be attacked at any moment. All night the soldiers toiled
over the sand while the prairie fire cast an eerie light upon them.
The dawn of August 8 found the exhausted troopers still traveling,
now over rolling prairie. At sundown, they made camp on West
Cache Creek.[14]

The next day Mackenzie and his men marched northwest over

Lieutenant Henry Ware Lawton, Fourth Cavalry (National Archives)

more prairie and in midafternoon reached Otter Creek, where Colonel Grierson and several companies of his Tenth Cavalry were waiting. They made camp immediately, but the wagons of the column did not arrive until after 8:00 P.M. The drivers had to stop to butcher several buffaloes which the scouts shot, load the meat, and then toil across several deep ravines to reach the campsite.

After several conferences, Mackenzie and Grierson decided to establish a supply camp on Otter Creek. From there they would scout for Kicking Bird's village, which had not reported in at Fort Sill since the capture of Satanta and Big Tree. Grierson was to explore the country between the Wichita Mountains and the North Fork of the Red River while Mackenzie would move into the badlands between the North Fork and the Salt Fork of the Red River. One of the Fort Sill interpreters, Matthew Leeper, went with Mackenzie.[15]

After resting his command, Mackenzie made a one-day trek to the North Fork on August 16, crossed the river the next day, and moved through a bleak, burned-over prairie. On August 18, as

103

Mackenzie's column marched in and out among the sand hills adja-
cent to the North Fork, a courier arrived with mail from the supply
camp. After reading the dispatches Mackenzie became very disturbed and irritable. His attitude toward the campaign changed no-
ticeably, and he seemed to lose all desire to find any Indians. He
never disclosed the contents of the correspondence to his staff officers, who were puzzled by his subsequent actions.[16]

What Mackenzie had received were copies of a letter from
General Sherman and a telegram from General Reynolds to the adjutant general:

Headquarters, Army of the
United States
St. Albans, Vermont.
July 29, 1871

Dear McCoy [Colonel James Culbertson McCoy],

I have received all the letters you have sent me, one of
this number being from Mackenzie in Texas. I wish this
letter to be shown [to the] secretary of war . . . with my
opinion that Genl Mackenzie should not cross the boundary
of Texas, into the Indian country, unless called on by Genl
Grierson. The latter has now an ample force to deal with
the Kioways, and can force them to surrender an equivalent
for the mules taken from Warren's train. I have already indicated to Genl Reynolds, that his Cavalry could be sent this
fall into that mountain country west of "Double Mountain
[Staked Plains]."

W. T. Sherman[17]

(Telegram)

Headquarters, Department of Texas
Adjutant General, United States Army
Washington, D.C.

Movement under Colonel Mackenzie, is in compliance
with Special Order 138, paragraph IV, July 5, 1871, Department Texas,—Extract copy of instructions mailed to Adjutant General, July 10.—No authority to enter reservations

unless in actual pursuit as authorized by recent instructions from Indian Bureau—

J. J. Reynolds[18]

The phrase "unless in *actual* pursuit" meant Mackenzie had no authority to be in Indian Territory. Up to this point he felt that he had been in pursuit of Kicking Bird, but to be safe, he decided to search the area west of the reservation on the chance he might find Kicking Bird outside Indian Territory boundaries.

Meanwhile, Grierson, who campaigned in a leisurely fashion, learned that Kicking Bird had delivered the promised forty-one mules to Lawrie Tatum. Grierson thereupon sent interpreter Horace P. Jones to warn Kicking Bird to move back to the reservation before Mackenzie's command could find him, then returned to Fort Sill. He left four companies of cavalry at Otter Creek to protect the supply camp.[19]

Mackenzie moved through the gypsum belt that extends between the North Fork and the Elm Fork of the Red River. The fine white gypsum powder covered everything, reflecting and intensifying the August sun's glare. The heat was so great that the men could not grasp the barrels of their carbines without blistering their hands. They put wet sponges in their hats to prevent sunstroke and carried an extra canteen to keep them damp. But the gypsum also permeated the water, which cut the men's lips, encrusted their canteens, and caused chronic diarrhea. The horses also suffered greatly, and many of the animals grew so weak they literally dropped dead in their tracks.

Meanwhile the Tonkawa scouts intercepted a small party of Kiowa hunters, but they refused to disclose the location of their village and soon set off at a dead run toward the Indian Territory. The officers wanted to pursue and capture them, but Mackenzie would not permit it.

That evening Mackenzie ordered a night march to confuse the Indian scouts he now knew to be shadowing the column. Mackenzie realized that this first Indian campaign was as much a training exercise for his regiment as it was a punitive expedition, and he wanted to give his men experience in such maneuvers. The colonel was already preparing for future campaigns.

A night march over rough, unknown country is perhaps one of the most difficult movements that cavalry can be asked to perform. This particular situation was aggravated by the large number of pack mules with the column and the relative inexperience of the troopers in leading mules. The animals balked at every arroyo or ravine they came to, and the men had to push them down one bank and tug and half-lift them up the other. The mules' packs frequently became stuck in the narrow defiles, and kettles, pots, pans, and other items were torn off, all crashing down with a great clattering, banging sound. The skittish mules responded with loud brays and squeals, as well as kicks and lashing hooves; the exasperated troopers retaliated with equally loud curses and numerous well-aimed kicks of their own. By morning, the exhausted command was allowed to make camp, having covered only seven miles during the turbulent night. The next day the Tonkawa scouts picked up fresh Indian signs which eventually led the column to Sweetwater Creek. Mackenzie rested his horses and allowed his weary troopers the almost forgotten luxury of bathing in the creek. Most of the grateful men responded by throwing themselves, fully clothed, into the cool water.

From this point, Mackenzie turned downstream. Had he moved nine miles in the opposite direction, up Sweetwater Creek, he would have discovered Kicking Bird's camp. However, having located no real traces of the Indian village and being uncertain of what he could do if he should discover it, Mackenzie gave up his search on August 28. By slow marches through a driving rain and then through steaming heat—forcing the abandonment of ten horses and two mules—he finally reached the Otter Creek camp on September 1.[20]

Mackenzie discovered the companies of the Tenth Cavalry living in regal luxury compared to the way the officers and men of the Fourth had passed the previous weeks. The colonel and his adjutant found Captain Louis Carpenter's camp pitched in a beautiful arbor near the stream. Tents, streets, latrines, and a kitchen were set up. Carpenter's tent boasted the almost incredible affluence of a wooden floor, and dinner was served in dishes on a table with a tablecloth and camp chairs. The meal climaxed with prune pie. Afterward, Mackenzie remarked over and over in astonishment: "Prune pie! Well I'll be damned! And in the field; what do you think of that?"[21]

At Otter Creek Mackenzie saw a copy of a letter from Lawrie Tatum to Grierson, stating that Kicking Bird had delivered the forty-one mules and was doing his best to stop his people from raiding and to persuade them to stay on the reservation.[22] There was no longer any reason for Mackenzie to remain in Indian Territory. He sent his men back to Richardson and Griffin and began to prepare for the autumn campaign Sherman had promised him.

Mackenzie's first expedition from Richardson had not been fruitless, for the troops had gained much hard-won experience and geographic knowledge of the terrain. Nonetheless, Mackenzie was bitterly disappointed over not finding Kicking Bird's camp, and his depression "seemed to possess his soul and disturb his peace of mind."[23]

Mackenzie returned to Richardson on September 13, ahead of Lawton's slow-moving column of wagons and mules. The next day Companies C, E, and I, Fourth Cavalry, and C, Eleventh Infantry, marched into the fort. The other troopers who had taken part in the August-to-September campaign against the Kiowas had concentrated at Fort Griffin to rest and resupply. On September 15, Company I returned to Concho, its home fort.[24]

Eager to be back in the field as soon as possible, Mackenzie had already set about organizing his next expedition. Satanta and Big Tree's imprisonment, plus Mackenzie's foray into Indian Territory, had definitely inhibited the raiding tendencies of the Kiowas. Lawrie Tatum's letter to Grierson, informing him that Kicking Bird had returned the mules, also provided the direction for Fort Richardson's second Indian campaign: "I would be very glad indeed if . . . General Mackenzie could . . . induce Mow-way and his band [Kwahadi Comanches] to come into the reservation and behave."[25]

Mackenzie, still disconsolate over the outcome of his summer expedition, looked forward to a more unhampered fall campaign.

And, indeed, there seemed to be at least three major differences between this forthcoming expedition and the one just concluded. First, Mackenzie had Sherman's complete approval for the fall excursion. There was no danger of his being recalled just as the chase heated up, which is what Mackenzie felt had happened earlier. Second, he would not be operating in Indian Territory where he had to answer to Tatum and Grierson. He was moving out onto the Staked Plains, or Llano Estacado, where there were no reservation or boundary lines. And finally, he would be striking at a declared hostile force which was operating far from the reservation and had, in fact, never been on the reservation—the Comanche bands of Mow-way and Parra-o-coom. These two chiefs had informed Tatum that not until the "blue coats" invaded their country and "whipped them" would they move onto the reservation and "walk on the white man's road."[26] Their lucrative trade with the Comancheros brought more in the way of "white man's goods" than did the reservation Indians' annuities and rations. The Comancheros would cross the Llano Estacado to meet the Comanches and trade cartloads of goods for stolen cattle at the Canadian River, Quitaque Springs, Laguna Sabines, and Cañon del Rescate.

On September 24, Mackenzie sent Captains Edward Heyl and Wirt Davis with Company K, Fourth Cavalry, and Company I, Eleventh Infantry, to old Camp Cooper, located five miles north of Fort Griffin on a bend of the Clear Fork of the Brazos. Camp Cooper was to serve as Mackenzie's staging area. The colonel arrived there early on the twenty-sixth. Companies A, B, D, F, G, H, K, and L of the Fourth Cavalry and Companies I and A of the Eleventh Infantry were poised for Mackenzie's second expedition of 1871.[27]

On October 3, after a scouting party moved ahead and selected a campsite, the command of six hundred men rode out of Camp Cooper singing their regimental song: "Come home, John, don't stay long; Come home soon to your own Chick-a-biddy."[28] Lieutenant Boehm and his Tonkawa scouts fanned out ahead of the column to search for trails. California and Paint creeks, both quicksand streams with steep banks, presented great problems for Quartermaster Lawton and his wagons. Several men were dispatched to help the wagons cross these streams and the numerous crevices and arroyos.

The next day's march took the command across the Double Mountain Fork of the Brazos and into camp near Flat Top Mountain. That evening a cold gale began to blow. Near midnight, a distant rumbling could be heard, and soon through the darkness the troops discerned a great moving mass: a buffalo stampede! By waving their blankets and yelling, the officers and men managed to turn the headlong charge from the camp and save their horse herd.

The following day, October 7, the cavalry column crossed the Salt Fork of the Brazos and moved through the immense herd of buffalo that had stampeded past the camp the night before. During the day's march the troopers passed several abandoned Comanchero "trading stations": natural caves or dugouts in the banks or bluffs supported by a framework of poles. Mackenzie encamped that night on Duck Creek, a small tributary of the Salt Fork. This became the site of Lawton's Camp Supply.[29]

That night, Mackenzie dispatched the Tonkawa scouts to search for signs of the Kwahadi Comanches' village. The next day a cavalry patrol, with the same mission, found no trails, not even of the Tonkawas. When the detachment returned, Mackenzie instructed his officers to prepare the column for a night march. He ordered the supply wagons corralled and left the infantry companies to guard them.

The men of the Fourth had suffered many trials and tribulations during their first night march in Indian Territory and did not relish another such excursion. Nevertheless, Mackenzie knew he was nearing Cañon Blanco, a great rift in the earth which begins where Catfish Creek runs into the Freshwater Fork of the Brazos, and he thought the canyon might be the hiding place of a Kwahadi camp, perhaps even that of Quanah Parker's[30] people. Therefore, during the moonless night of October 8, the Fourth Cavalry left their campfires blazing to deceive any unfriendly eyes and began their march.

After a great deal of confusion reminiscent of the August maneuver, including bumps, bruises, and profuse profanity directed at the cantankerous mules, the column found itself in a small box canyon with a great steep rock wall. Floundering among the ravines and arroyos, Mackenzie realized he was hopelessly trapped and ordered the command to bivouac quietly, without building fires.[31]

At dawn the colonel extricated his expedition from the box canyon and marched until around 9:30 A.M., when he reached the Freshwater Fork of the Brazos. The column made camp, and the weary troopers built fires and ate breakfast. Mackenzie ordered Captain Heyl and a small detachment to scout the area while the remainder of the men rested. Near midafternoon, the Tonkawa scouts arrived weary and famished. They had been traveling steadily since leaving the camp on Duck Creek. On their way to rejoin the command, they had surprised four Comanche warriors who were spying upon Captain Heyl's reconnassiance. The Comanches easily escaped the exhausted scouts, but, to Mackenzie's delight, the Tonkawas had come across a trail which they thought led to the enemy's camp.[32]

At 3:00 P.M. Mackenzie and his men crossed the Freshwater Fork and moved upstream toward the mouth of Cañon Blanco. After they had marched two miles, a shot rang out. Fearing the shot heralded an attack upon Captain Clarence Mauck's squad in the rear of the column, Mackenzie ordered the head of the column to countermarch to Mauck's aid. However, he soon discovered from scouts sent galloping back to investigate that a careless trooper had accidentally discharged his carbine. Mackenzie rescinded the command to countermarch, but, unfortunately, by this time the entire column was in disorder. A great deal of time was necessary to sort out the confusion, and, as darkness was almost upon the expedition, Mackenzie directed the men to make camp. The troopers settled down in the narrow entrance to Cañon Blanco, bordered by small hills on one side and the Freshwater Fork on the other. Mauck's detachment rejoined the column and, finding little room in the narrow enclosure, crowded in at the rear of the line. Mackenzie directed that the horses of the command be cross-sidelined by tying a hind foot to the opposite front foot and tying these sideline ropes to picket pins driven in the ground. Mackenzie later reported that "The horses were properly secured and guarded,"[33] but he was in error. He had not put out enough sentinels or sleeping parties around the horse herd.

Around 1:00 A.M., just as the moon set, the quiet night erupted with nerve-shattering yelling, shooting, and ringing of bells. A band of Comanches rode along the small hills bordering the camp, dragging buffalo robes from their racing mounts. Gun flashes from the rear guard and war whoops of the Tonkawa scouts mixed with the Comanches' demonic yelling to produce a fantastic cacophony. Barely audible shouts to stand to horses came too late. The frightened animals ripped out their stakes, and flying horses, picket pins, and ropes filled the night. Cursing troopers frantically dove for lariats and held fast to their mounts. Despite their efforts sixty-six horses disappeared into the darkness, including Mackenzie's fine gray pacer. At first light, the colonel sent two small scouting parties led by Captain Heyl and Lieutenant William Hemphill to find the trail of the horses.[34]

In the meantime, Parra-o-coom, the attacking chief, addressed his warriors, exhorting them to meet things straight ahead, to fight, to be brave. The Comanches donned their war shields, tied up their horses' tails, arranged sheets about their waists, and had a parade. When Parra-o-coom gave the word, they moved against the soldiers who followed their trail.[35] Lieutenant Robert Carter, who had warned the sentries to fire a shot if they saw anything, was at that moment completing an inspection tour of the picket posts. Suddenly a gunshot echoed down the rocky slopes of Cañon Blanco. Carter rode to the sound and met Captain Heyl and Lieutenant Hemphill, their scouting parties also attracted by the picket's shot. Down the valley they saw about a dozen Indians driving off several horses. Immediately the three officers and eleven enlisted men scattered out in pursuit. Closing to within pistol shot of the Indians, they opened fire, jumped a small ravine at full gallop, and chased the Indians for several hundred more yards up a hill to the summit. There the soldiers reined up quickly: arrayed before them was the entire Comanche horde. According to Carter, Heyl exclaimed: "Heavens, but we are in a nest! Just look at the Indians."[36] The trials of the campaign had worn down the soldiers' horses, and the just-completed furious chase had left them completely blown. Now they found themselves two miles from camp, exposed in the open with no cover whatsoever, and about to be

charged by a totally superior number of Indians. Carter shouted
that their only possibility for survival would be to dismount and
hold the Indians at bay with rapid fire, then to retreat slowly to the
ravine the troopers had crossed some thousand yards in the rear.
Once there, they should be able to hold out until Mackenzie could
come to their rescue.

Immediately the troopers dismounted, deployed left and right,
and began to fire into the Indians. Heyl galloped to the right to
direct the fire of Hemphill and the six Company K men. Five men
of Company G followed Carter. The soldiers began to retreat
slowly, shooting as they went, taking special care not to allow the
Indians to flank and encircle them.

The troopers' desperate volleys checked the Indians' advance.
Cohaya, one of the Comanche participants, later said:

> The bullets came toward us like the roar of a sling whirling
> through the air. Some of the soldiers were dismounted,
> some mounted. They were about 250 yards away. None of us
> got hit. Our medicine man must have been very powerful.[37]

The Indians were armed with muzzle-loading guns, a few
breech-loading rifles, bows, and lances. Still, the war whoops, the
fantastic colors of their war paint, the ringing bells, the waving
feathers, and the flashing mirrors would have produced a terrifying
effect even upon hardened veterans. Heyl's men, far from being veterans, were raw recruits, and this display of savage military splendor
proved to be more than they could face. They mounted their horses
and, with Captain Heyl and Lieutenant Hemphill in the lead,
dashed for safety.[38]

Lieutenant Carter and his five men were stunned. All their
curses, threats, entreaties, and pleas failed to affect the fleeing soldiers. Shocked and furious, Carter and his men appeared hopelessly
outnumbered, six men facing a hundred "Lords of the Plains."
Nevertheless, the troopers mounted and continued their organized
retreat, turning to fire every few feet. Bullets and arrows flew all
around them and struck several horses. The Indians also hit one
soldier in the hand. Unable to work the lever of his carbine, he
used his hunting knife to eject a spent shell, and just as the Indians

112

Lieutenant Robert G. Carter, Fourth
Cavalry, author and Medal of Honor
winner (National Archives)

Quanah Parker, Comanche chief
(National Archives)

closed upon him, he shot one from the saddle. Again and again the troopers' carbines checked the Comanches' charges. Almost at the ravine, Carter ordered his men to pump several shots into the Indians and make a dash for their lives.

The troopers' rapid, concentrated volleys emptied several Indian saddles and momentarily stemmed the Comanches' advance. Wheeling, the soldiers spurred their exhausted mounts for the ravine. Suddenly, Private William Gregg's horse began to stagger and sway. A large Comanche war chief whom Carter believed to be Quanah Parker raced in upon Gregg, keeping the soldier between himself and the other troopers. Carter fired several shots at the Comanche, and Gregg attempted to use his carbine, but the weapon apparently jammed. The Indian thrust a pistol near the soldier's head and fired, mortally wounding Gregg, who toppled from the saddle. Cohaya recalled, "One of the soldiers got behind. We killed and scalped him. The scalp was no good, but we had a big celebration over it anyway." [39]

The Comanches had almost closed upon Carter and the rest of his men when they abruptly pulled up short and began to fall back. The reason was quickly apparent, for from the direction of Mackenzie's camp came the Tonkawa scouts mounted on their fastest ponies. Yelling and shooting, they drove in upon the Comanches, their mortal enemies. In the midst of the galloping scouts, Carter saw Lieutenant Boehm with his white sombrero whipping in the wind.

When Boehm reined up, Carter was surprised to see Captain Heyl and Lieutenant Hemphill and their men with the scouts. Boehm had met the fleeing men and, using his carbine, had persuaded them to return with him. [40] Mackenzie and his entire command approached while the scouts pursued the retreating Indians. The warriors withdrew up Cañon Blanco, maintaining an irregular, large circle just out of effective rifle range.

A small group of Indians dispersed among the bluffs and boulders of the canyon and began a sniping action against the advancing troops. Quickly, Boehm and Carter and a dozen men engaged the Indians and dislodged them from the cliffs. During this action, Lieutenant Carter suffered an apparent fractured left leg when his horse stumbled into a large boulder. Incredibly, after the surgeon put his leg in splints, Carter spent the rest of that day, as well as all of the next three days, in the saddle leading his men. Only later was it determined that his leg was not broken after all, but only badly bruised.

Mackenzie's main force pursued the Indians through the broken ground above the canyon, but the Comanches mounted fresh horses and escaped into the brush. Realizing that his winded mounts could not possibly overtake the retreating hostiles, Mackenzie halted the advance, probably around 10:00 A.M. The column reformed in the valley, a detail buried Private Gregg's mutilated body, and the grim and weary troopers made camp.

Around 2:30 P.M. Mackenzie took up the chase. Following a fresh trail the Tonkawas had discovered he moved up the canyon until dark. The colonel recognized that the sixty or so men who had lost their horses in the raid could not keep up, and he ordered them to march back to Lawton's supply camp on Duck Creek.

The next day Mackenzie continued to follow the Indian trail through Cañon Blanco. Later that afternoon, he came to the site of the Kwahadis' village. Feeling that the campsite had just been abandoned, Mackenzie pushed onward. However, the Comanches, in typical Plains Indian fashion, crossed and recrossed their trail numerous times, making it difficult to follow. Darkness overtook the cavalry column not far beyond the village site, and Mackenzie went into camp.

The next morning the Tonkawas found the trail on the bluffs above the soldiers' position. The cavalrymen scaled the steep canyon walls and for the first time viewed the formidable Llano Estacado, "a vast, almost illimitable expanse of prairie. As far as the eye could reach, not a bush or tree, a twig or stone, not an object of any kind or a living thing, was in sight."[41]

The troopers wore light cotton clothing suited to summer on the plains of Texas. But they were now three thousand feet above sea level on a cold October 12, and a norther had begun to blow. The command moved along until noon, when the trail disappeared. The scouts soon found it again, on the opposite side of the canyon. The weary column moved down the sloping sides and then struggled up to the opposite plateau, where they found a distinct trail made by dragging lodgepoles and the hooves of two to three thousand horses. It headed west by northwest out onto the Llano Estacado. Mackenzie at once ordered the column forward and followed the fleeing Indian village into the "uninterrupted vastness" of the Staked Plains.[42]

All day Mackenzie pushed after the Indians, right into the teeth of a fierce, howling norther which pelted the soldiers and their animals with sleet and wet snow. Comanche warriors repeatedly appeared on the flanks of the column and harried the troopers, trying to draw their attention from the retreating village. Mackenzie moved his pack train from the rear of the formation to the middle, boxed his squadrons around it, and drove forward. As the day wore on, the cavalrymen passed discarded puppies, lodgepoles, buffalo skins, firewood, and stone hammers, all the precious articles of Indian life. Finally, as darkness approached, the fleeing villagers could be seen perhaps a mile or more in the distance.

Suddenly, however, the norther became a full blizzard. The sleet and snow drove in with numbing impact, and an inky darkness, like "a great black curtain," engulfed the command. So close to his goal, Mackenzie was compelled to halt the chase. The Comanche warriors formed up, dashed close and fired into the ranks of the troopers, then disappeared into the growing darkness. Mackenzie sent a hand-picked detachment galloping in pursuit of the warriors, but it was forced back by the storm. The command pitched camp on the spot. Tarpaulins, blankets, and buffalo robes were unpacked to keep the exhausted troopers from freezing, and they settled down to pass a thoroughly miserable night.[43]

The next day, October 13, dawned clear and beautiful, but after following the trail for a few more miles, Mackenzie turned back and camped on the site of his previous bivouac. The command had ventured about forty miles out on the Llano Estacado. Strangely, Mackenzie did not push on and assault the Comanche village when it seemed to be at his mercy. Perhaps he declined to launch an attack out of compassion for the women and children in the village, although in light of Mackenzie's subsequent attacks on Indian encampments at the North Fork of the Red River, at Remolina in

116

THE CAMPAIGNS OF 1871

Mexico, and at Palo Duro Canyon, this hardly seems likely. Certainly Mackenzie and the Fourth Cavalry never gained a reputation for bloodthirstiness like the Third Colorado Cavalry for their atrocities at Sand Creek or the U.S. Seventh Cavalry for their action at the Washita River and at Wounded Knee, and, indeed, Mackenzie would later capture a large number of noncombatants who proved useful in securing peace on the frontier. Nonetheless, the mute testimony of scores of burned villages and decimated populations left by the hard-striking cavalry regiments argues that, no matter what official policy might be, the relative safety of Indian women and children was never of great concern to the army in the field.

More probable is that Mackenzie feared the vicious blizzard which could destroy his weakened men and their winded mounts. The column was, after all, badly overextended for a unit of its size, being over a hundred miles from the supply base and operating in unknown territory. He may have thought that his troopers simply were not strong enough to fight a major engagement against a determined Indian foe after their exertions of the past three days, let alone survive a raging winter storm afterwards. Or, in light of future disciplinary problems, Mackenzie may even have feared not that his men *could* not fight, but that they *would* not fight. The Fourth was by no means a crack military unit yet, as Captain Heyl and his men had proven just three days earlier. Possibly Mackenzie thought his men simply could go no farther. Unfortunately, conjecture is all that can be offered. Mackenzie never made known his reasons for calling off the pursuit, either to his officers or in his reports.[44]

On October 15, the command moved back into Cañon Blanco and headed for the supply camp. During the march the Tonkawas discovered two Comanche scouts and chased them into a ravine alongside the canyon wall. Mackenzie ordered Lieutenant Boehm to take fifteen dismounted men and drive the Comanches from the ravine. Impatient at the length of time Boehm was taking, Mackenzie rode forward, dismounted, and began directing his movements. Suddenly, there was a swish, a thud, and Mackenzie was down with an arrow protruding from his right thigh. Several troopers helped him to the rear, where Surgeon Rufus Choate removed the barbed arrow and tended the wound. The Comanches wounded another man before Boehm forced them out of the ravine and shot them down. In a letter to the assistant adjutant general, Mackenzie stated that during his return two Indians were killed but only one soldier wounded; Mackenzie failed to mention his wound in the official report, either out of pride or embarrassment.[45]

The column camped at that spot and next day marched to the mouth of Cañon Blanco, where Lawton met them with supplies. Mackenzie allowed the men to rest for a few days. He reasoned that if the Indians he had pursued were indeed Quanah Parker's people, they might soon return to one of Quanah's favorite camping grounds near the headwaters of the Pease. Mackenzie intended to strike at him there, and on October 24, the command moved out in search of Parker. However, Mackenzie's wound became steadily worse, provoking a scene between him and one of the surgeons, Dr. Gregory. The good doctor, hoping to frighten Mackenzie into taking better care of himself, went to the colonel's tent to inform him that if he did not rest more it would become necessary to amputate the limb. No sooner had Dr. Gregory uttered the word "amputate" than Mackenzie "seized a crutch or big cane, and making for the doctor caused him to jump out from under the tent flap to save his own head from amputation." The scarlet-faced physician retreated to his own tent, and amputation was not mentioned again within the colonel's hearing. Nevertheless, Mackenzie reluctantly admitted that he could no longer lead the column and turned command over to Captain Mauck. On October 29 he returned to Lawton's Camp Supply.[46]

Mackenzie sent Lawton and his wagons to Griffin to obtain corn for Mauck's troops and directed Lieutenant W. A. Thompson to march Company A, two-thirds of whom were without horses, back to Richardson. He ordered Lieutenant Carter and the remainder of the men to Cottonwood Springs. Mackenzie then entered an ambulance and started for Fort Richardson, arriving there on November 8. Thompson and Company A came in the following day.[47]

Captain Mauck reached the Pease River and, finding no Comanches, returned to the Duck Creek supply camp through a driving snowstorm, losing several horses to the cold. Lawton reached

Camp Supply on November 7 with the desperately needed provisions, and on November 12, the expedition marched into Fort Griffin singing the regimental song. Mauck and Companies B, F, K, and L, Fourth Cavalry, and I, Eleventh Infantry, continued on to Richardson, arriving there on November 18.[48]

Thus ended Fort Richardson's second Indian campaign of 1871. Mackenzie's troopers had marched 509 miles, suffered greatly from the elements, and lost one man and many horses. Yet there was precious little to show for all their efforts. They had scored no major successes, and the escape of the Comanche village had ended the expedition on a particularly sour note. Still, there had been some progress, and that, perhaps, was all Mackenzie could hope for. Both he and the Fourth were learning, as Carter put it, "a perfectly new game . . . an absolutely new kind of warfare," and the knowledge and experience they needed could not be found in any books or journals. The geography of the land, the necessities of campaigning on the Texas plains in searing summer and numbing winter, the methods of finding and defeating the hostiles, all this and more they had to learn through trial and error, no matter how bitter the lessons proved to be. Slowly, Mackenzie and the Fourth Cavalry were mastering the skills needed to wage war upon the Indians.[49]

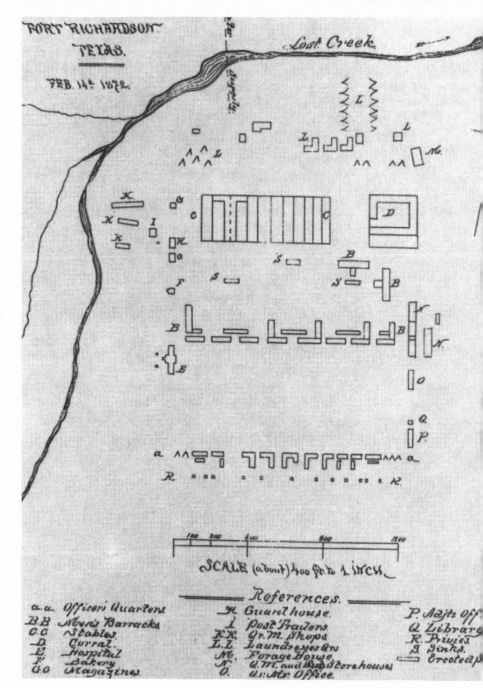

Map of Fort Richardson in 1872, Quartermaster General's Office (National Archives)

CHAPTER SEVEN

ALTHOUGH THE MEN OF
the Fourth Cavalry had quickly
proved themselves more adept
at Indian fighting than their
predecessors, the Sixth Cavalry,
they also proved more accomplished at one of the Sixth's less-
enviable pastimes: deserting.
From January 1868, when they
returned from Buffalo Springs,
until March 1871, when they
marched to Kansas, the Fort Richardson-based elements of the
Sixth Cavalry suffered 195 desertions. From April 1871 to December 1871, the Fourth Cavalry at Richardson lost 171 men to the
same cause, a ratio more than triple that of the previous regiment.
In July alone, sixty-three men left the ranks of the Fourth without
permission and with no intention to return.[1]

The Campaigns of 1872

As a result of their miserable living conditions, the health of
the men deteriorated. In November and December of 1871, ninety-
five men reported sick, a full 20 percent of the garrison. Their dis-
eases included typhoid fever, remittant and intermittent fever,
acute diarrhea and dysentery, and pneumonia.[3] Also, in December,
due to lack of adequate nutrition, scurvy set in. This is hardly surprising considering that the rations consisted of pork, bacon, salted
beef, flour, hard bread, beans, peas, rice, hominy, coffee, and tea.
The post surgeon suggested that pickles, onions, dried apples, and
vinegar be issued immediately, but none of these supplies could be
obtained until the next spring.[4] In the markets of Jacksboro milk
was available for 10¢ a quart, butter for 40¢ a pound, eggs for 75¢ a

121

dozen, and chickens for 75¢ each,[5] but for the average soldier, who made only thirteen dollars a month, such items were priced out of reach. Although thirteen troopers of the Sixth and Fourth cavalries died of disease at Richardson in 1871,[6] this is not a surprisingly high death toll in light of the medical knowledge of the era. The surgeons of the frontier cavalry were basically the same ones whose lack of ability allowed almost as many Union soldiers to die of dysentery and diarrhea in the Civil War as were killed outright on the battlefield[7] and who still blamed many sicknesses on "ill humours" and "bad air."[8]

The troops at Richardson also endured a rigid, disciplined daily schedule that drove a man from sunup to sundown, allowing no time for athletics and little time for recreation.[9] The soldiers sought relief from the dull routine in the saloons of Jacksboro, where their sometimes desperate desires for amusement or escape would usually earn them a stay in the guardhouse, a place where 9 percent of the total garrison of Richardson spent time in 1871.[10] Other punishments might find a soldier walking his beat with a thirty-pound log balanced on his shoulders, chained spread-eagle on a caisson wheel, tied up by the wrists, thrown into an icy pond, or confined in an iron "sweatbox." Only in extreme cases did Mackenzie order a court-martial.[11]

Finally, the troopers found themselves serving in a land where new opportunities were always presenting themselves, and the temptation for a man earning thirteen dollars a month to follow a get-rich-quick idea often proved too great.[12] More than one recruit from New York or Pennsylvania found Texas a land brimming with promise and a four- or five-year enlistment too long a wait to start exploring that promise.

On November 27, the combination of harsh post life, the rigors of the autumn Indian expedition, and deep frustration and loss of morale caused by the failure to capture Quanah Parker's village proved too much for ten men of Company B. They deserted en masse. Mackenzie, furious and determined to put an end to the increasing desertions, called Lieutenants Lawton and Carter to his quarters and ordered each to take a detail of two corporals and eleven privates and pursue the deserters until they were captured.

Mackenzie emphasized that the two officers were not to return without the fugitives, even if this meant trailing them to New Orleans or New York. Lawton and his detail left for Decatur, while Carter took the road to Weatherford.

Carter eventually found the deserters on a wagon train several miles east of Hillsboro. He arrested a civilian driver and eight soldiers. On a sweep through the country on the return to Richardson, Carter uncovered two more deserters, bringing his total haul to eleven. Lawton found no fugitives and, to his great embarrassment, had to report that one of his own patrol had deserted.[13]

Of course, desertions were a problem throughout the army of the 1870s, but there were several reasons why the units stationed at Richardson seemed so particularly hard-hit by them. The government had intended Fort Richardson to be one of a series of links in a defensive shield for the settlements. As such, the post had been designed to accommodate at most six companies of cavalry and two companies of support infantry. But the events of 1871 convinced many in the government, not the least of whom was General Sherman, that the answer to the Indian problem was not to be found in standing on the defensive but in taking the offensive against the hostiles. This, of course, required more men, and by the end of 1871 the garrison had been increased to eleven cavalry and three infantry companies. With the arrival of reinforcements and replacements in the spring of 1872, the adjutant general reported that 666 officers and men were stationed at the fort. No longer was Richardson just the largest post in Texas; it was now the largest military installation of any kind in the United States.[2] And it was terribly overcrowded and unsanitary.

Officers and their families experienced some inconveniences, being forced to share their frame and picket quarters or move into tent shelters. But, as always, the enlisted men were most affected. Barracks intended to house forty to fifty men now overflowed with a hundred or more. The soldiers slept three or four to a bunk on rarely-changed straw mattresses. In the hot months the buildings were stifling. Since only three windows on each side of the barracks had been provided for ventilation, the men suffocated in the close surroundings and oppressive heat. And since the picket walls of the barracks had began to warp almost as soon as they were put up, the cold months proved even worse. The men shivered as arctic winds gusted almost unimpeded through their quarters. Wet months meant leaking roofs and perpetually damp quarters, and dry months meant blowing, choking dust and swarming insects. No matter what the season, the enlisted men suffered.

Carter's massive arrest of the fugitives and their subsequent court-martial broke the back of the problem. Six men deserted in January, but three were recaptured. Immediately, those prisoners plus three of Carter's haul were bundled off to the federal penitentiary at Baton Rouge, and in early February seventeen more followed. These actions had the desired effect upon the enlisted men. There were no desertions in February and only one in March. In total, 1872 brought eighty-seven desertions, still a high number but less than half the total for the previous year.[14]

Once Mackenzie had the Fourth Cavalry's discipline problem reasonably in hand, the troopers settled down to a relatively uneventful winter. The Kiowas, still in shock over the imprisonment of Satanta and Big Tree, stayed on the reservation. But the soldiers were busy. Mackenzie kept an average of three full-scale scouts in the field every month during the winter of 1871–1872, although the countryside was so quiet that the excursions proved to be mere exercise for the soldiers. Several details were sent to Denton and to various sawmills near the post to obtain shingles and lumber, evidence of the never-ending struggle to keep the buildings at Richardson from falling into ruins. Also, an escort of armed soldiers accompanied most wagon trains leaving Richardson, a measure adopted the previous summer after the attack on Henry Warren's corn train.[15]

The relative calm of the early months of 1872 did not last. The Comanches renewed their raiding as soon as their ponies recovered from the winter's fast. The Kiowas resisted the temptation of the warpath for a while, probably through fear for the safety of Satanta and Big Tree, but at last the warm weather, the fat, sleek war ponies, and the inactivity of the reservation proved too much. They, too, resumed their raids with a fury. On April 24, 1872, Mackenzie wrote to the assistant adjutant general of the Department of Texas to complain about the perennial problem of the cavalry in

Texas: "From the vigorous manner in which Indian raids have opened in the last few days, it is of the utmost importance that the Companies should be kept well mounted to render them efficient."[16]

The Indian raids indeed opened in a "vigorous manner." On April 20, a band of Kiowas under White Horse and Big Bow swarmed over a government contractor's train at Howard's Wells in Crockett County, killing seventeen teamsters; eight were chained to the wheels of their burning wagons and roasted alive. Two companies of the Ninth Cavalry from Fort Concho overtook the Indians but were driven back, one officer losing his life in the fight. Other Kiowas attacked a civilian surveying party under L. H. Luckett near old Fort Belknap on May 19, killing one surveyor. The Indians lost two braves to the Texans' accurate fire; one was Kompaite, the young brother of White Horse.[17]

White Horse immediately organized a vengeance raid. On June 19, he and seven other Kiowas overran the small farm of Abel Lee and his family, on the Clear Fork of the Brazos, just a few miles from Fort Griffin. Lee died in his chair on the front porch while his wife was shot down inside the house, scalped, and mutilated. Their four children attempted to escape through a vegetable garden, but one was shot and killed and the rest captured. They were carried north to the reservation, where the participants in the raid claimed them as slaves. In great distress, agent Tatum was forced to report to the Commissioner of Indian Affairs a painfully obvious truth, "The Kiowas and a few bands of the Comanches are uncontrollable by me."[18]

With Indians in the vicinity, Mackenzie kept scouts out constantly. Eleven full-scale scouting parties left Fort Richardson in May in pursuit of raiders, but only two managed to find any. On May 18, Lieutenant John McKinney, with one officer, ten privates, and Henry Strong, the post scout, engaged twenty hostiles in a pitched battle near the center of present-day Wichita Falls. The Indians managed to slip away, but not unscathed. As Strong later wrote: "We never knew how many we killed, but while they held us off they tied three of their bucks on horses." The other patrol to encounter Indians that month was not as successful. The unlucky Captain Heyl, who had allegedly deserted Carter at Cañon Blanco, and a detachment from Companies A and B were encamped fifteen miles from Richardson on May 23 when they were attacked by an "overwhelming number" of hostiles. The Indians managed to shoot one of the enlisted men, Private Lawrence Henche, through the lungs and drive the entire command back to Richardson. Henche died shortly after reaching the post hospital.[19]

On March 28, 1872, a Fort Concho detachment of Fourth Cavalry, under the command of Sergeant William H. Wilson, intercepted a band of Comanchero raiders. The troopers killed two of the men and, most importantly, captured one. The captive, who said his name was Polonis Ortiz, confessed to being one of a band of cattle thieves operating from New Mexico in conjunction with the Kwahadi Comanches. The frightened Mexican proceeded to name his employers, to reveal the locations of several trading stations, and to claim that a good road with plenty of permanent water and grass crossed the Llano Estacado.[20] General C. C. Augur, a veteran Indian fighter who succeeded General Reynolds as commander of the Department of Texas,[21] ordered an investigation to determine the truth of Ortiz's statements. Nearly two months later, on May 13, Captain Napoleon Bonaparte McLaughlen returned to Concho from a sweeping scout to report that not only was everything Ortiz claimed true, but also a recently abandoned campsite of about two hundred lodges was discovered, with indications that at least a thousand head of horses and mules had been herded nearby.[22] On the basis of this information Augur summoned Mackenzie to San Antonio on May 20. After a short strategy meeting, the two officers agreed on a plan of action, and Mackenzie left San Antonio carrying Augur's orders for an immediate campaign against the Staked Plains Comanches.[23]

Mackenzie returned to Fort Richardson on June 2 and began to assemble his expedition. Previous experience, the information gained from Ortiz, and the best guesswork of his Tonkawa scouts suggested a number of possible Comanche lairs: Cañon Blanco, the Mucha Que Valley, the North Fork of the Red River, and Palo Duro Creek. Mackenzie intended to search these locations, one after another, until he found his quarry. He sent to Concho ordering Major Alfred Latimer and Companies D and I of the Fourth Cavalry to move to Camp Supply on Duck Creek. Lieutenant Colonel William Shafter received directions to march from Fort McKavett with three companies of the Twenty-fourth Infantry, including wagons, ambulances, and surgeons, and to be in camp on the Freshwater Fork of the Brazos by July 1. On June 19, Mackenzie left Richardson with Companies A, B, and L, wagons, and pack mules.[24] At Griffin he picked up Company F, Fourth Cavalry, and Company A, Eleventh Infantry, Lieutenant Boehm and twenty scouts, and more wagons and mules. Leaving Griffin on June 22, Mackenzie retraced his route of the previous year to Duck Creek, arriving on June 27 at Camp Supply, where he was met by Major Latimer's command from Concho.[25]

If any Indians lurked near Cañon Blanco, where Mackenzie had been wounded the year before, the Colonel wished to snare them. Expecting Shafter soon to be in position on the Freshwater Fork, Mackenzie ordered Major Latimer and Companies D and I to march up the river. Meanwhile, he and the rest of the command cut across the tablelands to Cañon Blanco and moved down the Freshwater Fork. He hoped that any Indians in the area would be driven into a trap between the three forces; however, on July 1, Mackenzie met Latimer's command moving up the river. Nothing had been seen of Shafter and his Twenty-fourth Infantry (unknown to Mackenzie, Shafter had gotten a late start from McKavett and was at that time still toiling towards the Freshwater Fork). The entrapment action was a failure.[26]

Mackenzie established a supply camp there on the Freshwater Fork of the Brazos and ordered more material, including 19,200 rounds of ammunition, from Fort Griffin. He dispatched two unsuccessful scouts south and southwest, about forty miles into the Mucha Que Valley, and then personally led a ten-day scout north as far as Mulberry Creek but found nothing.[27]

This reconnaissance convinced Mackenzie that the Comanches were either on the North Fork of the Red River or on Palo Duro Creek. Meanwhile, Ortiz, who had been brought along to help the scouts, discovered a wide, well-traveled road where none should have been, running westward onto the Staked Plains. The tracks of a large cattle herd were plainly visible. For one hundred years the white man had considered the Llano Estacado too vast and too arid even to explore, much less to move cattle across. Clearly this situation warranted investigation. In light of existing geographical knowledge of the area, Mackenzie decided to take an enormous gamble. On July 28, he turned westward along the road with a picked command of Companies A, B, D, F, and I—a total of 240 troopers of the Fourth—and Quartermaster Lawton with his supply train. The remainder of the command stayed behind to guard the supply camp.[28]

August 7 found Mackenzie and his men camped on the Las Cañadinas Arroyo, about twenty miles from Fort Sumner, New Mexico.[29] The march across the Staked Plains, which had been so daring in conception, proved quite ordinary in execution. Mackenzie simply followed the path which countless cattle hooves had made quite plain. He found water and good grazing all along the way, but no Comanches or Comancheros. Mackenzie rested and re-supplied at Fort Sumner, then turned the column north to Fort Bascom, New Mexico, arriving there on August 16.[30]

Ortiz told Mackenzie about a return route which ran east along Tierra Blanca Creek to Palo Duro Canyon, one of the two remaining sites where the Kwahadi Comanches might be camped. Mackenzie determined to try this new route and sent a detachment ahead to scout for Indian camps along Palo Duro Creek, which ran parallel to the Tierra Blanca and joined it at Palo Duro Canyon.

On August 18, Mackenzie headed east following Ortiz's new trail and executed another uneventful march. On August 23, he met his detachment at the junction of the Tierra Blanca and the Palo Duro, again without finding Indians. Disappointed, Mackenzie returned to his Freshwater Fork supply camp, arriving there on August 31. In thirty days of campaigning, his command had marched 640 miles, crossed the Staked Plains by two different routes both superior to the Pecos Trail (the major cattle trail in use at that time), and obtained invaluable information which contributed greatly to the exploration of the American West. Mackenzie had proven that troops could operate on the Llano Estacado, and the implications were enormous. The roads, water, and good grazing he had discovered would soon provide the means for the United States army to strike at the hostile Kiowas and Comanches in their last strongholds, and the trail he had blazed, already being called the Mackenzie Trail by the troopers, would soon be followed by countless pioneers and settlers. General Augur, in his annual report on September 28, 1872, wrote that the information and knowledge Mackenzie obtained was "well worth the summer's labor."[31]

Mackenzie, however, was not ready to rest on his laurels. He had accomplished much, but he had failed to discover any Indians or Comancheros. Ortiz had told him that the Kwahadis usually camped either on Palo Duro Creek or on the North Fork of the Red River. He now knew the Indians were not anywhere along the Palo Duro, so he made plans to move on the North Fork.[32]

For three weeks Mackenzie rested and resupplied his command at the Duck Creek camp. The horses, which had almost worn away their shoes, were reshod. They required good grazing to regain their strength. Quartermaster Lawton brought supplies and tended to repairing the wagons and harnesses. On Saturday, September 21, Mackenzie moved north with Companies A, D, F, I, and L of the Fourth Cavalry, Company I of the Twenty-fourth Infantry, Lieutenant Boehm and his Tonkawas, the post guide Henry Strong, Polonis Ortiz, and assorted medical and engineering personnel. In all, Mackenzie's force consisted of twelve officers and 272 enlisted men. Because of the poor condition of its mounts, Company B, Fourth Cavalry, returned to Fort Richardson.[33]

By September 28, Mackenzie was within twenty miles of the North Fork of the Red River. He detached his supply train, with the Twenty-fourth Infantry to guard it, and the next day marched on to the South Fork of McClellan's Creek, a tributary of the North Fork. About four miles above where the streams joined, Boehm's scouts found two trails, one of two horses, the other of a mule. The vines along the creek were loaded with grapes, and it appeared that the mule was used to carry a load of picked grapes. The scouts were sure a village was nearby. The command followed the trail of the mule for twelve miles until, in the distance, Mackenzie saw the object of his two-year search: a large Comanche village, situated in a beau-

Lieutenant Peter Martin Boehm, Fourth Cavalry. Courtesy Special Collections of the University of Texas at Arlington Libraries, Arlington, Texas.

Mow-way (Shaking Hand), Comanche chief (National Archives)

tiful valley some three to five miles away on the south side of the North Fork. It was the village of the Kotsoteka chief Mow-way, or Shaking Hand, and was the largest of many Kwahadi and Kotsoteka camps in the area.[34]

Mackenzie rested his horses for a few minutes, then formed his men in columns of four. The covers were removed from the flag and guidons, and the command galloped forward. The Indians, going about their daily routine, were caught completely by surprise. They could see the troopers' dust but apparently thought their own hunters were chasing buffalo.[35]

The troopers moved to within a half-mile of the village before the Indians became aware of them. Horrified squaws dropped ladles into cooking fires and bowls onto the ground at the sight of the advancing bluecoats. Warriors caught the glint of sunlight off polished carbines. The Indians scattered. Women grabbed up children and ran for the brush. Warriors snatched up weapons and sprinted for their war ponies. The camp was a mass of confusion when Mackenzie and his troopers slashed into the outer perimeter of teepees.

Company D veered just north of the camp and headed for the horse herd, one of the prime objectives of any Indian campaign. Company I overran a detached group of lodges to the south of the camp. Mackenzie and companies A, F, and L charged into the heart of the village, Spencer carbines, Smith-Wessons, and Colt pistols cracking and flashing in the dusty light.[36]

Company F rode in the middle of this attacking formation. The sergeant in charge of the rear set of fours in the company's column was John Charlton, who a year before as corporal had played a role in the death of old Satank. The order "Right front into line!" brought Sergeant Charlton's set of fours wheeling to form the right end of what was now a linear formation. Suddenly, several Indians who had been concealed in some nearby high grass rose and fired a volley with their rifles and bows into the turning troopers. The bullets and arrows brought down every trooper in the squad. Only Charlton escaped unharmed. He immediately returned fire, downing one of the ambushers; the rest fled.[37]

Company A pushed a group of Indians to the edge of the river where about eighty of them launched a desperate stand. The troopers twice deployed to flank the Indians' position. Each time the defenders charged to prevent the maneuver and were driven back with heavy losses. The warriors dumped their dead in a deep pool of water to prevent the Tonkawas from scalping and desecrating them. Company I swung around and came to the aid of Company A, pumping such a severe fire into the Indians' position that the warriors fled and the women surrendered.[38]

After a half-hour battle, Mackenzie's cavalry secured the village. The troopers began to round up prisoners and count the dead. Mackenzie lost one man, and two others would soon die. Three soldiers were wounded and ten horses killed.[39] The Comanches suffered heavily, although the exact number of dead is not certain: Mackenzie said twenty-four, while other estimates range from fifty to sixty-two. Among the dead were Kotsoteka Chief Kai-wotche and his wife. It was Kai-wotche's mule that Mackenzie had trailed to the village.[40]

The Tonkawas immediately began to scalp their dead foes, but Mackenzie put a stop to what he regarded as a disgusting practice. Tonkawa Henry, one of the lead trackers, was indignant at being denied his natural battle-won right: "What for you no Lette me scalp heme Comanche?"[41] he demanded. Mackenzie, however, was adamant, and, after being promised their pick of the captured Comanche horses, the frustrated scouts desisted.

Mackenzie's haul was impressive indeed. He took prisoner some 130 women and children and captured 175 large and 87 small teepees. But most important of all, he took the Comanche horse herd, which accounts placed at from 800 to 3000 animals.[42]

Mackenzie ordered all the lodges and most of the Comanche property that could be gathered burned. The soldiers herded the prisoners two miles from the smoking village and with the arrival of nightfall made camp. Mackenzie corralled the Indian ponies in a draw halfway between his camp and the ruins of the village and assigned Boehm and the still-annoyed Tonkawas to guard it. Unfortunately the Tonkawas' petulance gave way to exhaustion, and they were all soon fast asleep. Before long, the sound of shouts, war whoops, and bells split the night.[43] Mackenzie must have thought he was reliving his nightmare of a year before when Quanah Parker's Comanches ran off the last captured herd.

At first the Comanches failed, but later that night they struck again, more successfully. Not only did they regain most of their lost ponies but the mounts of Boehm and the Tonkawas also. The next day, Boehm and the scouts walked into camp "looking sheepish and woefully dejected."[44] Mackenzie reported that the Indians struck again the next night and ran off still more of the captured herd, until all he retained were fifty ponies and nine mules. As promised, Mackenzie allowed the Tonkawas to have their choice of the horses "to give them some encouragement" and turned the rest over to the quartermaster.[45]

Mackenzie moved back to his supply camp, arriving on October 8, 1872. He sent the captive Comanches under escort to Fort Concho where they were held in the post corral, well sheltered and fed. The companies were dispatched to their respective posts, A and L arriving at Richardson on October 23.[46]

Mackenzie's victory at the North Fork of the Red River has been called "one of the major Anglo-American triumphs over the Indians on the Southern Plains."[47] Congress awarded nine Medals of Honor for gallantry during the action.[48] Fort Richardson's commander was proving himself to be one of the finest Indian fighters of the West, and now even the Kwahadis began to respect and fear "Bad Hand" Mackenzie. He showed the Indians that the white soldiers could hunt them down and attack them even in the heart of their strongholds. The days of the "Lords of the Plains" were fast becoming numbered.

CHAPTER EIGHT

WHEN COLONEL MACKEN-
zie returned from General Augur's headquarters in San Antonio on November 5, 1872,[1] the
glory days of Fort Richardson
ended. Augur and Mackenzie
had decided that Richardson
was too far east to accommodate
expeditions to the Staked Plains,
and, since it appeared that the
final acts in the struggle for the

The Years of Decision, 1873–1875

Southern Plains would be fought out on that vast and bleak arena,
it seemed necessary to move the Fourth Cavalry to Fort Concho,
nearer to the theater of operations.[2] Although Richardson still had
a vital role in the defense of the Texas frontier, after 1873 the em-
phasis shifted more to civil matters, and no more Indian campaigns
originated from the fort.

On December 18, 1872, Lieutenant Colonel George Buell,
Eleventh Infantry, left Richardson to assume command of Fort
Griffin, and on December 28, Fort Griffin's former commanding
officer, Colonel William Wood, Eleventh Infantry, arrived at Rich-
ardson. After a brief meeting, Mackenzie handed over command of
the post to Colonel Wood, and he and Lieutenant Lawton left for
Fort Concho. Thus Richardson became the headquarters of the
Eleventh Infantry, as well as the home post for Companies B, C, D,
I, and K of that regiment.[3] Companies A, B, C, and E of the Fourth
Cavalry remained at the post until March 4, 1873, when the weather
improved enough for them to march to their new post, Fort Con-

cho. They were replaced at Richardson by Companies E, I, and L of the Tenth Cavalry, formerly stationed at Fort Sill.[4]

In all, seven companies of the Tenth were transferred to Texas, with Companies C and D taking post at Fort Griffin and A and F at Concho.[5] The townspeople were not happy with the change, for the Tenth Cavalry, as well as its sister regiment, the Ninth, was composed entirely of negro soldiers with white officers.

General Ulysses S. Grant had organized the Tenth in August 1866. As its first commander he appointed Colonel Benjamin Henry Grierson, who had gained acclaim throughout the North in April 1863 when he led three regiments of Union cavalry on a sixteen-day, six-hundred-mile raid from Memphis to Baton Rouge. Grierson's task with the Tenth Cavalry was not simple. Many superior officers discriminated against the black regiments in housing, equipment, mounts, and assignments. Junior officers often refused to accept transfers to the Ninth and Tenth because they believed the negroes to be inferior soldiers and commissions in the regiments to be socially degrading. Despite these very real problems and prejudices, Grierson managed to mold the ex-slaves and field hands into a first-class fighting unit.[6] Since arriving in Indian Territory, the Tenth had established an excellent regimental service record, engaging in almost constant skirmishing with the Indians and coolly arresting Satank, Satanta, and Big Tree in 1871. Because the Indians thought the black troopers' hair resembled that of the buffalo, they called the men of the Tenth "Buffalo Soldiers," a name they proudly accepted.[7]

At Fort Richardson, the three companies of buffalo soldiers posted a desertion rate one-tenth that of Mackenzie's "crack" Fourth Cavalry and one-sixth that of Colonel Wood's Eleventh Infantry companies. Desertion declined to a point where the Tenth enjoyed the lowest rate in the United States Army of the late nineteenth century.[8] The army offered a negro a better life at this time than he could achieve as a civilian. White soldiers felt underpaid and ill-cared-for; negro soldiers were generally delighted with any pay and seemed "accustomed to hard knocks."[9] They were certainly healthier. For instance, at Fort Richardson, only during one month in 1873 did more black soldiers than white report for sick call. In February 1873, out of 381 white officers and men present at the post, 24 reported sick; of the 156 black soldiers present, only 1 answered sick call.[10]

If the black soldiers expected to find a grateful civilian population, they were quickly disappointed. The heavy hand of Reconstruction had only recently been removed from the state, and the Republican government which had forced bitterly resented reforms upon the population was still in power. The hatreds engendered by the Civil War and Reconstruction were still fresh, and in many minds, ex-slaves carrying guns were all-too-painful reminders of southern defeat and northern victory. Too, social prejudices die hard. H. H. McConnell, who had retired from the army and returned to Jacksboro to live, wrote:

> A club of the officers and men . . . would occasionally give a ball to which the citizens were invited. They were enjoyable occasions, and no friction ever occured between the citizens and soldiers, as a rule. This don't apply to the colored soldiers; the citizens here had little use for the latter, and, in fact, the white soldiers hadn't either; they looked upon them as an *unnecessary* evil.[11]

Longtime Jacksboro resident Thomas F. Horton described the negro soldiers as "haughty, impudent and insulting. They usually came over to town in bunches of from thirty to forty. The private citizens had no protection from them, if one happened to say Negro in the hearing of one of these groups he was grossly insulted and against such numbers had to endure their scoffing."[12]

Such conduct, however, might not always be endured, for as Horton dryly noted, "Occasionally a horse-back man in town, if insulted by them would empty his six-shooter into them and hurriedly depart." This was the case with one Jack Horner, who was accosted by "a considerable bunch" of black soldiers in one of Jacksboro's numerous saloons. A shooting quickly followed, in which the soldiers sustained losses and withdrew. They soon returned, in greater numbers and with a white sergeant, and attempted to arrest Horner. The result was a rousing gun battle fought in the streets of the town, at the end of which Horner managed to make good his escape in a hail of bullets. A few days later he returned to Jacksboro with a lawyer, and together they visited the post commander where a treaty was negotiated. Supposedly Horner agreed "not to kill any more Negroes if the Negroes would not kill any more of him."[13]

In Texas in the 1870s, incidents between blacks and whites were inevitable. Shoving matches, harsh words, and fistfights among the soldiers were common and usually resulted in no more serious consequences than a stay in the guardhouse. However, the potential for real violence was always present: on August 1, 1872, for instance, several white soldiers of the Eleventh Infantry objected to the presence of a party of blacks at a dancehouse in Jacksboro. In the ensuing melee, a white, Sergeant William Lawrence, was shot to death and another, Corporal Zachery Ringiron, was seriously wounded. Their assailants were never apprehended.[14]

In spite of the problems generated by the ever-present racial prejudices of the times, the troopers of the Tenth performed their duties at Richardson admirably. They were constantly in the field, escorting literally hundreds of civilian contractors' trains and mail stages to Fort Griffin. They aided local law officers in making arrests, pursued and captured rustlers and horse thieves, and transported criminals to the District Court in Weatherford. Their escorts protected cattle herds moving west, and their hard-riding patrols kept open the Butterfield Trail.[15] The protection afforded by the cavalrymen's carbines had a marvelous way of transcending the issue of race.

During 1873 and 1874, the three companies of buffalo soldiers supported by three to five companies of Eleventh Infantry made up the entire garrison of Fort Richardson. The post adjutant complained in March 1873 that "the strength of the garrison [is] entirely inadequate for the performance of the duties required of it." The infantry units supplied all the demands for skilled labor at the post, which left the cavalry to handle guard duty as well as escort details. Under such conditions, more than one night's rest between guard duty shifts was considered a luxury.[16]

Fortunately, the spring and early summer of 1873 were relatively quiet on the Texas frontier. Seven details rode from Richardson "in pursuit of hostile Indians" during this time, a small number compared to the Fourth Cavalry's twenty-five scouts put in the field over a like period in 1871.[17] However, none of the Tenth Cavalry's scouts found Indians.

This period of unprecedented quiet can only be attributed to the calming effects of holding Indian hostages behind prison walls at Huntsville and in a corral at Fort Concho. In October 1872, a delegation of Kiowas led by Lone Wolf visited Washington at the request of the Indian Department and obtained the federal government's promise that if the peace were kept for six months, Satanta and Big Tree would be released from prison. A short time later, after Mackenzie's success at the North Fork, the famous Comanche war chief Parra-o-coom (Bull Bear) came to the Fort Sill agency and told agent Lawrie Tatum that the soldiers had defeated his people. He said he was ready to move to the reservation and raise corn. But first, Tatum must restore the women and children that Mackenzie had taken.[18]

Tatum believed that this would be a mistake. Since he had requested the arrest of Satank, Satanta, and Big Tree, the agent had come to favor a policy of prompt punishment for every crime the Indians committed, a view which brought him into direct conflict with the peace policy of his coreligionists. Using the leverage that the imprisoned Satanta and Big Tree gave over the Kiowas and Mackenzie's prisoners over the Comanches, Tatum had managed to free fourteen white captives and twelve Mexicans. But instead of thanks, his failure to support the peace policy brought him an official reprimand from the Executive Committee of the Friends. On March 31, 1873, Tatum resigned.[19]

His successor, James Haworth, was in full accord with the views of the Executive Committee: namely, that kind acts and good faith would have more effect upon the Indians than threats of retaliation. As a gesture of goodwill, one of Haworth's first acts was to ask the army to remove all its troops from the agency grounds. To further gain the confidence of their charges and to show the generosity of the government, the Quakers then asked for the release of the Comanche captives. General Augur agreed and ordered the prisoners taken by wagon to Fort Sill under military escort. There, on June 11, 1873, the captive women and children were returned to their tribesmen.[20] The grateful Comanche chiefs pledged to walk the white man's road forever, but no sooner had the Indians departed than a few Comanche raiders struck at the Texas settlements.

Meanwhile, Secretary of the Interior Columbus Delano, encouraged by the relative peace on the Texas frontier and by the Kiowas' assurances that they would keep that peace if Satanta and Big Tree were released, asked Governor Davis to free the chiefs. This sparked an immediate explosion of local public resentment. The Texas press attacked both Delano and the governor, and the state legislature voted unanimously against a pardon. The Quakers pressured Delano by reminding him that the government had promised to release the chiefs if the Kiowas stopped raiding. By all accounts, the Indians had lived up to their end of the bargain, and if the Quakers were going to win the full trust and cooperation of their wards, then the government must do likewise. Finally, despite public opinion and after many stops and starts, Governor Davis personally paroled the two chiefs to their people at Fort Sill on October 8, 1873.[21] In anger and disgust, General Sherman wrote to Davis:

> I believe in making a tour of your frontier with a small escort, I ran the risk of my life; and I said what I now say to you, that I will not again voluntarily assume that risk in the interest of your frontier, that I believe Satanta and Big Tree will have their revenge if they have not already had it, and that if they are to have scalps, that yours is the first that should be taken.[22]

Now that the captives were free, the grass was up, and the ponies were sleek and fat, the dire predictions of men such as Sherman and Tatum began to move towards grim fullfillment.

The quiet in Jack County was shattered in the early fall. Howell Walker, aged fifty; his son Henry, thirteen; and Mortimer Stevens were hunting deer at Thurman's Spring on Little Salt Creek, some seven miles southwest from Jacksboro and six miles from Fort Richardson, when they were surprised by a band of Indians, most probably Comanches. In a sworn deposition before Jack County Justice

140

of the Peace Moses Wiley, Mortimer Stevens described the events that transpired:

> We saw some deer coming in from the North, we were about forty yards apart, I had showed [Mr. Walker] the deer, and he looked . . . to the left, toward the bluff and started to run toward me and said "My God Steve the world is alive with Indians . . . the best thing we can do is to make that mountain." Him and his son started for the mountain . . . and I struck in behind them. We had made a little point of timber in there about two hundred and fifty yards from the Spring. About that time, here come the Indians charging us from the direction of the Spring. We fell down on our bellies and they charged all around us. They had passed us, and we all started for a bluff in the creek, and when we got in about one hundred yards of the creek bluff the Indians charged us again. When we got down in the creek the Indians came charging right along the edge of it and commenced shooting down the creek at us. I commenced shooting and then two run around the head of the branch and got in behind us. I was shooting at the Indians in front of us and he was watching the Indians behind us. He kept raising his gun to his face and taking it down again, and while he was doing that he was shot by the two Indians that got behind us. I think the shot went through him and wounded his son, they both sung out "wounded" about the same time.
>
> The old man fell right over backwards his son was lying on his belly, and the old man was setting on his knee watching the Indians on the other side of the creek. They were both gasping for breath.
>
> The old man said to me "Steve if you get out alive have me buried decent, and go to Mr. Ayres and get the money that is due on the hay" the boy said "My Lord Steve I am killed" while they were gasping I shot at an Indian and he gave a yell and I started down the creek in the direction I shot, they did not follow me.[23]

Stevens escaped into a blackjack thicket and eventually made his way to Fort Richardson. A detail under the command of Captain Thomas Little and a group of citizens recovered the bodies the next day. Little pursued the raiders but failed to overtake them.[24] One of the citizens, Jacksboro resident L. J. Valentine, wrote to Governor Davis immediately upon returning from Thurman's Spring:

> I have just returned from one of the most revolting sights I have ever witnessed—the mutilated bodies of Howell Walker, and his Son Henry . . . who were killed yesterday at "Thurman's Spring" about 7 miles S.W. from here.
>
> During the last month there has Scarcely a night passed without Some depredations being committed by the Indians in the vicinity of the town, and "Fort Richardson," and throughout the Country— Some, within half a mile of the military post. As many as 150 to 200 Horses and Mules, have been taken during this period . . .[25]

Even before the attack at Thurman's Spring, the units at Richardson increased their patrols and scouts. On August 15, Captain Theodore A. Baldwin and Companies E and I of the Tenth left Richardson to join Fort Sill's new commanding officer, Lieutenant Colonel John W. Davidson, in a major scout through southern Indian Territory. Davidson wanted to determine if the reservation Indians still raided in Texas. After covering some four hundred miles, Davidson returned to Sill on September 14 and reported that the entire reservation was a "city of refuge" for the raiders and that the only way to solve the problem was to dismount the Indians and make them answer a daily roll-call.[26]

In early October, Captain Baldwin and Company I discovered a band of Indians on the Salt Creek Prairie. After a long chase, the Indians abandoned nine of their ponies, which Baldwin herded back to Richardson. The post adjutant wrote a large "Successful" beside the report of the scout.[27]

Also in early October, a party of unscrupulous white men stole a large herd of Comanche ponies from near the Fort Sill agency. On October 24, Second Lieutenant Charles R. Ward and ten privates accompanied the United States marshal to a place identified only as "Paradise Prairie" to recover most of the stolen herd and arrest one of the ringleaders, a man named William P. Jackson. Ward and the marshal returned Jackson and the horse herd to Fort Sill early in November,[28] but the damage to the shaky peace already was done. Nine Kiowas and twenty-one Comanches used the theft as an excuse to invade Texas. All of the Kiowas were of the *on-de*, the aristocracy of the tribe, and their number included Tau-ankia (Sitting-in-the-Saddle), favorite son of Chief Lone Wolf, and Gui-tain (Heart-of-a-Young-Wolf), son of Red Otter and nephew of Lone Wolf. Actually, gaining replacements for the stolen horses was of minor importance compared to the thirst of these young Indian warriors to attain social prestige through brave deeds in combat. Before the release of Satanta and Big Tree, the Kiowa chiefs had restrained their tribesmen from raiding with the threat of killing any offender's horses and burning his teepee. But now that the army no longer held the two captives, the restraints upon the restless warriors dissolved. As one young warrior haughtily informed a Quaker council: "It matters not what the chiefs said in council with the whites. We, the young men, are the warriors, and shall not listen to them or any one else. We shall do as we please. Washington may be a big chief among white people but he is not our chief, and he has nothing to do with us. We shall not be controlled by him."[29]

Altogether, during the fall of 1873 Indians killed six civilians in the vicinity of Fort Richardson.[30] It seemed the promises made by the Comanches and the Kiowas were growing as cold as the passing days. In late November, Tau-ankia, Gui-tain, and their companions struck along the Nueces River in Texas, killing several ranchers. They then continued into Mexico, killed fourteen citizens on the Olmos River, and captured some 150 horses and mules. On December 7, the returning raiders were intercepted near South Kickapoo Springs in Edwards County by Lieutenant Charles L. Hudson and forty-one troopers of the Fourth Cavalry scouting out of Fort Clark. In the ensuing battle nine Indians died, among them Tau-ankia and Gui-tain. When the news reached Lone Wolf's camp, he went into deep mourning, slashed his body, burned his teepee, slew his ponies, and swore revenge upon the Texans. "The camp re-

143

sounded with the death-wail—the song of mourning for the unre-
turning braves—mingled with the war-whoop."[31]

As the number of raids stepped up, so too did the number of
interceptions by cavalry patrols. In February, a Tenth Cavalry patrol out of Fort Griffin attacked a party near Double Mountains,
killing eleven Comanches. All totaled, thirty Kiowas and Comanches died while on raids in Texas during the winter of 1873–1874.[32]
The tribes were furious, and hundreds of warriors joined Lone Wolf
in desiring revenge. Kicking Bird, always the advocate of peace,
found his path a lonely one.

Besides a burning desire for revenge, other factors spurred the
tribes onto the warpath. The quality and quantity of the rations
issued by the agents on the reservation was wanting. During the
previous winter, some Indians who had remained close to their
agencies had been forced to kill their horses and mules to supple-
ment their meager commissary supplies. Unfortunately, if there was
not always sufficient food available, there always seemed to be more
than enough whiskey bartered to the tribes by illicit white traders.
Various Indian agents and commissioners had complained of this il-
legal trade for years, without much effect. Henry Alvord, Special
Commissioner to the Kiowas and Comanches, called the problem
"the most dangerous evil of all."[33] The situation was further aggravated when horse thieves from Texas and Kansas enraged the Indians by stealing large numbers of ponies from the tribal herds.

While this combination of hatred, injured pride, empty bellies, and whiskey would have been more than sufficient in earlier
days to send the tribes down the warpath,[34] in 1874 there was an
even more pressing reason for action, a situation that demanded urgent attention. The completion of the transcontinental railroad
had provided, for the first time, the means for the New England
leather industries to tap the seemingly unlimited masses of buffalo
ranging the Southern Plains. Small armies of hunters, transported
by rail, descended upon the great animals. From 1872 to 1874,
hunters killed an estimated 3.7 million buffalo (although some historians believe the actual number to be twice as great) while only
150,000 were brought down by Indians. In 1873 alone, the Atchi-

Guipago (Lone Wolf), major chief of the Kiowas (National Archives)

son, Topeka and Santa Fe Railroad moved 251,433 robes, 1,617,600 pounds of meat, and 2,743,100 pounds of bone. The slaughter was so great that even the Texas legislature became concerned, but General Sheridan told them, "Let them kill, skin, and sell until the buffalo is exterminated, as it is the only way to bring lasting peace and allow civilization to advance."[35]

The buffalo supplied the Indians with food, clothing, shelter, weapons, tools—all the essentials of life. The buffalo hunt had acquired a spiritual connotation to the Plains Indians. The pursuit of the buffalo had led them to master the horse, and mounted, they soon had mastered their environment. One of the terms of the Medicine Lodge Treaty allowed the Indians to leave the reservation to hunt buffalo, and the meat brought back supplemented the deficient rations of the agency. Of all the various threats to the Plains Indians' way of life, by far the gravest was the impending extermination of the buffalo. Without the great herds the Indians could not exist free and wild on the plains. They would be forced to come to the reservation and take the white man's dole.

And there was the truth of it, a truth so apparent and simple that all the tribes seemed to grasp it at once. Accordingly, their anger lashed out at the buffalo killers. On June 27, 1874, seven hundred Indians led by Quanah Parker and a new Comanche prophet, Isatai (Rear-End-of-a-Wolf), fell upon a party of buffalo hunters at Adobe Walls, Texas. Isatai had preached a war to kill all the whites and save the buffalo and had promised to use his magic to make the warriors impervious to the white man's bullets. However, the Indians lost the element of total surprise, and the twenty-eight hunters managed to keep them at bay with their long-range rifles despite several fierce charges by the warriors. Much to their dismay, the Indians discovered that Isatai's magic did not work after all, and at the end of the day, they withdrew north, having lost thirteen to fifteen warriors and forty-six ponies. They killed only three of the white hunters.[36]

Lone Wolf may have been at the Battle of Adobe Walls,[37] but if so, the deaths of three buffalo hunters were not enough to assuage his grief. In April, he had traveled to Texas with a sizable number of companions to recover the bodies of Tau-ankia and Gui-tain. Hotly

146

pursued by units of the Fourth Cavalry, Lone Wolf buried his son and nephew in a cleft high up on a mountainside and then led his warriors in an attack upon a horse herd belonging to the Ninth Cavalry. The Indians killed one trooper, captured twenty-two horses, and escaped towards the Staked Plains.[38]

In early July, the Kiowas held their annual medicine dance, or Sun Dance, on the North Fork of the Red River, in Greer County, Indian Territory.[39] After the dance ended, Maman-ti, the medicine man who had been one of the leaders of the attack on Henry Warren's corn train, agreed to lead the revenge raid that Lone Wolf so desperately wanted.[40] The war party, about fifty strong, started south on July 10. In two days they reached the Salt Creek Prairie and passed over the open plain where the wagon teamsters had died. Maman-ti led them east towards one of the most picturesque spots in Texas, Lost Valley in northwest Jack County. The valley had an almost perfectly level floor hemmed in by rugged, heavily wooded hills.[41] At its northern end was a large ranch owned by a famous Texas cattleman, Oliver Loving.

Around 11:30 on the morning of July 12, the Indians sighted four cowboys riding in the direction of Loving's ranch. The Indians charged after them, but the white men (Oliver Loving himself and three of his ranch hands) managed to outdistance their pursuers and escape. Loving immediately wrote to the commanding officer of Fort Richardson to report the incident.[42] As the Indians were rallying, their scouts reported the approach of another, larger body of white men from the southwest. In classic Plains Indian fashion, Maman-ti left the main portion of the war party hidden along the wooded ridge of Lost Valley while he and another warrior, Ad-la-te (Loud Talker), rode out into the open, dismounted, and led their horses up the valley, hoping to lure the newcomers into an ambush. The moment the white men spied the two Indians, they rose to the bait and galloped into Maman-ti's trap.[43]

Unknown to the Indians, this was no ordinary party of settlers they were about to engage: it was a patrol of Texas Rangers led by Major John B. Jones, the commander of the Texas Frontier Battalion, and composed of his twenty-five man personal escort and ten men of Captain G. W. Stevens's company.[44] They were in the area

Major John B. Jones, Texas Rangers, commander of the Texas Frontier Batallion (Texas State Library)

because two days before, on July 10, a small party of Comanches had attacked Loving's ranch, killed a cowboy named John Heath, and made off with six horses.[45] Major Jones had received his commission just two months before, and since that time he had been touring the settlements, personally supervising the organization and deployment of his six Ranger companies. On July 11, he was sixty miles south of Loving's when he got word of the attack. He and his men rode all that day to reach Captain Stevens's camp just south of the Salt Creek Prairie. The next morning, the combined command set out to track the raiders and instead discovered the

148

Typical Ranger frontier defense company, ca. 1880 (Texas State Library)

broad trail left by Maman-ti's party. Many of the Rangers were young and inexperienced, and as the trail grew fresher, they grew more restless and excited. Finally, when two Indians were spotted in the distance, on foot, leading their ponies, all the words of caution and orders to stay in formation were ignored, and several men galloped to the attack.

Almost immediately, the Rangers came under fire from all sides. Lee Corn, a member of Jones's escort, was hit in the arm and knocked off his horse. A comrade named Wheeler dismounted and dragged Corn into some brush where they remained concealed for the rest of the battle.

Major Jones realized that, caught out in the open with no cover and with bullets flying from seemingly all directions, his force was in danger of being annihilated. Immediately, he led his men in a desperate charge back down the valley to a dry gully where they could take shelter. Along the way two more Rangers, George Moore and William Glass, were wounded and several horses were lost, but Jones's quick decision proved to be the correct one. From the cover of the gully the heavily armed Texans managed to keep the Indians at bay for the rest of the afternoon.

After a few hours of desultory skirmishing, Maman-ti was forced to recognize that the white men's position was too strong to be carried by assault. He decided to try another stratagem. Figuring that the besieged men would soon need water, he ordered most of his warriors to make a great display of departing north up the valley, while a few selected Kiowas with the fastest ponies remained in hiding near Cameron Creek, the closest water hole. If any of the white men took the lure, Lone Wolf would have his revenge.

For the second time that day Maman-ti's plans worked perfectly. Two of the Rangers, Mel Porter and David Bailey, believing that the Indians had gone, left the gully laden with canteens and against orders rode about a mile north to the water hole on Cameron Creek. Bailey remained mounted and kept watch while Porter filled the canteens. Suddenly, the Indians who had been hiding nearby burst upon the two men. Porter mounted and rode frantically north but was knocked off his horse by a Kiowa warrior. He rolled into Cameron Creek and swam underwater until, desperate for air, he was forced to surface, and found himself looking straight into the gun barrels of fellow Rangers Corn and Wheeler. By sheer chance, Porter had stumbled upon their hiding place. The three men remained concealed until well after dark, then made their way to Loving's ranch. Bailey, however, was not so fortunate. He tried to ride south back to the Rangers' position, but the Indians easily cut him off. His horse was wounded and he was lanced from the saddle. Lone Wolf dismounted and, using his hatchet-pipe and hunting knife, hacked Bailey's head to pieces and disemboweled his body. Other Indians shot arrows or sank their lances into the lifeless corpse. Then, with the death of Tau-ankia avenged and the honor of the revenge raid satisfied, the Kiowas mounted their ponies and rode north.

As evening approached, Major Jones sent one of his men to Richardson with the following dispatch:

July 12th

To the Commanding Officer of U.S. Troops at Ft. Richardson,

Sir,

I was attacked today four miles South of Lovings Ranch by about one hundred well armed Indians. Had only thirty-five men and lost one man killed, one wounded and five missing. Fought them three hours and drove them off, but have not force enough to attack them. Can you send me assistance to Lovings. The Indians are still in the valley. Lost twelve horses.[46]

Jno. B. Jones

Maj. Comdg. Frontier Battalion

Jones then had the body of William Glass, who had died during the day, tied to a horse, and the Rangers limped into Loving's ranch under the cover of darkness. Early the next morning Captain Baldwin and Companies I and L of the Tenth arrived at the ranch. They recovered David Bailey's body, and then the Rangers and Baldwin's troopers together scoured the surrounding countryside. They could find no sign of the raiders.[47]

Other war parties struck all along the frontier, and as word of each new depredation came in, the pressure on the federal government increased. Finally, Generals Sherman and Sheridan saw that the situation had become intolerable. Late in 1872, these two men had formulated plans for one huge campaign to drive the Indians onto the reservation.[48] Now that a general outbreak seemed at hand, Sherman asked Secretary of War William Belknap for authorization to carry out these plans. Belknap recognized that conditions on the frontier had not really changed: despite promises by the Indians and assurances from the Indian agents, the Indians still raided as much as ever. He conceded the failure of the Quaker peace policy and in July 1874 ordered the chastisement of guilty Indians wherever found, regardless of reservation lines or agency boundaries.[49]

The campaign, soon to be known as the Red River War, called for five columns of troops to descend upon the Panhandle of Texas and drive any Indians encountered back to the reservation. From the north, Colonel Nelson A. Miles was to march from Fort Dodge, Kansas, with eight companies of the Sixth Cavalry and four companies of the Fifth Infantry to scout along the headwaters of the Red River. From Fort Union, New Mexico, Major William R. Price was to move east with four companies of the Eighth Cavalry and drive all hostiles from along the Canadian River into Miles's expedition. Colonel Mackenzie was to march north from Fort Concho with eight companies of his Fourth Cavalry, four companies of the Tenth Infantry, one of the Eleventh, and thirty Indian scouts, and scout along the Mackenzie trail and the eastern Llano Estacado. Lieutenant Colonel George Buell was to lead four companies of the Ninth Cavalry, two of the Tenth, two companies of the Eleventh Infantry, and thirty scouts from Fort Griffin to Fort Sill and then west to operate along the Salt Fork of the Red River, slightly north of Mackenzie. Finally, Lieutenant Colonel John Davidson was to sweep north and then west from Fort Sill, roughly between the Washita River and Buell's column, with six companies of the Tenth Cavalry, three companies of the Eleventh Infantry, and forty-four Indian scouts. In short, forty-six companies, nearly three thousand men under five commanders, were to converge upon the Staked Plains, attack the hostile Indians, destroy their camps and animals, and herd them back to the reservation where their leaders were to be arrested and the rest held as prisoners of war.[50]

On August 14, 1874, Companies E and L of the Tenth Cavalry and Companies E and F of the Eleventh Infantry marched from Richardson to form part of Davidson's command in the forthcoming campaign.[51] Upon arriving at Sill, Companies E and L, along with C and H (also of the Tenth), received orders to move immediately on to Anadarko, where a dangerous situation was developing.

On July 26, Colonel Davidson had been directed to enroll all "friendly" Indians in order to protect them during the roundup of their more warlike brothers. The idea of answering a daily roll call was odious to the Plains Indians, but some complied; by August 8, 173 Kiowas, 108 Kiowa-Apaches, and 83 Comanches[52] had re-

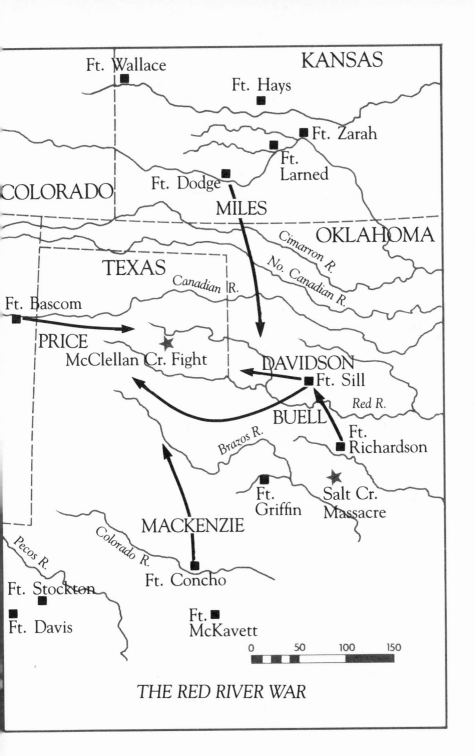

KANSAS

Ft. Wallace

Ft. Hays

Ft. Zarah

Ft. Larned

COLORADO

Ft. Dodge

MILES

OKLAHOMA

Cimarron R.

TEXAS

Canadian R.

No. Canadian R.

Ft. Bascom

PRICE

McClellan Cr. Fight

DAVIDSON

Ft. Sill

Red R.

BUELL

Ft. Richardson

Brazos R.

Ft. Griffin

Salt Cr. Massacre

MACKENZIE

Colorado R.

Pecos R.

Ft. Stockton

Ft. Davis

Ft. Concho

Ft. McKavett

0   50   100   150

THE RED RIVER WAR

ported in at Fort Sill. Davidson then closed the enrollment and declared all Indians not on his lists to be hostiles. Included in this category were several bands of Comanches, including the Nokonis of Chief Big Red Food (Pe-arua-akup-akup) and some Kiowas under Lone Wolf. On August 21, these chiefs and their people arrived at the Caddo and Wichita agency at Anadarko and began to cause trouble,[53] demanding supplies from the commissary and plundering the crops of the so-called "tame" Indians.[54] A frantic message to Fort Sill from the official in charge brought Davidson and the four companies of buffalo soldiers galloping into Anadarko around noon on August 22.

Davidson confronted Big Red Food and told him that he and his people must surrender all their weapons and return with the soldiers to Fort Sill. Big Red Food was on the verge of agreeing when some of Lone Wolf's men began to taunt the Comanches, calling them women. "Act like men," they called. "If you have trouble with the soldiers, we'll help you." Upon hearing this, Big Red Food gave a loud whoop, somersaulted from his pony, and made a mad dash for the nearest brush. The soldiers fired at him unsuccessfully, and the Kiowas and Comanches immediately returned their shots, starting a wild, ten-minute melee in which hundreds of bullets were discharged but no one on either side was injured.

Davidson was anxious not to harm any of the friendly Indians camped at the agency, so he decided to try to drive the hostile Comanches and Kiowas from the grounds. Company L dismounted and proceeded to clear the commissary and corral of Kiowa snipers. As the Indians withdrew, Captain Louis Carpenter and his Company H made a daring and gallant charge which scattered the hostiles in all directions. Davidson then regrouped his men and returned to protect the agency, stopping only briefly to set fire to the abandoned Nokonis camp. All the Indians' lodges and property, including their precious winter provisions—several tons of dried buffalo and deer meat—were destroyed. Throughout the night, the troopers and the agency staff (who had been armed and pressed into service) traded shots with Indian skirmishers while the sputtering fires from the remains of Big Red Food's camp illuminated the entire scene with an unreal, perhaps even hellish, glare.

The next morning, about three hundred warriors attempted to gain some high ground overlooking the agency, but Captain Carpenter led Companies E and L of Richardson and his company H in a quick ascent of the opposite slope and succeeded in driving the Indians away just as they reached the crest. Then, in retaliation for burning their camp, several Comanches fired the dry grass north of the agency, hoping a strong north wind would carry the flames onto the grounds. The troopers set counterfires which quickly got out of control, and they spent the rest of the morning frantically trying to save both the buildings and themselves from destruction. Eventually the soldiers brought the grass fires under control, and the Indians, no doubt much chagrined, withdrew.

The Anadarko fight was over. Insofar as military engagements go, it was of minor significance. But it did have one very positive result: it separated the friendly Indians from the unfriendly ones. Those camped at Sill and Anadarko and the Cheyenne Agency at Darlington who were registered and answered the daily roll call were friendly, and all others were not. In the following weeks 585 Kiowas, 479 Comanches, and 306 Kiowa-Apaches,[55] fearing the consequences of opposing the army's might, came to Fort Sill to register. This represented about one-half the total number of those tribes. The rest fled west. Now the army had what it had always wanted: a clear, precise line between peaceful and hostile Indians and the freedom to act against the latter.

And act it did. Throughout the fall and winter of 1874–1875, the soldiers crossed and recrossed the plains, driving the Indians before them, allowing the fugitives and their animals no rest. Change, against which the Indians had stood so long, was now utterly and irrevocably upon them, and they were powerless to prevent it. In some ways, they themselves were even responsible for it. But the time for fixing blame was past, as was the time for negotiation and compromise. The time also was gone for such things as gallantry and honor, if these conceits had ever truly existed at all on the frontier. This flight to the Staked Plains was an act of desperation, the act of a people whose world was crumbling, and there was nothing glorious or honorable in its inception nor its inescapable conclusion.

Two units from Richardson, Company E of the Tenth Cavalry

and Company F of the Eleventh Infantry, marched with George Buell's column north from Fort Griffin to Fort Sill. On October 3, Buell headed west for the Canadian River, then on to the Washita and the Sweetwater before returning to Sill on December 13. While in the field Buell drove his men to the limits of their endurance, and his command suffered intensely from the onslaught of winter. But the Indians suffered more. In his merciless advance, Buell captured and burned over six hundred lodges and destroyed tons of supplies and camp equipage. His unrelenting pursuit physically broke down many of the Indians' ponies, already weakened from a lack of adequate forage in the cold months. But as debilitating as these blows certainly were, even more devastating was the mental fatigue produced by the constant threat of attack. Before bad weather and sheer exhaustion forced Buell to break up his expedition and return to Griffin, his campaign without respite had managed to crush the will of the resisting tribes.[56]

Meanwhile, two more Richardson-based companies, L of the Tenth Cavalry and E of the Eleventh Infantry, marched from Fort Sill on September 12 as part of Colonel Davidson's command. Davidson scouted up the North Fork of the Red River, then turned south to Mulberry Creek and returned to Sill on October 10, with nothing to show for his five-hundred-mile trek but the loss of thirty-six horses and twenty-two mules. Within eleven days Davidson was rested and refitted and again in the field, only now he scored almost immediate results. On October 24, he struck a large party of Indians who were fleeing from Buell's column. Over the space of three days Davidson managed to capture 45 Kiowas, 314 Comanches (including Big Red Food, the chief who had escaped at Anadarko), and over two thousand horses. Davidson pushed on to McClellan Creek, where he discovered and destroyed seventy-five Cheyenne lodges. But a heavy blizzard began blowing on November 15, ending Davidson's campaign just as it did Buell's. Davidson struggled back into Fort Sill on November 29, having lost one hundred horses and mules to exhaustion and cold and with twenty-six men suffering from frostbite.[57]

Buell's return to Sill on December 13 ended the direct participation of Richardson-based units in the Red River War. The men had performed admirably under extremely adverse conditions. They had suffered much, but much had been accomplished. Together, Davidson and Buell had marched more miles, captured more hostiles, and destroyed more property than any other commands that winter, all without the death of a single trooper. Buell wrote of his men, "I cannot give them too much credit for manly endurance without complaint."[58]

Of the other commanders in the field during this period, Colonel Miles was the most active. Pushing south and east along the Canadian River, he drove many of the hostile Cheyennes toward their agency at Darlington. He then turned southwest toward the Staked Plains, where, in early September, he linked up with Major Price and his column. Price had made a rather leisurely march east from New Mexico and had accomplished little. Therefore, the commander of the Department of the Missouri, General John Pope (who, along with the commander of the Department of Texas, General Augur, was responsible for implementing the grand strategy devised by Sherman and Sheridan), ordered Miles's and Price's expeditions to consolidate under the command of Colonel Miles.[59]

While Miles reorganized and resupplied his enlarged force, the aggressive Colonel Mackenzie and his Fourth Cavalry scored the single most spectacular success of the entire Red River campaign. On September 26, 1874, he discovered "the Place of Chinaberry Trees" in Palo Duro Canyon, where a majority of the Kwahadi Comanches and Lone Wolf's Kiowas had sought refuge. Mackenzie swept through a forest of teepees on the canyon floor, burning the shelters and the food supplies. He captured almost the entire Indian pony herd and drove the animals onto the plains. He then allowed the Tonkawa scouts to select 376 of the best and ordered the remainder, well over a thousand, shot by his soldiers. Mackenzie had learned that he could not hold a captured herd.[60]

Throughout the autumn and into the winter Mackenzie prowled the area around Palo Duro and the southern Staked Plains, while Miles swept the fringes of the Staked Plains east to the present border of Oklahoma. They fought many sharp engagements, destroyed hundreds of lodges and thousands of pounds of property, and suffered desperately from the weather. But by the time Macken-

zie quit the field in December and Miles finally disbanded his expedition in February, the war, for all practical purposes, was over.

Seven months of hostilities had left the Indians destitute.
Their winter food supplies were destroyed, their shelters burned,
their ponies killed. Without mobility and weak from hunger and
exposure and the harassment of the relentless soldiers, the Kiowas,
Comanches, and Cheyennes began to struggle back to the reservation as early as October. Lone Wolf and 252 Kiowas surrendered at
Fort Sill in February; some 1,600 Cheyennes capitulated in March;
Mow-way and 200 Comanches came in in April; and 407 of the
once-mighty Kwahadis submitted in early June. A satisfied General
Sheridan wrote, "This campaign was not only very comprehensive,
but was the most successful of any Indian campaign in this country
since its settlement by the whites."[61]

Among the early arrivals were Satanta and Big Tree. They had
fled the reservation after the Anadarko fight, but Big Tree slipped
into the Cheyenne Agency in late September. He informed the
agent that Satanta and his band were nearby and wished to surrender. They had been visiting the Wichita Agency when the fight
between Big Red Food and Davidson started, had panicked and
fled, and had spent the time since then dodging cavalry patrols. Satanta and his people came in on October 3, and both he and Big
Tree declared they were innocent of any wrongdoing. Said Satanta:
"I have done no fighting against the whites, have killed no white
men and committed no depredations since I left Fort Sill. When
the fight commenced at Wichita Agency . . . I picked up and left,
and took no part." Sherman, however, would have no excuses. Although he released Big Tree, he ordered Satanta returned to Huntsville for breaking the terms of his parole. There on October 11,
1878, the "Orator of the Plains," who once told the Medicine
Lodge Treaty commissioners that if a Kiowa could not roam free
over the prairie he grew pale and died, threw himself from a high
window and died.[62]

Secretary Belknap and General Sherman, following the prece-
dent set by the trials of Satanta and Big Tree in Jacksboro in 1871,
ordered trials and punishments for the ringleaders of the more re-

cent raids. As Sherman said, "To turn them loose to renew the same old game in the Spring seems folly."[63] The "trials" turned out to be nothing more than a process of identifying the troublemakers, who were to be sent to Saint Augustine, Florida, and held in military confinement in the old Spanish Castillo de San Marcos, known as Fort Marion. Kicking Bird was given the loathesome task of selecting the most guilty Kiowas. From the chiefs he chose Lone Wolf, Maman-ti, White Horse, Woman Heart, Swan, Eagle Chief, and Buffalo Bull's Entrails. He then singled out nineteen others, mostly young warriors of little note and Mexican captives. Eventually, thirty-four Cheyennes, nine Comanches, two Arapahoes, and one Caddo were also chosen to go to Fort Marion. Kicking Bird told Indian Agent Thomas Battey, "I am grieved at the ruin of my people."[64]

On May 2, 1875, as the seventy-two prisoners were being loaded into wagons to begin the journey to Florida, Kicking Bird rode up on a fine gray horse which had been given to him by one of the officers at Sill. He told the shackled warriors that he was sorry for them, but they had brought this trouble upon themselves. Nevertheless, he loved them and would work for their release. Maman-ti replied, "You think you have done well, Kicking Bird! You remain free, a big man with the whites. But you will not live long. I will see to that!"[65]

Two days afterward, Kicking Bird died at his camp near Fort Sill. The post surgeon suspected "strychnia," but the Kiowas believed that Maman-ti, the Sky Walker, had willed it. A few days after learning of Kicking Bird's death, Maman-ti also died, in atonement, the Kiowas said, for using his powers to kill one of his own people.[66] The captives were held in the damp confines of Fort Marion until 1878, at which time the survivors, seven Comanches and thirteen Kiowas, including Lone Wolf, were released to return to the reservation. The subdued chiefs and warriors arrived home on May 1 to be met by their tribesmen and their new agent, P. B. Hunt, who wrote, "There has been a very great change in those people, a complete and thorough reformation in every particular. Their professions of reform I believe to be sincere." Lone Wolf had contracted malarial fever in Florida and by the next spring was dead, at the age of 56.[67]

Thus the Red River War ended, and so too did many other things. The great Indian leaders were dead or in chains; the buffalo was gone; the power of the Southern Plains tribes was broken forever; a way of life was over. The army had waged total war against the Indians and had defeated them totally. The day of the lance, bow, and shield was finished.

CHAPTER NINE

The Years
of Decline,
1876–1878

ON DECEMBER 2, 1874, THE haggard and bone-weary men of Companies E and F, Eleventh Infantry, and Company L, Tenth Cavalry, returned to Fort Richardson from the Red River War. Company E of the Tenth came in on January 6, 1875. These units were joined by Companies A, F, H, I, K, and L of Mackenzie's Fourth Cavalry, which struggled in over a nineteen-day period from December 24 to January 12. The Indian Territory had been unofficially divided into districts, and Colonel Mackenzie was responsible for an area bounded by McClellan's Creek, the Red River, and the Canadian. Fort Sill was the most convenient post to this locale, but as it was already overcrowded, Mackenzie and Augur directed part of the Fourth Cavalry south to winter at its old regimental headquarters, Fort Richardson.[1]

These returning soldiers were proud of the roles they had played in the 1874 campaigns, and so were their leaders. General Sheridan would later write, "No men have ever worked harder or shown a higher sense of duty. No body of men of the same size was ever before so hardly taxed, mentally and physically, or compelled to make such hazardous and exacting marches . . . in their unequal contest with the wily savages. The hard work and wear and tear upon both men and animals can be fully appreciated only by those who are familiar with the country operated in."[2] These troopers had endured the almost indescribable hardships of autumn and winter

161

operations on the Staked Plains and had struck some of the heaviest blows of the war against the hostiles. And no doubt the sight of Jacksboro, even with its dilapidated log houses and propped-up frame buildings, was as good to the cold, dirty, and exhausted soldiers as the sight of them was to the townspeople who turned out to welcome them home. Soon the ramshackle barbershops began to fill with men who came for much-needed shaves and haircuts and to luxuriate in the almost forgotten pleasures of hot baths in the tin tubs out back. Amusement, escape, or just oblivion beckoned in the dozens of saloons, dance halls, and gambling dens which were once more in full swing. For a time, Jacksboro was a red-hot town again.

But while the men campaigning on the Staked Plains had been pushed to the limits of their endurance, Company I of the Tenth Cavalry, which had remained at Richardson, was not on a holiday. The depletion of the fort's garrison caused all the daily routines to devolve upon the men of this one company, and they probably spent as many hours in the saddle from August to December as did those who were on campaign. A constant stream of food and ordinance stores was in motion from the railhead in Fort Worth, through Weatherford to Richardson to Fort Griffin, and then to the columns in the field. Every wagon train, mail or passenger stage, and cattle herd that left Richardson heading west required an escort. The troopers also had to assist the Jack County sheriff in arresting horse thieves, recovering Indian ponies stolen from Fort Sill, and chasing down deserters.[3] Had there been any Indian activity in the vicinity of Richardson during the fall of 1874, the garrison, stretched as thin as it was, would have found it impossible to respond effectively. It was therefore fortunate for the settlers that all was quiet in Jack and the surrounding counties that season. The Southern Plains Indians were having far too many difficulties trying to hunt food for their families, to graze their stock, or even to sleep a night through in safety and security, to contemplate raiding in the settlements.

In January 1875, Companies I and L of the Tenth transferred to Fort Concho, which became the unit's new regimental headquarters. In March, Company E moved to Fort Griffin, and in April, when Colonel Benjamin Grierson, who had been on detached duty in the East during the Red River War, resumed command of the Tenth Cavalry, Colonel Davidson replaced Colonel Buell as Griffin's commanding officer. A few diehard bands of Comanches remained active in the Concho and Griffin areas, and the Kickapoos and Lipans still raided along the Rio Grande. In addition to these tribes, the Mescalero and Warm Springs Apaches began to make their presence felt, and Mexican and American bandits quickly took over cattle rustling where the Southern Plains Indians left off. There was still plenty for the cavalry to do on the frontier of West Texas.[4]

The departure of the Tenth Cavalry helped alleviate the serious overcrowding at Fort Richardson. For a time in January, over five hundred officers and men were living at the fort, many of them bivouacked in tents or quartered in picket barracks so rickety that "a good gust of wind might knock them down." In other words, conditions were much the same at Richardson as many of these soldiers had experienced in 1871 and 1872. This is hardly surprising since many of those buildings, considered unsafe just a few months after being constructed, had been standing unused and unattended since 1872. In June 1875, Assistant Inspector General N. H. Davis reported that the buildings at Richardson were "much dilapidated and growing worse. To repair properly is to rebuild."[5]

Despite the condition of their lodgings, the Fourth Cavalry companies who remained at Richardson passed an uneventful winter. Their duties included forming escorts for the regular visits of the paymaster, making a few scouts of the Salt Creek area, and helping the local authorities in routine civil matters, but mostly the troopers rested and refitted. Details traveled to Dallas and Dennison to buy replacements for horses broken down or worn out in the fall campaign, while damaged or lost equipment was repaired and replaced. Gradually men, animals, and equipment recovered from four months of arduous service, and the Richardson-based troopers of the Fourth readied themselves for duty in the spring.

In March, Companies F, K, and L were ordered to Fort Sill, where Colonel Mackenzie had assumed command and the Fourth Cavalry now had its regimental headquarters. In April, Companies

A and I followed, and Company H left for the Oklahoma post in May. With the departure of the last unit of the Fourth Cavalry, Fort Richardson, for the first time since its establishment, was garrisoned solely by foot soldiers, the men of Companies B, E, and K, Eleventh Infantry. And, from being seriously overcrowded, the post went to a condition of being undermanned. A traveler passing through Jacksboro at the time wrote: "Colonel Woods is here in command of the skeleton of three companies of the Eleventh Infantry, which are barely enough to do post duty and preserve government property."[6]

During that spring, the troops at Richardson began work on a new project—building the United States military telegraph line in North Texas. As early as 1869, the assistant adjutant general of the Department of Texas, General J. J. Reynolds, had requested that a telegraph line be established to aid in the interception of Indian raiders.[7] Two of these long-overdue lines eventually converged at Fort Richardson. The eastern line would run from Dennison to Jacksboro, a distance of 114 miles, while the northern line would stretch 105 miles from Jacksboro to Fort Sill. From Jacksboro, the line would continue to Fort Griffin, 71 miles southwest, then to Concho and Stockton and the Rio Grande forts.[8]

In April 1875, Richardson's post adjutant detailed sixteen men of the Eleventh as a fatigue party to assist the Twenty-fourth Infantry in the project. On May 8, the army completed the line from Dennison to Richardson and opened an office in Jacksboro. Construction crews completed the line from Fort Sill to Richardson on June 22, when parties working south from Sill and north from Richardson met at the Red River. When Second Lieutenant Albert L. Myer of Company G, Eleventh Infantry, and thirty of his men finished the line to Griffin on July 12, Richardson became connected directly to the outside world.[9] Until the military telegraph system, the nearest telegraph had been at Corsicana. Correspondence often required days to be carried across the prairie. The new system represented a vast leap forward in military operations. Of course, the line also represented another chore for the garrison. Details left every few months to clear the grass from around the poles and to replace the ones that were burned down by prairie fires or struck by lightning.[10]

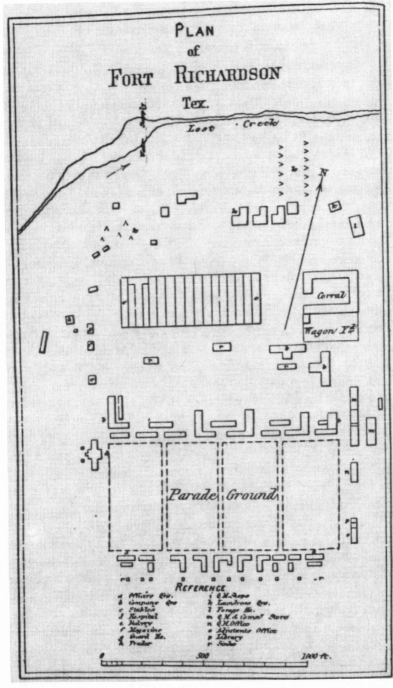

Map of Fort Richardson in 1876 (from *Outline Descriptions of the Posts in the Military Division of the Missouri, 1876*)

By transferring the cavalry from Richardson to other posts, the army in essence was declaring Jack County to be a secure area, safe from further Indian incursions. However, this proved not to be the case. In early May 1875, a Comanche named Isa-toho (Black Coyote) along with his wife and four braves left the reservation and stole several horses from Oliver Loving's ranch. Major John B. Jones and a detachment of twenty Texas Rangers were in the vicinity[11] and, upon learning of the raid, searched out and found the Indians' trail at the head of Lost Valley, in almost the same spot where Jones had discovered Lone Wolf and his party a year before. After about five miles of hard riding, the Rangers overtook the Indians and in a desperate running fight killed five of them, including Isa-toho and his wife (who, Major Jones reported, "handled her six-shooter quite as dexterously as did the bucks").[12] Major Jones asked for a party of soldiers from Richardson to verify the identity of the bodies, since many settlers at that time believed that the cattle and horse stealing in the area was being done by whites disguised as Indians. Appallingly, the soldiers cut off the heads of the dead thieves and sent them in jars of alcohol to Washington as gruesome proof that Indians, not whites, were the culprits. This deed prompted the anthropologist James Moody to note that in the troubles between the Texans and the Plains Indians, "atrocities were not confined to one side."[13] After this incident, the Eleventh Infantry settled down to a quiet life at Richardson, the monthly visits of the paymaster and the meager attractions of Jacksboro providing the only excitement. This period of quiet lasted well over a year.

In early July 1876, the men of Richardson had just finished celebrating the centennial of the birth of the United States of America when the shocking news arrived via the new telegraph that, on June 25, Colonel George Armstrong Custer and 215 officers and men of his Seventh Cavalry had been annihilated at the Little Bighorn River by the warriors of the Sioux chief Sitting Bull. In August, Companies B, E, and K of the Eleventh received orders to march to Fort Worth and there to entrain for the Dakota Territory, for service in General Alfred H. Terry's campaign against the Sioux. In November, Colonel William Wood, his headquarters, regimental band, and the remaining elements of the Eleventh were transferred to the Dakota Territory.[14] As had been the case five years before, when the Sixth Cavalry had been transferred to Kansas, some townspeople regretted the move. Said the local newspaper on November 17, 1876: "The command has been here for so long that they had become identified with our people and universal regret is expressed at their leaving."[15] However, the men of the Eleventh Infantry were replaced on August 27 by familiar faces: Captain Theodore A. Baldwin and the eighty-five buffalo soldiers of his Company I, Tenth Cavalry, returning after a nineteen-month absence, replete with baggage train and Gatling gun.[16]

Four months later, probably much to the chagrin of all the officers and men of Company I, Lieutenant Colonel John Davidson came riding into the fort to assume command. Richardson had had its share of unusual commanding officers—the catankerous Starr, the stern Oakes, the humorless, almost monastic Mackenzie—but Davidson was the most unstable of the lot. Lieutenant Richard Platt, Tenth Cavalry, wrote that, "The General had trouble with his head because of a previous sunstroke," but another Tenth Cavalry officer, Lieutenant Samuel Woodward, was less kind and far more candid. "The truth of the matter is . . . Gen'l Davidson is, without a doubt, crazy at times. He says himself he has had a sunstroke which seriously affects his brain and I have noticed he has . . . violent spells during which it is impossible to tell what fool thing he will not do. I must confess it ain't pleasant to serve under a lunatic." While at Fort Sill, Davidson had reportedly ordered major roads diverted to decrease traffic and dust near his quarters and directed that huge holes be knocked in the foundation of his house to increase ventilation. Although there is no record of any such erratic behavior during Davidson's stint at Richardson, a wave of apprehension certainly must have swept over Captain Baldwin and his men when they learned that they would once more be under Davidson's command.[17]

Together, the new commandant and his wary charges passed what proved to be an uneventful winter repairing telegraph poles and escorting the paymaster on his monthly visits—not to save his scalp from Indian raiders, as would have been the case just a few years before, but to prevent his being robbed by American bandits.[18] Indeed, thievery had grown so bad in the area that not even the confines of the fort itself could provide sanctuary. Around 2:00 A.M. on the morning of February 20, 1877, a gang of unknown culprits attempted to create a diversion by setting fire to one of the unoccupied buildings on the line of officers' quarters. The night sentry discovered the blaze and turned in the alarm. The troopers rushed from their quarters and, as there was no fire engine at the fort, pressed the post water wagon into service to carry water from the springs behind the officers' quarters. The soldiers ignored the burning structure and concentrated on saving the adjoining buildings. Flames leapt high in the air and sparks floated dangerously away on the wind, but amazingly, there were no other fires. Meanwhile, during all this confusion, the arsonists attempted to break into the storehouse and corral but were discovered and fled empty-handed. At first light, details of bleary-eyed buffalo soldiers assisted by the Jack County sheriff and his deputies fanned out across the countryside, searching for the trail of the would-be thieves. However, no arrests were ever made.[19]

In June 1877, Captain Baldwin led forty men on a twenty-five day scout along the southern edge of the Red River. His instructions from Colonel Davidson were to cut the trail of any Indians passing into or out of the state and to follow and attack them. He was also to determine the extent of settlement in the area. Baldwin returned to Richardson on June 29, having covered 489 miles. He intercepted only one small band of Indians, and they possessed a hunting pass from Fort Sill. Instead of hostiles, Baldwin discovered many settlers in the countryside around Beaver's Creek, Wanderer Creek, the Upper Wichita and the Pease rivers. With the Indian troubles in North Texas subsiding, the frontier seemed to be advancing rapidly and the country filling up with people. A traveler in Jack County at this time wrote: "We found farm homes thick where fifteen months ago one might travel half a day and see no human habitation. Ten Mile Prairie, situated in the north part of this county, has a new farm house on nearly every quarter section. The inhabitants are mostly of the kind who come to stay."[20]

However, the menace from the reservation was not totally at an end. In the early spring of 1877, a band of about forty Comanches under Chief Black Horse (Po-da-do-ah) fled the reservation to live on the Staked Plains. They attacked several bands of hunters and prowled along the line of settlement. In addition several small bands of Mescalero Apaches also operated in the area. On August 20, Baldwin was again in the saddle, with orders to march west with a detachment of thirty-five troopers and scout along the 101st meridian, from Cañon Blanco to Big Spring. He returned on September 21, having covered 658 miles without finding any sign of Black Horse or the Mescaleros.[21]

On September 23, Lieutenant James S. Jouett led twenty-five men of Company I onto the Staked Plains to hunt for Black Horse. Jouett did not return to Richardson until December 4, 1877, having covered an amazing total of 1,360 miles. Despite the efforts of Jouett and his men, Black Horse managed to elude his pursuers and eventually crossed the Staked Plains to join the Apaches in their war with the United States.[22]

Jouett's monumental effort was the last scout to originate from Richardson and, in many ways, it emphasized some obvious truths about the place. Richardson anchored a defensive line of forts that looked north towards the Indian Territory. But except for rare outbreaks, such as that of Black Horse and his followers, the Indians at Fort Sill had been quiet for two years. Obviously, the war for which Richardson had been constructed was over, and now the post was too far east to support the army as it engaged new enemies on new battlefields far to the west. The line of settlement which Richardson once guarded had, like a wave, washed far beyond it, and for an army that was chronically undermanned, undersupplied, and underfunded, the place was simply too costly to maintain. Richardson had performed very well in its intended function, and because of this, it became unnecessary. Despite the protests of the Jack County citizens, who sent a petition to General Reynolds asking that the fort be kept open,[23] orders came down to prepare to abandon the installation.[24]

On January 16, 1878, Lieutenant Robert P. Wilson, with a detachment of three officers and eighteen enlisted men of the Tenth Infantry, arrived from San Antonio to assume command of Fort Richardson and to begin a complete inventory of all supplies and

W.S.INGRAM
GROCERIES.

View of Fort Richardson from Jacksboro town square, ca. 1880 (Russell Jones Collection)

material at the post. Three days later, Colonel Davidson, Captain Baldwin, and the men of Company I, Tenth Cavalry, departed for Fort Sill.[25]

The last man to die at Fort Richardson was the commanding officer, Lieutenant Wilson. On March 22, 1878, while he was hunting near the post, his double-barrel shotgun burst, severely wounding him in the left arm and leg. He was taken to the post hospital where Dr. A. A. Yeomans, the army surgeon, and two civilian doctors from Jacksboro attended to his wounds. Despite this care, Lieutenant Wilson died two days later. The command of the post fell to Lieutenant Sumner H. Lincoln, Tenth Infantry.[26]

On April 16, 1878, Richardson's chaplain, B. L. Baldringer, was transferred to Fort Stockton. The fort had existed for ten years before the army had gotten around to assigning it a chaplain, and with no chapel or funds allocated to build one there had been little for him to do.[27] This was entirely in keeping with the government's

view that Richardson was only a temporary installation and as little money as possible should be put into it. Indeed, the government did not even furnish the post with a flagpole or with the funds to purchase one, and none existed at the fort until June 1877, when the officers and men of Company I, Tenth Cavalry, pooled their own funds, bought a flagstaff in Weatherford, and erected it themselves.[28]

On April 24 and 26, the soldiers moved most of the quartermaster stores and the surgeon and his medical supplies to Fort Griffin. The army ordered the remaining government equipment to be sold at a large public auction on May 1 and 2, 1878. Army paymaster Major Alfred Bates paid the twenty-eight men of Richardson for the last time on May 20, and three days later the post adjutant made the final entry in Fort Richardson's post returns: "The post is this day abandoned under Special Order 67, paragraph 3, Headquarters, Department of Texas, and the troops marched to Fort Griffin, Texas."[29]

Fort Richardson, ca. 1900 (Russell Jones Collection)

AFTERWORD

AND SO ON A BRIGHT spring morning in 1878, the United States Army abandoned Fort Richardson. During the post's ten years of active military existence, it had been home to more than five thousand officers and men and headquarters for three different regiments. Over that period, three officers and fifty-nine enlisted men died of  disease, one officer and two enlisted men were accidentally killed, and three troopers were murdered in nearby Jacksboro. Three major Indian campaigns and hundreds of scouts and patrols were launched from Richardson, resulting in thirteen troopers and an estimated one hundred fifty hostiles being killed in action. For gallantry in these engagements, Congress awarded twenty-four Medals of Honor to the men of Richardson. The post also lost 646 soldiers through desertion.

Considering the initial building costs and the expense of maintaining the post and paying the troops, the government probably spent between six and eight million dollars on the Jack County fort. Insofar as encouraging the settlement of Northwest Texas is concerned, it was money well spent. The Southern Plains Indians waged and lost a desperate war to stop the extension of white civilization and to save their way of life. The soldiers of Richardson helped blunt the fury of the Indians' assaults and played a major role in the pacification of the Southern Plains. Historian Carl Coke Rister wrote: "Fort Richardson was one of the most important posts in Texas," and without doubt, the contributions of Richardson and her men form a proud part of the distinguished history of American arms.

However, the story does not end there. Richardson's days of martial glory were certainly gone, but its usefulness to the community continued. Settlers moving into Jacksboro found in the abandoned buildings welcome refuge until they could find more suitable homes. Ranchers used the barracks as bunkhouses for their cowhands and the storehouses as barns and stables. The parade ground became at various times a football, baseball, and polo field, as well as county fair grounds. In 1898, the railroad finally came; the Chicago, Rock Island & Pacific built a depot inside the northern edge of the reservation. Still, by the turn of the century, most of the picket structures at the post had deteriorated beyond repair and had literally fallen into ruins. Newcomers to the area detraining at the depot must have wondered at the desolation, for anyone who read the newspapers during the 1870s was familiar with the dateline "Fort Richardson, Texas" that had begun so many important stories. Fort Richardson seemed destined for oblivion.

Happily, that was not to be. In the 1920s, Battery F, 131st Field Artillery, Texas National Guard, obtained a lease for some thirty acres of the site. The hospital was renovated, wired for electricity, and turned into the battery's headquarters; several other buildings were also stabilized. In 1936, primarily through the efforts of local citizens, the Texas Centennial Commission allocated money to purchase the forty-one acres upon which the surviving buildings stood. This site was turned over to the City of Jacksboro and the Jack County Historical Society to maintain, a task they performed nobly for three decades. Then, in 1963, the National Parks Service returned Fort Richardson once again to national prominence by declaring the post a National Historic Landmark, at that time one of only twelve such sites in the state. Five years later, the Texas Parks and Wildlife Department took over operation of the post, and in February 1973, Fort Richardson State Park was formally opened. Today, upwards of one hundred thousand people a year visit the park to share in Richardson's history. They tour the restored buildings, listen to lectures by park guides, and walk the manicured parade ground. And probably more than one pauses to conjure up imaginary columns of troopers wheeling and prancing in formation, practicing for the next campaign. The days of proud pennants and guidons streaming and snapping in the wind are gone, but for a new generation of Texans and visitors to Texas, Fort Richardson and its storied past lives on.

NOTES

Abbreviations Used in Notes:

AAGDT – Assistant Adjutant General, Department of Texas
AAGDM – Assistant Adjutant General, Department of the Missouri
CIA – Commissioner of Indian Affairs
DT – Department of Texas
GPO – Government Printing Office
NA – National Archives
OHS – Oklahoma Historical Society
PHPHR – *Panhandle-Plains Historical Review*
PMH – Post Medical Histories, Fort Richardson
RFR – Records of Fort Richardson
RG – Record Group
SHQ – *Southwestern Historical Quarterly*
SW – Secretary of War
TMH – *Texas Military History*
WHQ – *Western Historical Quarterly*
WTHAYB – *West Texas Historical Association Yearbook*

Chapter One

[1] Carl Coke Rister, *The Southwestern Frontier, 1865–1881* (1928), 74. Indians characteristically raided with the full moon, according to many references. One of the resolutions passed by "The Weatherford Convention," a gathering of citizens at Weatherford, Texas, to discuss frontier defense was "[resolved] that two companies of 50 men . . . be raised . . . to scout along the frontier during the present 'light moon'" (reported in the Dallas *Herald*, April 11, 1860). Even today a full moon in the Southwest is called a "Comanche Moon."

[2] See W. C. Holden, "Frontier Defense, 1846–1860," *WTHAYB* 6 (1930): 35–64, and Walter Prescott Webb, *The Texas Rangers: A Century of Frontier Defense* (1935).

[3] Rupert N. Richardson, *The Frontier of Northwest Texas, 1846 to*

1876 (1963), 61.

⁴ Ibid.

⁵ Robert M. Utley, *Frontiersmen in Blue* (1967), 71.

⁶ Holden, "Frontier Defense," 42.

⁷ Utley, *Frontiersmen in Blue*, 71.

⁸ The San Antonio *Daily Express*, quoted in Ernest Wallace, *Texas in Turmoil* (1965).

⁹ Oliver Knight, *Following the Indian Wars* (1960), 17–18.

¹⁰ Rister, *Southwestern Frontier*, 46.

¹¹ Richardson, *Frontier of Northwest Texas*, 61–75; see also William H. Leckie, *The Military Conquest of the Southern Plains* (1963), 16.

¹² W. W. Dennis, *Fort Richardson, Texas* (*1867–1878*) *and the Mackenzie Trail* (1964), 7; Ida Lasater Huckabay, *Ninety-Four Years in Jack County* (1949), 13–18. Jack County was officially established by act of the legislature on August 27, 1856. In the first county election on July 4, 1857, Los Creek was chosen to be the location of the county seat. The name Los Creek was changed first to Mesquiteville, and then to Jacksborough on February 6, 1858. According to Huckabay the spelling change to Jacksboro was not made until 1889, although it appears regularly in the present form on documents as early as 1866 and on the masthead of the *Frontier Echo* in 1875; see also Seymour V. Conner, *The Peters Colony of Texas* (1959), 160. Jack County was originally part of the huge Peters Colony grant.

¹³ Joseph Kennedy, *Population of the United States in 1860; the Eighth Census*, 488 (1861); Huckabay, *Ninety-Four Years*, 18. Huckabay places the Jack County population at well over a thousand. Captain B. B. Paddock, ed., *A Twentieth Century History and Biographical Record of North and West Texas* (1906), 1: 94, places the 1860 population of Jack County at 1688 and the 1870 figure at 1000.

¹⁴ Lena Clara Koch, "Federal Indian Policy in Texas," *SHQ* 28 (January 1925): 281, and 29 (July 1926): 123; James M. Day and Dorman Winfrey, eds., *Texas Indian Papers, 1860–1916* (1961), 3: 209–210; Randolph B. Marcy, *Thirty Years of Army Life on the Border* (1886), 170–223; Marcy and Robert Neighbors jointly surveyed the sites for the reserves, which were carved out of lands belonging to the state. A discussion of the Texas Indian reservations can be found in Kenneth F. Neighbours, "Robert S. Neighbors and the Founding of the Texas Indian Reservations," *WTHAYB* 31 (1955): 65–74. See also Rister, *Southwestern Frontier*, 38.

¹⁵ Rupert N. Richardson, *The Comanche Barrier to South Plains Settlement* (1933), 253–256. Troops from Camp Cooper prevented the settlers

178

from attacking the reservation on March 20, 1859, but a small skirmish took place on May 23, 1859. Quote in Paddock, *Twentieth Century History of North and West Texas*, 1: 94.

[16] Kenneth F. Neighbours, "Indian Exodus Out of Texas in 1859," *WTHAYB* 36 (1960): 84.

[17] Quoted in Holden, "Frontier Defense," 63.

[18] Utley, *Frontiersmen in Blue*, 71.

[19] The Texas Secession Convention of 1861 raised two cavalry regiments. John R. Baylor was elected lieutenant colonel of the Second Regiment, Texas Mounted Rifles; see Martin Hardwick Hall, "Planter vs. Frontiersman: Conflict in Confederate Indian Policy," *Essays on the American Civil War*, ed. William F. Holmes and Harold M. Hollingsworth (1968), 47.

[20] About peace purchasing, Hall, in "Planter vs. Frontiersman," 51, says: "Hostiles . . . after having gone on raids during the spring and summer, would frequently then sue for peace. Treaties would . . . be signed, and the Indians would be given their presents. Later, when the next spring arrived, these same Indians would take to the warpath again, knowing that later they could sue for peace and get presents anew." This Indian tendency to pledge peace during the fall and winter months and then wage war during the spring and summer was one of the major causes of aggravation between the tribes and the federal government.

[21] W. C. Holden, "Frontier Defense in Texas during the Civil War," *WTHAYB* 4 (1928): 19–21. For muster rolls of the North Texas companies (including one from Jack County) in the Frontier Regiment see Huckabay, *Ninety-Four Years*, 82–88.

[22] Wallace, *Texas in Turmoil*, 237–239.

[23] This was a general uprising in Colorado which continued after the Kiowas and Comanches departed. It was during this war that Major Jacob Downing and Colonel John M. Chivington executed savage attacks upon Cheyenne villages at Cedar Bluff, on May 3, 1864, and Sand Creek, November 29, 1864. See Stan Hoig, *The Sand Creek Massacre* (1961).

[24] Richardson, *Frontier of Northwest Texas*, 246–247; Colonel W. S. Nye, *Carbine and Lance, The Story of Old Fort Sill* (1943), 35. Brit Johnson, a brave negro, later managed to ransom six of the captives, including his wife and two children, from the Kiowas and Comanches.

[25] B. W. Aston, "Federal Military Reoccupation of the Texas Southwestern Frontier, 1865–1871," *TMH* 8 (Summer 1970): 125; Carl Coke Rister, "Fort Griffin," *WTHAYB* 1 (1925): 16. Rister says the frontier was driven back 150 to 200 miles at this time.

[26] Theronne Thompson, "Fort Buffalo Springs, Texas, Border Post,"

WTHAYB 36 (1960): 156.

²⁷Aston, "Federal Military Reoccupation," 125; Charles William Ramsdell, "Presidential Reconstruction in Texas," *SHQ* 11 (April 1908): 299.

²⁸Ramsdell, "Presidential Reconstruction in Texas," 299; Carl Coke Rister, *Border Command, General Phil Sheridan in the West* (1944), 23–24. Sheridan feared that state troops might be used against freedmen. SW, *Annual Report,* 1866, 48.

²⁹Wallace, *Texas in Turmoil,* 245; Robert Utley, *Frontier Regulars* (1973), 166.

³⁰SW, *Annual Report,* 1866, 1; Utley, *Frontier Regulars,* 15; William Addlemann Ganoe, *History of the United States Army* (1924), 303, 307.

³¹"The Act to Increase and Fix the Military Peace Establishment of the United States," July 28, 1866, and the "Army Appropriation Act," March 3, 1869, as quoted in Utley, *Frontier Regulars,* 11, 15, 36–37.

³²SW, *Annual Report,* 1866, Report of the Adjutant General, 4–5.

³³SW, *Annual Report,* 1878, 36, 38.

³⁴*Army and Navy Journal,* January 3, 1891, 317.

³⁵SW, *Annual Report,* 1882, 60–63; H. H. McConnell, *Five Years a Cavalryman, or Sketches of Regular Army Life on the Texas Frontier, Twenty Odd Years Ago* (1889), 212–213, 220–221, 237. For a history of the black units see William H. Leckie, *The Buffalo Soldiers: A Narrative of the Negro Cavalry in the West* (1967), and Arlen Fowler, *The Black Infantry in the West* (1971).

³⁶McConnell, *Five Years a Cavalryman,* 13, 16–17, 88, 106–108; Utley, *Frontier Regulars,* 22. See especially the chapters on desertion and alcoholism in Don Rickey, Jr., *Forty Miles a Day on Beans and Hay* (1963). Very little of Rickey's book deals with the army in Texas, but it is nonetheless a good description of the general problems of military life on the frontier.

³⁷Utley, *Frontier Regulars,* 13; Leckie, *Military Conquest,* 28. For reductions in rank, see Francis B. Heitman, *Historical Register and Dictionary of the U.S. Army* (1903), vol. 2.

³⁸Utley, *Frontier Regulars,* 19, 38.

³⁹*Army and Navy Journal,* October 6, 1877, 138–139.

⁴⁰Utley, *Frontier Regulars,* 22.

⁴¹Arcadi Gluckman, *United States Muskets, Rifles, and Carbines* (1948), 273–293, 406–409, 438–440; McConnell, *Five Years a Cavalryman,* 114. For a detailed discussion of the 1873 Springfield carbine, see Kenneth Hamner, *The Springfield Carbine on the Western Frontier* (1970);

Fort Richardson Post Returns, May 1868. Each trooper was responsible for the loss of his rifle to the amount of fifty dollars.

[42] Arcadi Gluckman, *United States Martial Pistols and Revolvers* (1939), 213–217, 233–236.

[43] Utley, *Frontier Regulars*, 71; Knight, *Following the Indian Wars*, 14.

[44] Utley, *Frontier Regulars*, 72, 78.

[45] McConnell, *Five Years a Cavalryman*, 230; Rickey, *Forty Miles a Day*, chapter 11; Donald E. Kloster, "Uniforms of the Army Prior and Subsequent to 1872," *Military Collector and Historian* 14 (1962): 103–112. Rollie Burns, a Wise County cowboy, related how prized the greatcoats were by the citizens: "Blue army overcoats were woven so tightly they turned the rain. They were hard to get, could not be purchased in a legitimate fashion at all. One had to barter for them clandestinely from the soldiers [of Fort Richardson]. The soldiers would tell their commanding officer they had lost their coats and get new ones issued . . . the usual price of a coat was a quart of whiskey." From William C. Holden, *Rollie Burns, or An Account of the Ranching Industry on the South Plains* (1932), 43.

[46] *Army and Navy Journal*, August 12, 1876, 4.

[47] Quote from Colonel Randolph B. Marcy's testimony in Senate Report 555, 45th Cong., 3d sess. 1878, 273; McConnell, *Five Years a Cavalryman*, 55; Knight, *Following the Indian Wars*, 63; Utley, *Frontier Regulars*, 48.

[48] McConnell, *Five Years a Cavalryman*, 14, 43, 117, 241. During the first few years of operations, the post returns consistently show a lack of serviceable mounts. See Fort Richardson Post Returns, 1866–1872.

[49] Melbourne Chandler, *Of Garryowen in Glory: The History of the 7th U.S. Cavalry* (1960), 29.

[50] Leckie, *Military Conquest*, 7.

[51] See Frank Gilbert Roe, *The Indian and the Horse* (1955).

[52] George Catlin, *Letters and Notes on the Manners, Customs, and Conditions of the North American Indians*, 2: 66.

[53] Walter Prescott Webb, *The Great Plains* (1931), 48, 53, 58–61.

[54] Marcy, *Thirty Years of Army Life*, 24–25; Richard Irving Dodge, *The Hunting Grounds of the Great American West* (1877), 330–331; SW, *Annual Report*, 1876, 500. See also Reginald and Gladys Laubin, *American Indian Archery* (1980).

[55] Richard Irving Dodge, *Our Wild Indians: Thirty-Three Years' Personal Experience Among the Red Men of the Great West* (1890), 451.

[56] Military societies abounded in the Plains tribes. Typical were those of the Kiowas: the Rabbits, Young Mountain Sheep, Horse Caps, Black

Legs, Crazy Legs, and Chief Dogs. The Rabbit society was composed of young boys, the next four were about equal in power and prestige, and membership in the Chief Dogs, or Koitsenkos, was limited to the ten bravest warriors in the tribe. See Dodge, *Hunting Grounds*, 353–354, 389–390; Frederick W. Hodge, *Handbook of American Indians North of Mexico, Bureau of American Ethnology, Bulletin No. 30* (1912), 1: 354.

⁵⁷ Dodge, *Hunting Grounds*, 400–401; Marcy, *Thirty Years of Army Life*, 23–24.

⁵⁸ W. W. Newcombe, Jr., *The Indians of Texas, from Prehistoric to Modern Times* (1961), 181–182. Newcombe says, "The most gamelike aspect of [Plains Indian] warfare was the practice of counting coup. The recognition of coups was roughly parallel to our system of awarding various medals for various deeds of valor in battle. The highest coup was awarded for the act of greatest bravery . . . [which] was to touch or strike a living enemy. Killing an enemy with a bullet or arrow from a distance was not such a great feat. Scalping an already-dead enemy hardly counted as a coup, but scalping an enemy (alive or dead) under perilous circumstances was appropriately rewarded. Stealing horses staked in an enemy camp, or under other equally dangerous circumstances, also rated high on the list of war honors. For a deed to count, it had to be witnessed by other warriors, and after a battle the chief gathered the participants so that the honors claimed could be adjudged."

⁵⁹ The Comanches lived in twelve bands, the most important of which were the Kwahadis (Antelopes), the Yamparikas (Root-Eaters), the Kotsotekas (Buffalo-Eaters), the Nokonis (Wanderers), and the Penatekas (Honey-Eaters). The Kiowas recognized five tribal bands: the Kata (Biters), the Kogui (Elks), the Kaigwu (Kiowas), the Kingep (Big Shields), and the Kongtalyui (Black Boys). Bureau of American Ethnology, *Fourteenth Annual Report* (1896), 2: 1044–1045, 1087; Hodge, *Handbook of American Indians*, 1: 327; James Mooney, "A Calendar History of the Kiowa," *Seventeenth Annual Report of the Bureau of American Ethnology 1895–1896*, 153–164.

⁶⁰ For a discussion of the buffalo and the Indian's use of it, see Francis Haines, *The Buffalo* (1970); William T. Hornaday, "The Extermination of the American Bison," *Annual Report of the United States National Museum* (1889); Larry Barsness, *Heads, Hides and Horns: The Compleat Buffalo Book* (1985). The fact that the Indians' ponies subsisted totally on prairie grass and were therefore entirely adapted to the plains environment accounts for a great deal of the advantage in mobility which the tribesmen enjoyed over the cavalry. Knight, *Following the Indian Wars*, 63.

[61] Marcy, *Thirty Years of Army Life,* 47–48; CIA, *Annual Report,* 1869, 553.

[62] SW, *Annual Report,* 1878, 38. The actual cost in lives has been roughly calculated. The army's records show that from January 1866 to January 1891, 932 officers and enlisted men were killed in action and 1,061 wounded in 1,065 engagements with hostile Indians. During that same period the army counted 461 civilians killed and 116 wounded, for a total of 2,570 white casualties. Indians killed and wounded were estimated at 5,519. "Chronological List of Actions, etc., with Indians from January 1, 1866, to January 1, 1891," in Joseph Peters, comp., *Indian Battles and Skirmishes on the American Frontier, 1790–1898* (1966), 2–56.

Chapter Two

[1] McConnell, *Five Years a Cavalryman,* 47, 50.

[2] Ibid., 50. No one can say just how great the depopulation of the frontier was during and after the Civil War, but the 1870 federal census records only 694 citizens living in Jack County in that year. Frances Walker, *Statistics of the Population of the United States, 1870; the Ninth Census,* p. 64.

[3] Fort Richardson Post Returns, June 1866.

[4] Ernest William Winkler, ed., *Journal of the Secession Convention of Texas, 1861* (1912), 80. The Jack County vote was fourteen in favor of secession, seventy-six opposed. Union sentiment was strong in the Red River counties, which contained a tenth of the population of Texas but cast more than a fourth of the votes against secession. Either the northern-born people exercised great influence in these counties, or the locations of the counties, the occupations of the people, and other factors made secession less appealing there. Richardson, *Frontier of Northwest Texas,* 226–227; James Alex Baggett, "The Constitutional Union Party in Texas," *SHQ* 82 (1979): 252.

[5] Rister, *The Southwestern Frontier,* 101–102. Dragoons were mounted infantrymen who generally dismounted to fight.

[6] Fort Richardson Post Returns, July-September 1866.

[7] Day and Winfrey, eds., *Texas Indian Papers,* 4: 97.

[8] Ibid., 101–103.

[9] Also spelled cavyyard. Robert G. Carter, *On the Border with Mackenzie, or Winning West Texas from the Comanches* (1961), 58.

[10] Wallace, *Texas in Turmoil,* 244; J. Evetts Haley, "The Comanchero

Trade," *SHQ* 38 (January 1935): 161. According to a tabular statement of Indian depredations prepared by the state of Texas and submitted to the Secretary of War Edward Stanton, from the close of the Civil War until July 1867, hostile Indians killed 7 white people in Jack County and stole 5000 head of cattle and 100 horses. Overall, during this period, 162 Texas citizens were killed, 43 carried into captivity, and 24 wounded by Indian raiders, and 31,000 head of cattle and 3800 horses were stolen. Day and Winfrey, eds., *Texas Indian Papers*, 4: 232–236.

[11] Fort Richardson Post Returns, September 1866; Day and Winfrey, eds., *Texas Indian Papers*, 4: 109. The victim's name here appears as Emmet Jones.

[12] Fort Richardson Post Returns, December 1866.

[13] McConnell, *Five Years a Cavalryman*, 49–50; Starr to AAGDT, January 7, 1867, Letters Received, DT, RG 393.

[14] McConnell, *Five Years a Cavalryman*, 60–61. Pine-top whiskey was described as a clear, white corn-based moonshine which the local merchants purchased for twenty-five cents a gallon and sold to the soldiers at prices ranging from three to five dollars a canteen full. Its effects can be imagined.

[15] Fort Richardson Post Returns, July-December 1866.

[16] Ibid., January 1867. Among the newly arrived recruits was H. H. McConnell, whose book *Five Years a Cavalryman* is the most accurate account of Fort Richardson's early years.

[17] McConnell, *Five Years a Cavalryman*, 53–54.

[18] A comment penned by Captain Robert G. Carter in a rare first edition copy of *Five Years a Cavalryman*, in the library of the late Mr. Fred Cotten of Weatherford, Texas.

[19] McConnell, *Five Years a Cavalryman*, 53.

[20] Ibid., 49–50, 77–79; Heitman, *Historical Register of the U.S. Army*, 1: 917; McConnell, 146.

[21] McConnell, *Five Years a Cavalryman*, 55; Fort Richardson Post Returns, February 1867.

[22] Fort Richardson Post Returns, February 1867.

[23] Assistant Surgeon Carlos Carvallo, "Zoology of Vicinity of Post," PMH, 1: 53; McConnell, *Five Years a Cavalryman*, 113–115.

[24] Fort Richardson Post Returns, March 1867.

[25] Day and Winfrey, eds., *Texas Indian Papers*, 4: 188–195, 240–241.

[26] Colonel James Starr to Oakes, April 20, 1867, Letters Received, DT, RG 98.

[27] McConnell, *Five Years a Cavalryman*, 59.

²⁸See Kenneth F. Neighbours, "Tonkawa Scouts and Guides," *WTHAYB* 49 (1973): 90–113; Carter, *On the Border with Mackenzie*, 133.

²⁹Fort Richardson Post Returns, April 1867.

³⁰Starr to Major General L. Thomas, April 27, 1867, Letters Received, DT, RG 393; Fort Richardson Post Returns, March-April 1867. Company G, Sixth Cavalry, joined the regiment at Jacksboro in early April, just in time for the move to Buffalo Springs. Company D was ordered to Sherman on March 1, 1867, to protect that settlement from Indian raiders, and Company F left Jacksboro March 20, 1867, on a long-range scout of the northwestern frontier.

³¹Thompson, "Fort Buffalo Springs," 158. In May 1867, Captain B. T. Hutchins reported that half of his men of Company A were dismounted. Hutchins to AAGDT, May 18, 1867, Letters Sent, RFR, 66.

³²SW, *Annual Report*, 1867, 378. Most of the skilled mechanics were brought from San Antonio. H. Allen Anderson, ed., "Indian Raids on the Texas Frontier: The Personal Memoirs of Hugh Allen Anderson," *WTHAYB* 51 (1975): 92.

³³Thompson, "Fort Buffalo Springs," 160–161.

³⁴This reference to bugle blowing from among the Indians appears in Lieutenant Matheny's report. This incident would seem to indicate the presence in the war party of one of the most famous Indians on the Texas frontier, Satanta (White Bear), a Kiowa chief who was noted for always carrying a bugle on his person and using it at the slightest provocation.

³⁵The official report of the siege of Buffalo Springs appears in Hutchins to AAGDT and Matheny to AAGDT, July 23, 1867, Letters Sent, RFR, 66. The only other first-hand account surviving is Sergeant H. H. McConnell's narrative in *Five Years a Cavalryman*, 93–99. McConnell gives himself a major role in the events, but he is not mentioned at all in the official reports.

³⁶McConnell, *Five Years a Cavalryman*, 100.

³⁷Hutchins to AAGDT, October 11, 1867, and October 24, 1867, Letters Sent, RFR, 66.

³⁸"Extract of Report of Lieutenant Colonel C. S. Strong, Assistant Quartermaster, USA," SW, *Annual Report*, 1868, 862–864.

³⁹Ibid., 868; McConnell, *Five Years a Cavalryman*, 127. McConnell estimates that around $100,000 was spent on Buffalo Springs, which is considerably more than the $41,769.94 claimed by the government.

⁴⁰Special Order No. 20, Post of Jacksboro, February 23, 1868, and Special Order No. 46, Fort Richardson, April 11, 1868, Special Orders, RFR, 92.

[41] McConnell, *Five Years a Cavalryman*, 81; Circular No. 4, Surgeon General's Office: "Barracks and Hospitals, with Descriptions of Military Posts," 184.

Chapter Three

[1] Special Order No. 27, Fifth Military District, New Orleans, Louisiana, February 6, 1868, in Special Orders, RFR, 92.

[2] Robert G. Ferris, ed., *Soldier and Brave* (1971), 12: 332.

[3] Hietman, *Historical Register of the U.S. Army*, 1: 828; Stephen W. Sears, *Landscape Turned Red: The Battle of Antietam* (1983), 242, 254–255.

[4] Assistant Surgeon J. N. Patzki, "Locality and History of Post," PMH, 1: 3; Circular No. 4, Surgeon General's Office, 184; Dennis, *Fort Richardson, Texas*, 12.

[5] McConnell, *Five Years a Cavalryman*, 104.

[6] Ibid., 162. This remark of McConnell's has been repeated in practically every work ever done on Richardson. As the original plans cannot now be located, its validity must remain conjectural. Had more stone been used in the construction, the appearance of the post certainly would have been better. As it was, the picket structures began to deteriorate almost immediately, warping so badly that nails could not be driven into them, but nail holes had to be bored. Every inspection report after 1870 speaks of the dilapidated condition of the buildings.

[7] Circular No. 4, 187; General Order No. 12, March 19, 1870, General Orders, RFR, 98.

[8] Circular No. 4, 187; Assistant Surgeon J. N. Patzki, "Description of Post," PMH, 1: 10.

[9] Patzki, "Description of Post," PMH, 1: 10.

[10] Captain James Curtis, Acting Assistant Inspector General, Special Report, April 2–5, 1870, Letters Received, Records of the Office of the Inspector General, RG 159.

[11] Captain W. B. Russell, Acting Inspector General, to AAGDT, March 8, 1875, Letters Received, DT, RG 393.

[12] Circular No. 4, 187; Carter, *On the Border with Mackenzie*, 69, 111–112.

[13] Carter, *On the Border with Mackenzie*, 321–322.

[14] Fort Richardson Post Returns, December 1869; Circular No. 4, 187; Patzki, "Description of Post," PMH, 1: 16.

[15] Circular Order No. 28, August 25, 1868, Special Orders, General

Orders, and Circulars, RFR, 92; Circular No. 4, 188; Patzki, "Description of Post," PMH, 1: 20; McConnell, *Five Years a Cavalryman*, 210.

[16] Circular No. 4, 188; Captain David Madden to Headquarters, February 17, 1868, Letters Received, DT, RG 393; SW, *Annual Report*, 1868, 869; Colonel W. N. Wood to AAGDT, July 6, 1875, Letters Sent, RFR, 72.

[17] The two larger barracks were 114 by 27 feet and 100 by 20 feet. Circular No. 4, 186; Patzki, "Description of Post," PMH 1: 13; Post Surgeon W. H. Forwood, "Monthly Sanitary Report," December 31, 1873, PMH, 2: 41–46.

[18] Forwood, "Monthly Sanitary Report," PMH, December 31, 1873, 2: 45; Patzki, "Description of Post," PMH, 1: 13–14. The moveable zinc-lined troughs were replaced in 1871 with a dry-earth system suggested by post surgeon Colonel John F. Hammond.

[19] The two stable buildings varied in width: one was thirty feet wide, the other thirty-five. Patzki, "Description of Post," PMH, 1: 67; Assistant Inspector General N. H. Davis, Inspection Report, June 16–18, 1875, Letters Received, Records of the Office of the Inspector General, RG 159; Captain T. A. Baldwin to AAGDT, October 26, 1877, Letters Sent, RFR, 73.

[20] McConnell, *Five Years a Cavalryman*, 164.

[21] Circular No. 4, 188; Patzki, "Description of Post," PMH, 1: 34; the plan was taken from Circular No. 4, April 27, 1867.

[22] Jack Van Gordon Anderson, *Recollections and Reflections of a Texian* (1966), 2.

[23] Patzki, "Description of Post," PMH, 1: 34. The dimensions of the hospital and its rooms, as well as those of some other buildings at Richardson, vary from one source to another. One possible explanation for these inconsistencies could be that some writers actually went to the trouble of measuring the existing structures, while others were merely copying information from a set of standard plans, not allowing for deviations due to inept construction and shoddy materials. It is quite possible that the finished buildings at Richardson (as well as at many other posts in the West) corresponded more to the spirit of Washington's standardized plans than to the exact letter. Therefore, all measurements quoted in the text must be considered as approximates. Even the buildings still standing, such as the hospital, have undergone extensive renovations, and many original flaws have been corrected.

[24] Ibid., 34–36; Assistant Surgeon Carlos Carvallo, "Description of Post," PMH, 1: 20; Forwood, "Monthly Sanitary Report," April 30, 1875,

PMH, 2: 129, and "Monthly Sanitary Report," November 30, 1875, PMH, 2: 160.

²⁵ The washroom and privy were both nine by eleven feet. Patzki, "Description of the Post," PMH, 1: 35–36; Circular No. 4, 189.

²⁶ Patzki to Post Adjutant, September 23, 1870, Miscellaneous Materials, RFR; Post Surgeon David Weisel, "Record for the Month of June, 1872," PMH, 1: 270; Forwood to Post Adjutant, September 23, 1873, PMH, 2: 30; Inspector General Davis, Inspection Report, June 16–18, 1875; Post Surgeon A. A. Yeoman to Medical Director, DT, August 22, 1877, Letters Received, DT, RG 363.

²⁷ Patzki, "Description of Post," PMH, 1: 33–34, 67; Circular No. 4, 189; Forwood, "Monthly Sanitary Report," December 31, 1873, PMH, 2: 42.

²⁸ Patzki, "Description of Post," PMH, 1: 15; J. N. Patzki, "Miscellaneous," PMH, 1: 75; Circular No. 4, 187; McConnell, *Five Years a Cavalryman*, 211. The post surgeon, Dr. Patzki, reported that "amongst these vestials [sic] of the Temple of Venus there is [not] a single one free from venereal disease." Patzki, "Miscellaneous," PMH, 1: 97.

²⁹ Circular No. 4, 187.

³⁰ Patzki, "Description of Post," PMH, 1: 9; Circular No. 4, 187, 190.

³¹ Patzki, "Description of Post," PMH, 1: 9; Circular No. 4, 185; Post Surgeon J. F. Hammond to Post Adjutant, April 24, 1871, Records of the Office of Judge Advocate General, RG 153; Patzki, "Miscellaneous," PMH, 1: 72; Llerena Friend, ed., *M. K. Kellogg's Texas Journal, 1872*, 89.

³² Patzki, "Miscellaneous," PMH, 1: 73; Circular No. 4, 190; Fort Richardson Post Returns.

³³ McConnell, *Five Years a Cavalryman*, 159; Fort Richardson Post Returns, June–September 1868, September 1869.

³⁴ Jack County *Herald* (Jacksboro, Texas), Centennial Edition, August 1955. Brigadier General J. D. Bingham of the Quartermaster Department stated in his inspection report of February 24, 1869, that the "improvements" made at Fort Richardson had already cost the United States government $130,000; Bingham to Holobind, Department Quartermaster General, Letters Received, Office of the Quartermaster General, RG 92. The first six months of construction at Richardson, which resulted in the completion of two storehouses, one hospital with two wards, one kitchen, and one bakery, cost the government $70,602.34; SW, *Annual Report*, 1868, 869, 871.

³⁵ Patzki, "Miscellaneous," PMH, 1: 76.

³⁶ Thomas F. Horton, *History of Jack County*, 119; Huckabay, *Ninety-*

Four Years, 109; McConnell, *Five Years a Cavalryman,* 160; Henry Strong, *My Frontier Days and Indian Fights on the Plains of Texas* (1924), 79–82; *Frontier Echo* (Jacksboro, Texas), November 19, 1875.

³⁷ McConnell, *Five Years a Cavalryman,* 161.

³⁸ Strong, *Frontier Days,* 80.

³⁹ McConnell, *Five Years a Cavalryman,* 161; Horton, *History of Jack County,* 120.

⁴⁰ Huckabay, *Ninety-Four Years,* 107; *Frontier Echo* (Jacksboro, Texas), May 18, 1877. A traveler passing through Jacksboro in 1876 noted the relationship between the town and the fort: "Jacksboro has improved but little for several years. The location of one of the military posts here in 1867 had the effect to add materially to the town's importance as a trading post for the frontier settlers, but since the cessation of Indian troubles the troops have nearly all been withdrawn, resulting in a perceptible decrease in prosperity;" Paddock, ed., *Twentieth Century History of North and West Texas,* 1: 222.

Chapter Four

¹ Ernest Wallace, *Ranald S. Mackenzie and the Texas Frontier* (1964), 24. There were also a few Frenchmen in the Sixth Cavalry. During the summer and fall of 1870, while the Franco-Prussian War raged in Europe, tensions grew between the French and German soldiers at Fort Richardson. Most of the regimental band were Germans who insisted on playing their national tunes on every available occasion. The Frenchmen would respond by singing the "Marseillaise." These displays of nationalism often ended in blows. Finally, the officers had to forbid the playing and singing of such aggravating tunes. McConnell, *Five Years a Cavalryman,* 221.

² Fort Richardson Post Returns, January 1868–March 1871. Innumerable small scouting parties were constantly in the field, but as these detachments did not consist of more than four men and never ventured far from the post, they are not documented in the post returns.

³ Ibid.

⁴ Fort Richardson Post Returns, July 1870.

⁵ SW, *Annual Report,* 1870, 41–42.

⁶ McConnell, *Five Years a Cavalryman,* 49–50, 145–146, 229. Sergeant McConnell wrote that he did not come to love Major Starr while serving with him, but "I surely learned to respect his integrity and honor."

Colonel Oakes, by contrast, is mentioned by name only once in McConnell's book, probably because Sergeant McConnell spent the summer and most of the fall of 1870 under close arrest, accused by Colonel Oakes of misappropriating company funds. Although he was never convicted, the experience so soured McConnell on military life that when his enlistment expired, soon after the Sixth Cavalry transferred to Kansas, he left the army and returned to Jacksboro to become a permanent resident.

[7] Heitman, *Historical Register of the U.S. Army*, 1: 754.

[8] Fort Richardson Post Returns, April-May 1869; Oakes to AAGDT, May 21, 1869, Letters Sent, RFR, 67.

[9] Fort Richardson Post Returns, May 1869; Oakes to AAGDT, May 29, 1869, Letters Sent, RFR, 68; Special Order No. 79, May 24, 1869, Special Orders, RFR, 93. General Reynolds authorized the formation of citizen companies in April 1869. Twenty-three men were enrolled in Jack County by Lieutenants Hall and Overton of the Sixth Cavalry. Edward Wolffarth (see McConnell, *Five Years a Cavalryman*, 222) was elected the first captain. Before the company could pursue the marauding Indians, it was necessary for Oakes to furnish them with carbines, revolvers, and horses.

[10] "Memorial of Three Hundred and Fifty Citizens of the Northwestern Frontier of Texas," House Misc. Doc. 142, 41st Cong., 2d sess., 1870; "Petition to the Secretary of War," copy in Miscellaneous Files, RFR; Oakes to William Belknap, Secretary of War, February 20, 1870, Letters Sent, RFR, 68; SW, *Annual Report*, 1868, xvii.

[11] For the official report of the government commission investigating the massacre at Sand Creek see House Ex. Doc. 97, 40th Cong., 2d sess., 1867, Serial 1335. Of the seven hundred Indians encamped at Sand Creek, perhaps five hundred were slain, many of them mutilated and tortured. See n. 23, chapter one.

[12] For a complete discussion of the various public groups that wanted to rescue the American Indian from what was perceived to be a state of savagery, see Robert Winston Mardock, *The Reformers and the American Indian* (1971); CIA, *Annual Report*, 1865, 711–715; Mooney, "Calendar History," 181. Satanta attended the meeting but was not a signatory of the treaty.

[13] SW, *Annual Report*, 1870, 10; Mooney, "Calendar History," 178–180.

[14] Douglas C. Jones, *The Treaty of Medicine Lodge* (1966), 130–133.

[15] Mooney, "Calendar History," 187; CIA, *Annual Report*, 1869, 833; George A. Custer, *My Life on the Plains, or Personal Experiences with Indians* (1962), 270–274.

[16] SW, *Annual Report*, 1870, 10.

[17] H. Smythe, *Historical Sketch of Parker County and Weatherford, Texas* (1877), 122–124.

[18] CIA, *Annual Report*, 1869, 478; Lawrie Tatum, *Our Red Brothers and the Peace Policy of President Ulysses S. Grant* (1899), 48, 133; Leckie, *Buffalo Soldiers*, 55.

[19] SW, *Annual Report*, 1869, 144.

[20] Ibid., 1870, 76–77.

[21] Fort Richardson Post Returns, August-September 1868, August 1870, September-November 1876. Under the command of Lieutenant Gilbert E. Overton, Company D, Seventeenth Infantry built the post guardhouse in the summer of 1868. SW, *Annual Report*, 1868, 764–765; 1869, 214; 1870, 76–77; 1876, 66.

[22] Fort Richardson Post Returns, July 1867–July 1873; Starr to AAGDT, May 6, 1868, Letters Sent, RFR, 66.

[23] Fort Richardson Post Returns, June 1870; Oakes to AAGDT, September 12, 1870, Letters Sent, RFR, 69; McConnell, *Five Years a Cavalryman*, 215–216.

[24] The Austin *Daily Journal*, May 14, 1871, reports fifteen deaths in Jack County alone. The petition given General William T. Sherman by the citizens of Jack County during his visit in May 1871 lists eleven deaths in the area (see n. 49, below). Colonel Oakes reports fifteen citizens killed "in the vicinity of the post" in the preceding twelve months; Oakes to AAGDT, September 12, 1870, Letters Sent, RFR, 69.

[25] Fort Richardson Post Returns, June 1870.

[26] Thomas C. Battey, *The Life and Adventures of a Quaker Among the Indians*, 102–103.

[27] Nye, *Carbine and Lance*, 112–113.

[28] Special Order No. 131, July 6, 1870, Special Orders, RFR, 94.

[29] Captain C. B. McClellan, "Report of Engagement with Indians at Rock Station, Texas," July 12, 1870, Reports of Scouts, RFR, 119 1/2. This report is quoted in full in W. H. Carter, *From Yorktown to Santiago with the Sixth U.S. Cavalry*, 141–146.

[30] Heitman, *Historical Register of the U.S. Army*, 1: 676.

[31] McClellan, "Report of Engagement."

[32] Ibid.; Jack Loftin, "Kicking Bird's Face-Saving Battle," WTHAYB 51 (1975): 76–85; Nye, *Carbine and Lance*, 112–113. Nye got the story of Kicking Bird leading the first charge and killing a soldier with his lance from one of his Indian informants, Hunting Horse, a Kiowa participant. Nye also reports that twenty cowboys who were camped nearby joined the soldiers late that night after the battle ended. This event was related to

him in 1935 by J. B. Terrell, who claimed to be a member of the cattle outfit. McClellan does not mention the cowboys in his report either. As both Hunting Horse and Mr. Terrell were reporting details which occurred sixty-five years before, it is possible that one or even both of the men were mistaken. It is also possible that McClellan purposefully omitted the incidents, chagrined that an enemy could approach close enough to his lines to strike a soldier and then escape unharmed, and too prideful to admit that his professional soldiers would need help from cowhands.

[33] McClellan, "Report of Engagement"; McConnell, *Five Years a Cavalryman*, 216–217. McConnell gives an interesting contemporary account of Indian tactics on pages 217–218.

[34] Nye, *Carbine and Lance*, 113; McClellan, "Report of Engagement."

[35] The two dead soldiers were Corporal John Given and Private George Blum, both of K Company. Their bodies were abandoned in the retreat. Five of the men, including Dr. Hatch, were badly wounded. Patzki, "Record for the Month of July, 1870," PMH, 1: 177, 179.

[36] McClellan, "Report of Engagement."

[37] Patzki, "Record for the Month of July, 1870," PMH, 1: 179.

[38] Nye, *Carbine and Lance*, 113; Hugh D. Corwin, *The Kiowa Indians, Their History and Life Stories*, 101–104.

[39] Medals of honor went to Sergeants George Eldridge, Thomas Kerrigan, John Kirk, John May, Alonzo Stokes, and William Winterbottom, Corporals John Conner, John Given, Charles Smith, and James Watson, Private Solon Neal, Farrier Samuel Porter, and Bugler Claron Windus. *The Medal of Honor of the United States Army* (1948), 13–14. There were many early abuses in the awarding of the Medal of Honor. Overzealous officers often recommended large numbers of their men for the medal. This practice reached its height when the entire relief column for the Little Big Horn in 1876 was recommended for Medals of Honor. General Alfred Terry wrote that "Medals of Honor are not intended for ordinarily good conduct, but for conspicuous acts of gallantry." Thereafter a review board was set up to screen applicants for the medal. Fort Richardson Post Returns, October 1870; General Order No. 57, September 26, 1870, General Orders, RFR, 98.

[40] McConnell, *Five Years a Cavalryman*, 240. Just how many a "heap" would be is not known. Lawrie Tatum, the agent for the Kiowas and Comanches, mentioned the battle in his annual report but did not say if any of his charges were killed in the fight. Certainly none of the major chiefs who participated were harmed.

[41] Oakes to AAGDT, September 10, 1870, Letters Sent, RFR, 69.

[42] Medal of Honor winners were Sergeant Michael Welsh, Corporals Samuel Bowden and Daniel Keating, and Privates James Anderson and Benjamin Wilson. Fort Richardson Post Returns, October 1870; General Order No. 79, January 10, 1871, General Orders, RFR, 99; Carter, *From Yorktown to Santiago*, 148–149; *Medal of Honor*, 215–216; McConnell, *Five Years a Cavalryman*, 220.

[43] Fort Richardson Post Returns, November 1870; Carter, *From Yorktown to Santiago*, 152–153.

[44] Nye, *Carbine and Lance*, 123; Starr to Hagen, March 8, 1869, Letters Sent, RFR, 69.

[45] Report of Vincent Calya, United States Special Indian Commissioner, CIA, *Annual Report*, 1869, 528–529. Calya mistakenly reported Johnson's name as Jackson in his narrative.

[46] Nye, *Carbine and Lance*, 123. One of the Indian participants, Quitan, later reported that the Kiowas playfully tossed the kinky-haired scalps at one another and then threw them away, as the hair was too short to be of any value. Mooney, "Calendar History," 328; Borthwick to Post Adjutant, February 10, 1871, Miscellaneous Files, RFR. The wagon, "a light brown Studibacker with yellow running gear," was borrowed from Alfred Green of Weatherford. J. W. Robinson, Deposition, Jack County, February 1, 1871, Miscellaneous Files, RFR.

[47] Borthwick to Post Adjutant, February 10, 1871, Miscellaneous Files, RFR; Fort Richardson Post Returns, January 1871.

[48] Nye, *Carbine and Lance*, 124; Carter, *On the Border with Mackenzie*, 69; Special Order No. 23, January 26, 1871, Special Orders, RFR, 95; Borthwick to Post Adjutant, February 10, 1871, Miscellaneous Files, RFR.

[49] A complete list of the murders committed by hostile Indians in Jack County and the surrounding area appears in a petition the citizens of Jack County presented to General William T. Sherman during his visit to Fort Richardson. Petition, Citizens of Jack County to General Sherman, May 2, 1871, Letters Received, 1824–1880, Kiowa Agency (W489, M234, R377), RG 75, NA.

[50] Carter, *From Yorktown to Santiago*, 158. The public's contempt probably stemmed more from frustration with the government's Indian policy and with the performance of the Sixth Cavalry than from hatreds lingering from the Civil War.

[51] Fort Richardson Post Returns, March 1871; Oakes to AAGDT, March 19, 1871, Letters Sent, RFR, 70; Special Order No. 47, March 6, 1871, Special Orders, RFR, 95.

[52] McConnell, *Five Years a Cavalryman*, 233, 296.

Chapter Five

[1] Mooney, "Calendar History," 211; Wallace, *Mackenzie*, 9.

[2] Wallace, *Mackenzie*, 15; Carter, *On the Border with Mackenzie*, xii–xiii, 536–541.

[3] Mackenzie's service record appears in Ernest Wallace, editor, *Ranald S. Mackenzie's Official Correspondence Relating to Texas, 1871–1873*, 11–15.

[4] Ulysses Simpson Grant, *Personal Memoirs of U. S. Grant* (1887), 2: 541.

[5] Carter, *On the Border with Mackenzie*, 537; Wallace, *Mackenzie*, 14.

[6] Carter, *On the Border with Mackenzie*, 69. General Mackenzie noted: "Passed a mount on which two wooden crosses are erected with the remark 'three Negroes killed by Indians January 3rd, 1871' carved on the wood," in "Mackenzie's Journal of Move to Fort Richardson," Wallace, ed., *Mackenzie's Correspondence, 1871–1873*, 17–22.

[7] Carter, *On the Border with Mackenzie*, 69.

[8] Mackenzie to AAGDT, April 10, 1871, Letters Sent, RFR, 70.

[9] Fort Richardson Post Returns, April 1871.

[10] Ibid.; Special Orders No. 92 and 93, April 20, 1871, Special Orders, RFR, 95; Mackenzie to AAGDT, April 22, 1871, RFR, 70.

[11] The inspection tour is recorded in R. B. Marcy, "Extracts from Inspector General R. B. Marcy's Journal of an Inspection Tour while Accompanying the General in Chief during the Months of April, May, and June, 1871," 185–191, copy in the Phillips Collection, University of Oklahoma.

[12] House Ex. Doc. 97, 40th Cong., 2d sess., 2–3; General Order No. 8, Department of the Missouri, June 29, 1867, copy in Kiowa Files, Military Relations, OHS; General William T. Sherman, *Memoirs of General W. T. Sherman*, 2: 144; SW, *Annual Report*, 1867, 37.

[13] Leckie, *Military Conquest*, 134; CIA, *Annual Report*, 1869, 5–7.

[14] CIA, *Annual Report*, 1867, 314–315; 1870, 449.

[15] Quoted in Nye, *Carbine and Lance*, 124.

[16] "Extract of Marcy's Journal," 191.

[17] Ibid., 188–190; Benjamin Capps, *The Warren Wagontrain Raid*, 41, 263–265. Capps maintains that despite Sherman's refusal of reinforcements, patrols were dispatched to shadow him without his knowledge. Captain Clarence C. Mauck (incorrectly spelled as Manck by Capps) and Company B, Fourth Cavalry, did arrive at Richardson from Concho the day after Sherman, and another patrol under the command of Lieutenant Peter M. Boehm was dispatched from Richardson to "scout between Fort Richardson and Fort Griffin" on May 10. It would seem only natural that

local commanders would go to great lengths to protect the general-in-chief of the army from what they knew to be a clear and present Indian menace; see Fort Richardson Post Returns, May 1871.

[18] Nye, *Carbine and Lance*, 124.

[19] Leckie, *Military Conquest*, 146–148. The Indians traded with outlaws called Comancheros in the Staked Plains, those arid stretches where Texas, Oklahoma, Kansas, and New Mexico converge. See also J. Evetts Haley, "The Comanchero Trade," *SHQ* 38 (1935): 157–176.

[20] Nye, *Carbine and Lance*, 126–130, 135. Satank translated as Sitting Bear, Satanta as White Bear. Big Tree's name in Kiowa was Addo-etta, but whites always referred to him with the English translation of his name.

[21] The Koitsenko (Chief Dogs or Real Dogs), the most noble of the six or so Kiowa military societies, was "a select body of ten of the bravest warriors, who were pledged to lead every desperate charge and to keep their place in the front of battle until they won victory or death." As their senior member, Satank was allowed the honor of wearing a black elkskin sash, his badge of office; Hodge, *Handbook of American Indians*, 1: 354, 862; Mooney, "Calendar History," 284–285.

[22] Tatum, *Our Red Brothers*, 48.

[23] Jones, *Treaty of Medicine Lodge*, 204. This book is a thorough discussion of the treaty negotiations and the newspaper coverage it received at the time.

[24] Ibid., 111, 156.

[25] Ibid., 156–157.

[26] Ibid., 157.

[27] Mooney, "Calendar History," 327–328. Satank always spoke of his son as if he were sleeping, and he frequently placed food and water near the platform. The dead youth, who had the same name as his father, had already risen to the office of tonhyopda, the pipe-bearer who went in front of the young warriors on a raid. In April 1870, Colonel B. H. Grierson, the commanding officer at Fort Sill, wrote to the commandant at Fort Richardson, informing him of the death of Satank's son and warning that Satank would surely seek revenge upon the settlers. Grierson to Commanding Officer, April 20, 1870, Miscellaneous Files, RFR.

[28] Benjamin Capps's book, although titled *The Warren Wagontrain Raid*, is in reality an apologist's biography of Satanta. For contemporary and far different views of the chief, see Tatum, *Our Red Brothers*; Custer, *Life on the Plains*; and Carter, *On the Border with Mackenzie*.

[29] Corwin, *The Kiowa Indians*, 62. Satanta once showed up for an important council with General Winfield Scott Hancock with his body painted a brilliant red color. Hancock made him a present of a major gen-

eral's coat and a yellow sash, and the chief "rode grandly away, a riot of barbaric color." Custer, *My Life on the Plains*, 59; Mooney, "Calendar History," 210.

[30] Satanta's bugle is plainly visible in several photographs of him. He would play "the battered instrument at the slightest provocation." Jones, *Treaty of Medicine Lodge*, 51, 204; Mooney, "Calendar History," 177, 327.

[31] Capps, *Warren Wagontrain Raid*, 6–7, 11.

[32] Mooney, "Calendar History," 180–183; Leckie, *Military Conquest*, 33.

[33] Jones, *Treaty of Medicine Lodge*, 114.

[34] Ibid. Two Quaker Indian commissioners, John Butler and Achilles Pugh, met the Kiowa chief in 1870 and wrote, "Satanta . . . is a daring and restless personage." CIA, *Annual Report*, 1869, 565.

[35] Jones, *Treaty of Medicine Lodge*, 204; Mooney, "Calendar History," 206. Mooney accepts the title at face value, saying that Satanta's "eloquence and vigor of expression in his native tongue, a peculiarly forcible one," gained him the accolade. Jones, who studied the reporters who covered Medicine Lodge, says that Satanta "became somewhat of a bore after having been on his feet throughout most of the first day of speech making," and that "Orator of the Plains" was a sarcastic jibe, not a compliment.

[36] Corwin, *The Kiowa Indians*, 53.

[37] Ibid., 62.

[38] Ibid.

[39] J. W. Wilbarger, *Indian Depredations in Texas* (1935), 563.

[40] Nye, *Carbine and Lance*, 127.

[41] Ibid. About the Kiowa medicine men in general, Corwin says: "The Kiowa Medicine Man was a curious mixture of physician, religious leader and magician. Along with these accomplishments he was a good student of psychology and became learned in the art of guiding the thoughts and anticipating the desires of his people. They were, generally speaking, the real leaders rather than the Chiefs or War Chiefs." Corwin, *The Kiowa Indians*, 32. Some controversy has developed in recent years over who the actual leader was of this raid. Satanta would later claim the credit, and most contemporary sources identify him as the leader. However, in the 1930s, Wilbur S. Nye interviewed many old Indians, including Yellow Wolf, a participant; Ay-tah, the wife of Set-maunte, another participant; and George Hunt, who obtained his information from Big Tree and others. Nye was told that Satanta took a leading part, but that Maman-ti was *the* leader of the raid. Benjamin Capps dismisses these accounts as attempts by the old Kiowas to warp their own history and downgrade Satanta and other militant chiefs; see *Warren Wagontrain Raid*, 267–268.

[42] Nye, *Carbine and Lance*, 127–128. The testimony Nye obtained in the 1930s is the only in-depth firsthand account of the raid itself and of the Indians' actions prior to and after the fight.

[43] As noted, Capps claims that patrols followed Sherman from Fort Griffin without his knowledge in order to protect him should he be attacked, and that the Indians surely detected their presence and remained hidden. *Warren Wagontrain Raid*, 263–264, 267.

[44] Ibid., 41.

[45] Major John K. Mizner to AAGDT, May 20, 1871, Letters Sent, RFR, 70.

[46] Ibid.; Nye, *Carbine and Lance*, 131. The men who escaped, besides Brazeal, were Dick Motor, Hobbs Carey, Charles Brady, and R. A. Day. Behind them they left N. S. Long, James Elliott, Samuel Elliott, M. J. Baxter, Jessee Bowman, John Mullins, and James Williams.

[47] Nye, *Carbine and Lance*, 127–131; Capps, *Warren Wagontrain Raid*, 50–54. Nye's account is accepted as the standard since it is based on firsthand testimony. Capps offers a more dramatic recreation of the fight, much of it conjecture.

[48] Carter, *On the Border with Mackenzie*, 76–80.

[49] Jack County Citizens' Petition, May 1871.

[50] Hammond, "Record for the Month of May, 1871," PMH, 1: 217. The attending surgeon indicated the bullet entered under the external melialus [sic] of Brazeal's left foot.

[51] Ibid. Sherman dictated his orders to Mackenzie while in the ward of the hospital, and the Post Surgeon, J. F. Hammond, wrote them down; General Sherman to Colonel Mackenzie, May 19, 1871, Miscellaneous Files, RFR. The other four surviving drivers also reached Richardson that morning. In his letter of instructions to Mackenzie, Sherman wrote: "On reaching the abandoned train this afternoon, you can judge of the truth of the statement of the five men who escaped from the train and reported its capture to us this morning." And, in a letter to Colonel William Wood, the commanding officer of Fort Griffin, General Sherman reported: "A pretty strong party of Indians have attacked and captured a train of twelve (12) wagons this side of Salt Creek, ten (10) miles this side of Fort Belknap, killed seven (7) men, and five (5) have escaped to this Post—one wounded." Sherman to Wood, May 19, 1871, Letters Sent, RFR, 70.

[52] Fort Richardson Post Returns, May 1871.

[53] Patzki to Mackenzie, May 19, 1871, Miscellaneous Files, RFR; Nye, *Carbine and Lance*, 131. Patzki's report mentions only five bodies. The remains of the two men killed near the woods were not found immediately.

[54] Mizner to AAGDT, May 20, 1871, Letters Sent, RFR, 70.

[55] In the winter of 1872, Captain Wirt Davis and Company F, Fourth Cavalry, built a monument—constructed of oak, pyramidal in shape, and painted olive with the inscription in black—at the site of the burial. M. K. Kellogg wrote in summer 1872 that he "Came to monument to 7 men massacred . . . inscribed as follows: 'sacred to the memory of seven brave men killed at this place on Thursday, May 18, 1871, while in discharge of their duty defending their wagon train against 150 Comanche Indians.'" The state of Texas erected a stone monument at the site in 1936. Friend, ed., *Kellogg's Texas Journal,* 150; Huckabay, *Ninety-Four Years,* 169–170.

[56] Nye, *Carbine and Lance,* 131–132.

[57] Mizner to AAGDT, June 11, 1871, Letters Sent, RFR, 70; Fort Richardson Post Returns, May 1871. Boehm's patrol, Company A, Fourth Cavalry, was ten days out from Richardson on a thirty-day scout.

[58] Sherman to Pope, May 24, 1871, in Wallace, *Mackenzie's Correspondence, 1871–1873,* 25–26.

[59] Tatum, *Our Red Brothers,* 116.

[60] Satanta is referring to an incident that took place in December 1868, just after the Battle of the Washita, in which he and Lone Wolf were arrested by Major General Philip H. Sheridan and Lieutenant Colonel George Custer. Custer threatened to hang them both within forty-eight hours if their people did not come in to the reservation. Satanta and Lone Wolf were allowed to send runners to tell their tribesmen of their plight, and within the time limit, most of the Kiowas complied and came in. The chiefs were released not in the "several days" Satanta remembers, but in mid-February, at which time a subdued and grateful Satanta told Sheridan: "Whatever you tell me I mean to hold fast to it. . . . After this, I am going to have the white man's road, to plant corn. . . . You will not hear of the Kiowas killing any more whites." Leckie, *Military Conquest,* 109–113; Custer, *My Life on the Plains,* 298–311.

[61] The dead warriors were Tson-to-goodle, Hau-tau, and Tomasi. There were also four wounded Indians.

[62] Tatum, *Our Red Brothers,* 116–117; Lawrie Tatum to Jonathan Richards, May 30, 1871, Kiowa Files, Trial of Satanta and Big Tree, OHS; Tatum to James Mooney, April 7, 1896, in Mooney, "Calendar History," 331–332.

[63] Tatum to Grierson, May 27, 1871, Kiowa Files, Trial of Satanta and Big Tree, OHS.

[64] Nye, *Carbine and Lance,* 136.

[65] Tatum to Mooney, in Mooney, "Calendar History," 332; "Extract

of Marcy's Journal," 196; Tatum, *Our Red Brothers*, 118; "General William T. Sherman's Testimony before the Committee on Military Affairs,"
in House Report No. 384, 43rd Cong., 1st sess., 1874, 268–279; Tatum
to Richards, May 30, 1871, Kiowa Files, Trial of Satanta and Big Tree,
OHS; Nye, *Carbine and Lance*, 136–139; Sherman to Townsend, May 28,
1871, in Wallace, ed., *Mackenzie's Correspondence, 1871–1873*, 27–28;
Richard H. Pratt, *Battlefield and Classroom: Four Decades with the American
Indian, 1867–1904*, ed. Robert Utley (1964), 45–46.

⁶⁶ Nye, *Carbine and Lance*, 139.

⁶⁷ Tatum to Richards, May 30, 1871, Kiowa Files, Trial of Satanta
and Big Tree, OHS; Tatum, *Our Red Brothers*, 118; "Extract of Marcy's
Journal," 196; Nye *Carbine and Lance*, 136–142. Regarding the tense
meeting on Grierson's front porch, General Sherman later matter-of-factly
reported, "We had an angry council on General Grierson's porch, at Fort
Sill, which came near to resulting in a hand to hand fight." House Report
No. 384, 43rd Cong., 1st sess., 1874, 275. See also "Arrest of Satanta,
Satank, and Big Tree. General Sherman's Letter," *New York Times*, June 8,
1871.

⁶⁸ Mackenzie to Sherman, June 16, 1871, Letters Sent, RFR, 70.

⁶⁹ Nye, *Carbine and Lance*, 144; Leckie, *Military Conquest*, 152 fn.
Leckie says that Big Tree helped restrain Satank because he feared the old
Indian's actions would result in their all being shot.

⁷⁰ Robert G. Carter, *The Old Sergeant's Story* (1926), 78–79.

⁷¹ Nye, *Carbine and Lance*, 145–146; Corwin, *The Kiowa Indians*,
60–63.

⁷² Mooney, "Calendar History," 329; Thurston to Mackenzie, June 17,
1871, Miscellaneous Files, RFR. Lieutenant George A. Thurston, Fourth
Cavalry officer of the day, later reported: "I heard Satank chanting in the
Indian style what I now suppose to have been his 'death song.'"

⁷³ Pratt, *Battlefield and Classroom*, 47.

⁷⁴ Thurston to Mackenzie, June 17, 1871; Mooney, "Calendar History," 329–330; Nye, *Carbine and Lance*, 145–147; Mackenzie to Sherman, June 16, 1871, Letters Sent, RFR, 70; Carter, *On the Border with
Mackenzie*, 91–95; Carter, *Old Sergeant's Story*, 81; Tatum, *Our Red Brothers*, 118–121; Tatum to Richards, May 30, 1871. The civilian teamster,
Antonio Burrel, who was driving the wagon in which Satank rode, fell
victim to two of the bullets meant for the old warrior. He toppled from the
wagon seat, seriously wounded, but later recovered. See "Setank [sic]
Shot," *New York Times*, June 22, 1871.

⁷⁵ Carter, *Old Sergeant's Story*, 81; Mackenzie to Sherman, June 16,
1871; Fort Richardson Post Returns, June 1871; Dallas *Herald*, June 24,

1871; Carter, *On the Border with Mackenzie,* 97–98; Mizner to Sherman, June 9, 1871, Letters Sent, RFR, 70.

[76] Mizner to AAGDT, June 6, 1871, Miscellaneous Files, RFR.

[77] Huckabay, *Ninety-Four Years,* 179.

[78] "Indictment returned against Satanta and Big Tree by the Grand Jury of the District Court of Jack County," as quoted in ibid., 179–180.

[79] Ibid., 180; Fort Richardson Post Returns, July 1871.

[80] Fort Richardson Post Returns, July 1871; Huckabay, *Ninety-Four Years,* 181–183. Court records have disappeared; what exists is a ten-page summary of the trial, dated September 8, 1871, and addressed to the sheriff of Jack County by County Clerk James Robinson. Capps says: "It purports to be a warrant . . . ordering the sheriff to convey the two prisoners to the penitentiary at Huntsville, but . . . this document was [undoubtedly] Jack County's answer to the federal government's demand for trial records." Capps, *Warren Wagontrain Raid,* 289. Capps refers to the document as the "Warrant Minutes," which is as good a title as any. There are two copies, one in the Southwest Collection at Texas Tech University, the other in the Miscellaneous Files, RFR.

[81] The jurists were Daniel Brown, John H. Brown, Lucas P. Bunch, John Cameron, James Cooley, Samuel Cooper, Peter Hart, William Hensley, Evert Johnson, Peter Lynn, H. B. Verner, and T. W. Williams, foreman. "Warrant Minutes," Miscellaneous Files, RFR.

[82] Minutes of the Thirteenth Judicial District Court, State of Texas, July 5 and 6, 1871, as quoted in Huckabay, *Ninety-Four Years,* 183–186, and in Smythe, *Historical Sketch of Parker County,* 273–277. The "Warrant Minutes" do not contain speeches, only motions, pleas, etc. It is interesting to note that Brazeal was not discharged from the Fort Richardson hospital until June 23. It is possible that he testified in return for treatment or, as the state's star witness, that he was retained in protective custody until no longer needed. Hammond, "Record for the Month of June, 1871," PMH, 1: 223.

[83] Smythe, *Historical Sketch of Parker County,* 272–273.

[84] Ibid., 273–274.

[85] "Warrant Minutes," Miscellaneous Files, RFR.

[86] Tatum to Sherman, May 29, 1871, Miscellaneous Files, RFR.

[87] "Commutation for Satanta and Big Tree," August 2, 1871, Miscellaneous Files, RFR; Captain A. E. Latimer to AAGDT, September 2, 1871, Letters Sent, RFR, 70.

[88] Special Order No. 241, October 14, 1871, Special Orders, RFR, 95.

[89] See Carl Coke Rister, "The Significance of the Jacksboro Indian Affair of 1871," *SHQ* 29 (1926): 181–200.

[90] CIA, *Annual Report*, 1871, 419.

[91] Quoted in Wood to Mackenzie, July 6, 1871, Miscellaneous Files, RFR.

Chapter Six

[1] Mackenzie to Sherman, June 16, 1871, Letters Sent, RFR, 70.

[2] Reynolds to Mackenzie, July 6, 1871, Miscellaneous Files, RFR; Leckie, *Military Conquest*, 156.

[3] Leckie, *Military Conquest*, 156–157.

[4] See General Order No. 8, Department of the Missouri, June 29, 1869, in Kiowa Files, Military Relations File, OHS.

[5] Fort Richardson Post Returns, July 1871.

[6] Carter, *On the Border with Mackenzie*, 106–114. See also Richard Snow, "Henry Ware Lawton," *American Heritage* 33 (April/May 1983): 40–42.

[7] Fort Richardson Post Returns, July 1871.

[8] Fort Richardson Post Returns, July–August, 1871; Carter, *On the Border with Mackenzie*, 115.

[9] Carter, *On the Border with Mackenzie*, 116.

[10] Henrietta was a small village founded in 1860 and subsequently overrun by Indians. Destroyed after its abandonment, the town was later rebuilt.

[11] Carter, *On the Border with Mackenzie*, 118.

[12] Ibid., 119.

[13] Ibid., 119–120.

[14] Ibid., 120–121.

[15] Ibid., 122–123.

[16] Ibid., 123.

[17] Sherman to McCoy, July 29, 1871, copy in Wallace, ed., *Mackenzie's Correspondence, 1871–1873*, 38–39.

[18] Reynolds to Adjutant General, August 3, 1871, copy in ibid., 39.

[19] Carter, *On the Border with Mackenzie*, 144; Nye, *Carbine and Lance*, 149.

[20] Carter, *On the Border with Mackenzie*, 136–141.

[21] Ibid., 143.

[22] Ibid., 144. Forty mules and one horse were returned to Lawrie

Tatum to replace Henry Warren's lost stock. In November 1871 Mr. Warren traveled to Fort Sill, took possession of thirty-five mules, and returned with them to Weatherford. The next month, Captain W. L. Howell of the Quartermaster's Department noticed that two of the mules bore a US brand and, much to Warren's chagrin, confiscated them as government property. Mizner to Warren, August 26, 1871, Letters Sent, RFR, 70; Warren to Mackenzie, December 18, 1871, Miscellaneous Files, RFR.

[23] Carter, *On the Border with Mackenzie,* 147. In retrospect, it is fortunate that Mackenzie did not find Kicking Bird's village. Unknown to the colonel, the Kiowas had fragmented into a war faction led by Lone Wolf and a peace faction led by Kicking Bird. If Mackenzie had attacked the latter's camp, as he surely would have if he had located it, then much of the good Kicking Bird was able to accomplish in later years probably would have been lost.

[24] Ibid., 145–147; Fort Richardson Post Returns, September 1871.

[25] Quoted in Richardson, *Comanche Barrier to South Plains Settlement,* 346. The Kwahadis were generally considered to be the fiercest of all the twelve major Comanche bands. See n. 59, chapter one.

[26] Tatum, *Our Red Brothers,* 134.

[27] Fort Richardson Post Returns, September 1871; Carter, *On the Border with Mackenzie,* 158.

[28] Carter, *On the Border with Mackenzie,* 159.

[29] Ibid., 159–160; Leckie, *Military Conquest,* 159. Leckie places the site of Mackenzie's supply camp at Catfish Creek, not Duck Creek.

[30] Quanah Parker, a Comanche chief, was the half-breed son of Cynthia Ann Parker, a kidnapped white woman, and Peta Nokona, chief of the Nokonis Comanches. See Zoe Tilghman, *Quanah, The Eagle of the Comanches* (1938), and Clyde L. and Grace Jackson, *Quanah Parker* (1959).

[31] Carter, *On the Border with Mackenzie,* 162.

[32] Ibid., 163.

[33] Mackenzie to AAGDT, November 15, 1871, in Wallace, ed., *Mackenzie's Correspondence, 1871–1873,* 42.

[34] Ibid.; Carter, *On the Border with Mackenzie,* 165–168.

[35] Nye, *Carbine and Lance,* 151. Nye interviewed the surviving Indian participants of the Cañon Blanco fight.

[36] Carter, *On the Border with Mackenzie,* 170.

[37] Nye, *Carbine and Lance,* 151.

[38] Carter, *On the Border with Mackenzie,* 171–174.

[39] Ibid., 175–177; Nye, *Carbine and Lance,* 151. Contrary to Carter's account, Cohaya claimed there were no Indian casualties on that day.

[40] This version does not appear in the official report, scanty as it is, and is open to question. However, in May 1872, when Mackenzie launched his third campaign from Richardson, Captain Heyl and Company K were left behind to guard a railroad surveying party. Many years later Carter received the Medal of Honor for his actions at Cañon Blanco. He remained grateful to Boehm; after Boehm's death, Carter had his remains transferred to the Arlington National Cemetery. Carter, *On the Border with Mackenzie*, 179, 185–186.

[41] Ibid., 187–188.

[42] Ibid., 188–189.

[43] Ibid., 189–196.

[44] Ibid., 193–194; Mackenzie to AAGDT, November 15, 1871, in Wallace, ed., *Mackenzie's Correspondence, 1871–1873*, 41–42. Mackenzie's reports are notorious for their brevity. See also Mackenzie to Tatum, November 23, 1871, Kiowa Files, Depredations, OHS.

[45] Carter, *On the Border with Mackenzie*, 197–198; Mackenzie to AAGDT, November 15, 1871, in Wallace, ed., *Mackenzie's Correspondence, 1871–1873*, 41–42.

[46] Carter, *On the Border with Mackenzie*, 202.

[47] Fort Richardson Post Returns, November 1871; the post surgeon noted in his monthly report: "Colonel Mackenzie returned from scout with arrow wound, middle of right thigh, in front, to the bone." Hammond, "Record for the Month of November, 1871," PMH, 1: 240.

[48] Fort Richardson Post Returns, November 1871.

[49] Wallace, *Mackenzie*, 56; Carter, *On the Border with Mackenzie*, 535.

Chapter Seven

[1] Fort Richardson Post Returns, January 1868–March 1871, April–December 1871.

[2] SW, *Annual Report*, 1872, 61–62.

[3] Hammond, "Record for the Month of November-December, 1871," PMH, 1: 240–242.

[4] Ibid.

[5] Patzki, "Miscellaneous," PMH, 1: 73.

[6] Hammond, "Record for the Month of December, 1871," PMH, 1: 242; Fort Richardson Post Returns, January-December 1871.

[7] James I. Robertson, Jr., *The Civil War* (1963), 26.

[8] The sanitary reports filed by the post surgeons are full of references

to "noxious vapors" and so on. See especially Forwood, "Monthly Sanitary Report, December 31, 1873," PMH, 2: 44–45.

[9] A trooper's day was planned from reveille at 5:15 A.M. until taps at 8:15 P.M., six days a week. See Chapter Four for typical daily schedule. The dull routine was broken on holidays, such as the Fourth of July, when games would often be held at the post. During July 4, 1872, artist M. K. Kellogg witnessed foot and sack races, hunting the bottle, and fireworks at the fort. The day was topped off with cards and claret punch at an officer's quarters. Friend, ed., Kellogg's Texas Journal, 93. Other non-holiday activities were encouraged, such as the post library, a drama club for officers, and a glee club for enlisted men. Musical instruments were soon procured for the glee club members, who adopted the name "Jolly Blues Band" and played at both military and civil affairs throughout North Central Texas. McConnell, Five Years a Cavalryman, 163.

[10] Fort Richardson Post Returns, January-December 1871.

[11] Carter, On the Border with Mackenzie, 221; McConnell, Five Years a Cavalryman, 197.

[12] Knight, Following the Indian Wars, 26.

[13] Carter, On the Border with Mackenzie, 222–243; Carter, Old Sergeant's Story, 20–46.

[14] Fort Richardson Post Returns, January-December 1872.

[15] SW, Annual Report, 1871, 34; Fort Richardson Post Returns, November 1871–March 1872.

[16] Mackenzie to Augur, April 24, 1872, Letters Sent, RFR, 71. Part of the problem in keeping the troopers "well mounted" was the poor quality of stock available to the army. Mackenzie sent several detachments of officers to East Texas to purchase horses. One reported: "The people of Texas are accustomed to seeing nothing but an inferior grade of horse, and therefore, when they do raise horses superior to the common prairie stock they have an idea that their horses are very valuable and they ask enormous prices." Lieutenant W. A. Thompson to Carter, June 30, 1871, Miscellaneous Files, RFR.

[17] Nye, Carbine and Lance, 152–153; Leckie, Military Conquest, 161–162.

[18] E. C. G. Galbreath's Report, June 11, 1871, in Wallace, ed., Mackenzie's Correspondence, 1871–1873, 77–79; Tatum to Richards, June 7, 1872, Kiowa Files, Depredations, OHS; Battey, Quaker Among the Indians, 150; Nye, Carbine and Lance, 153–154. Of the four Lee children, Frances, fourteen, was killed outright, and Millie, nine, Susanna, seventeen, and John, six, were carried off. The Kiowa chief Kicking Bird was able to re-

cover all three within three months. CIA, *Annual Report,* 1872, 631–632.

[19] Fort Richardson Post Returns, May 1872; Strong, *Frontier Days,* 32. In his report of the action, dated May 20, 1872, Lt. McKinney praised the "cool bravery" of scout Strong. McKinney to Post Adjutant, May 20, 1872, Reports of Scouts, RFR, 119. Private Henche died of a .50-caliber bullet wound in the chest. Dr. W. A. Wolf, "Record for the Month of May, 1872," PMH, 1: 266–267.

[20] SW, *Annual Report,* 1872, 56; Hatch to Granger, March 30, 1872, in Wallace, ed., *Mackenzie's Correspondence, 1871–1873,* 45–46.

[21] Fort Richardson Post Returns, May 1872. Augur had specific instructions from Generals Sherman and Sheridan to give Mackenzie a free hand in quieting the Kiowas and Comanches. Mackenzie was primarily responsible for General Reynolds being replaced. As early as 1869, Mackenzie had suspected that Reynolds was guilty of fraud in awarding contracts for army supplies. In June 1871, Mackenzie put his suspicions in writing and sent them to General Henry Halleck, the commander of the Division of the South. Reynolds immediately sought to have Mackenzie court-martialed for disobedience of orders and contempt and disrespect towards his commanding officer. The judge advocate general declined to prosecute, however, and Sherman and Sheridan contrived to have the Department of Texas put in the Division of the Missouri. They then replaced Reynolds with General Augur, who proved to be more interested in solving the Indian problem than in seeking kickbacks from civilian contractors. See Wallace, *Mackenzie,* 62–64, and General Order No. 66, "Reorganization of the Department of Texas," November 1, 1871, in Wallace, ed., *Mackenzie's Correspondence, 1871–1873,* 40–41.

[22] Major John P. Hatch to AAGDT, May 16, 1872, and "N. B. McLaughlin's Report of Scout," April 27–May 13, 1872, in Wallace, ed., *Mackenzie's Correspondence, 1871–1873,* 63–71.

[23] Special Order No. 102, May 31, 1872, in ibid., 71–72.

[24] Special Order No. 102, June 14, 1872, Special Orders, RFR, 96; Fort Richardson Post Returns, June 1872; Ernest R. Archambeau, ed., "Monthly Reports of the Fourth Cavalry, 1872–1874," PPHR 38 (1965): 101.

[25] Carter, *On the Border with Mackenzie,* 367–377; Wallace, *Mackenzie,* 65–66; Mackenzie to AAGDT, June 20 and June 28, 1872, in Wallace, ed., *Mackenzie's Correspondence, 1871–1873,* 90–91, 94–95; Archambeau, "Monthly Reports of the Fourth Cavalry," 102.

[26] Mackenzie to AAGDT, July 5, 1872, in Wallace, ed., *Mackenzie's Correspondence, 1871–1873,* 100–101.

[27] Mackenzie to AAGDT, July 22, 1872, in ibid., 110–111; "Reports and Journals of Scouts," in ibid., 112–123.

[28] Wallace, *Mackenzie*, 69–70.

[29] Mackenzie to AAGDT, August 7, 1872, in Wallace, ed., *Mackenzie's Correspondence, 1871–1873*, 127–128.

[30] Mackenzie to AAGDT, August 15, 1872, in ibid., 127–128; Mackenzie to Granger, August 15, 1872, in ibid., 129–130; Strong, *Frontier Days*, 33–34.

[31] Wallace, *Mackenzie*, 73–74; Mackenzie to AAGDT, September 3, 1872, in Wallace, ed., *Mackenzie's Correspondence, 1871–1873*, 133–134; Carter, *On the Border with Mackenzie*, 376; SW, *Annual Report*, 1872, 56.

[32] Mackenzie to AAGDT, September 19, 1872, in Wallace, ed., *Mackenzie's Correspondence, 1871–1873*, 134–135.

[33] Mackenzie to AAGDT, October 12, 1872, in ibid., 141–145; Carter, *On the Border with Mackenzie*, 376–377; Wallace, *Mackenzie*, 78; Carter, *Old Sergeant's Story*, 82; Fort Richardson Post Returns, September-October 1872; Archambeau, ed., "Monthly Reports of the Fourth Cavalry," 104.

[34] Mackenzie to AAGDT, October 12, 1872; Carter, *On the Border with Mackenzie*, 377–379; Nye, *Carbine and Lance*, 161–162.

[35] W. A. Thompson, "Scouting with Mackenzie," *Journal of the United States Cavalry Association* 10 (1897): 430.

[36] Mackenzie to AAGDT, October 12, 1872.

[37] Ibid.; Thompson, "Scouting with Mackenzie," 430; Archambeau, "Monthly Reports of the Fourth Cavalry," 104; Carter, *On the Border with Mackenzie*, 378; Carter, *Old Sergeant's Story*, 85. Private John Dorcas was hit in the neck and died almost immediately. Private John Kelly was also hit in the neck and died shortly after the battle. Private William Rankin was shot in the spine, and Private Beals was hit in the thigh. All are mentioned in Mackenzie's report except Beals, who suffered a wound similar to the colonel's in the previous campaign, which also was not reported.

[38] Thompson, "Scouting with Mackenzie," 431; Nye, *Carbine and Lance*, 162; Strong, *Frontier Days*, 38–39. The Plains Indians were mortal enemies of the Tonkawas and believed that not only would the Tonkawas scalp their victims but would practice cannibalism upon them also. Hence, they went to great lengths to see that their dead did not fall into Tonkawa hands.

[39] Mackenzie to AAGDT, October 12, 1872; Archambeau, ed., "Monthly Reports of the Fourth Cavalry," 104. Corporal Henry McMasters of A Company died of wounds before reaching Richardson.

⁴⁰Mackenzie to AAGDT, October 12, 1872; Strong, *Frontier Days,* 38–39; Carter, *On the Border with Mackenzie,* 378; Thompson, "Scouting with Mackenzie," 431–432; Archambeau, ed., "Monthly Reports of the Fourth Cavalry," 104. Chief Kai-wotche was in charge of the camp, as Mow-way, the principal chief, was attending a peace council near Anadarko; see Nye, *Carbine and Lance,* 159–163.

⁴¹Strong, *Frontier Days,* 39.

⁴²Ibid., 38; Carter, *On the Border with Mackenzie,* 378; Carter, *Old Sergeant's Story,* 86; Thompson, "Scouting with Mackenzie," 431; Archambeau, ed., "Monthly Reports of the Fourth Cavalry," 104.

⁴³Mackenzie to AAGDT, October 12, 1872.

⁴⁴Carter, *On the Border with Mackenzie,* 379.

⁴⁵Mackenzie to AAGDT, October 12, 1872.

⁴⁶Ibid.; Carter, *On the Border with Mackenzie,* 389; Archambeau, ed., "Monthly Reports of the Fourth Cavalry," 105; Fort Richardson Post Returns, October 1872. Mackenzie took 130 prisoners but many were badly wounded. He brought away 124. On October 12, there were 116 in his custody, and by the time the captives arrived at Concho, they numbered 115. See Wallace, *Mackenzie,* 85.

⁴⁷Wallace, *Mackenzie,* 86.

⁴⁸*Medal of Honor,* 217–218; General Order No. 99, November 2, 1872, General Orders, RFR, 100. Medal of Honor winners were Sergeants William Foster and William McNamara, Corporal William O'Neal, Privates George Smith and William Rankin, Farrier David Larkin, and Blacksmith James Pratt. Sergeant William Wilson was awarded *two* Medals of Honor for his gallantry in action.

Chapter Eight

¹Fort Richardson Post Returns, November 1872; Special Order No. 193, October 29, 1872, Special Orders, RFR, 96.

²Special Order No. 291, December 3, 1872, Special Orders, RFR, 96; Mackenzie to AAGDT, December 21, 1872, Letters Sent, RFR, 70.

³Fort Richardson Post Returns, December 1872; SW, *Annual Report,* 1873, 29.

⁴Fort Richardson Post Returns, March 1873; SW, *Annual Report,* 1873, 29; Archambeau, "Monthly Reports of the Fourth Cavalry," 110–111. Company K, under the command of the unfortunate Captain Heyl, was performing escort duty for a surveying party of the Texas and Pacific Railroad when the move to Concho was made. This task was not com-

pleted until early May, at which time the Company joined the regiment at its new duty station, Fort Clark, on the Rio Grande. It was from this post that Mackenzie and the Fourth (again minus the unreliable Company K) launched their famous raid into Mexico against the Kickapoos and the Lipan Apaches in May 1873.

Carter, *On the Border with Mackenzie*, 397–410, gives a colorful account of the problems involved in moving a cavalry regiment, wives, laundresses, camp women, and baggage five hundred miles in horse-drawn wagons which were "in the last stages of consumptive decay." Carter took along his pet dog "Tippy" but makes no mention of the dozens of camp dogs which belonged to the regiment collectively. Nor does he comment on the fate of the regiment's less traditional pets, which included a deer, two fawns, three bear cubs and three grown bears, two wolf pups, a coyote, an eagle, a buffalo calf, and two wildcats (330–331).

[5] Leckie, *Buffalo Soldiers*, 72.

[6] Ibid., 7–8; Marian T. Place, *Rifles and War Bonnets* (1968), 9–16.

[7] Leckie, *Buffalo Soldiers*, 26.

[8] Ibid., 72; Fort Richardson Post Returns, April 1871–December 1872.

[9] McConnell, *Five Years a Cavalryman*, 212.

[10] Records of the Adjutant General's Office, filed in PMH, 1: 301.

[11] McConnell, *Five Years a Cavalryman*, 163.

[12] Horton, *History of Jack County*, 120.

[13] Ibid., 121–122. Horner changed his name to Frank M. Canton and later became the first Adjutant General of Oklahoma. See Edward Evertt Dale, ed., *Frontier Times: The Autobiography of Frank M. Canton* (1966).

[14] Hammond, "Record for the Month of August, 1872," PMH, 1: 279.

[15] Fort Richardson Post Returns, April 1873–January 1878.

[16] Ibid., March 1873. At no time in 1873 were there more than 420 men present for duty at Richardson, and the number frequently dropped below 300. Richardson fell from the rank of largest post in the U.S. to fifth place in Texas. SW, *Annual Report*, 1873, 62–63.

[17] Fort Richardson Post Returns, March–September 1871, March–September 1873.

[18] Mooney, "Calendar History," 192–195; Tatum, *Our Red Brothers*, 132, 137–138; Nye, *Carbine and Lance*, 162–163; Battey, *Quaker Among the Indians*, 197–198.

[19] Tatum, *Our Red Brothers*, 133–134; Mooney, "Calendar History," 311.

[20] CIA, *Annual Report*, 1873, 587; Tatum, *Our Red Brothers*,

167–168. Captain Robert MacClermont, in charge of delivering the captives to Fort Sill, was forced to make a wide detour around Jacksboro, where "armed citizens, many of them drunk" had gathered to stop the return. The same story also appears in Battey, *Quaker Among the Indians,* 161–165, who says three thousand armed citizens gathered in Jacksboro. Battey obviously was not familiar with the population totals of Jack and the surrounding counties and was misled by exaggerated reports.

[21] CIA, *Annual Report,* 1872, 486, 512–533, and 1873, 375, and 1874, 320; Mooney, "Calendar History," 195–197, 337–338; Tatum, *Our Red Brothers,* 173–177; Battey, *Quaker Among the Indians,* 199–202; Nye, *Carbine and Lance,* 168–177; Day and Winfrey, eds., *Texas Indian Papers,* 4: 349–363.

[22] Sherman to Edmund Davis, Feb. 16, 1874, as quoted in Carl Coke Rister, "Satanta, Orator of the Plains," *Southwestern Review* 17 (1931): 97–98.

[23] Day and Winfrey, eds., *Texas Indian Papers,* 4: 338–342.

[24] Fort Richardson Post Returns, September 1873; Fort Worth *Democrat,* September 13, 1873. Dr. R. L. McClure examined the bodies and reported "the breast of Howell Walker perforated by bullet holes and . . . the entire scalp stripped off—the right ear gone and an incision extending about one half round the body on the right side from near the backbone to a little beyond the middle line in front, cutting into the abdomen— wounding the intestines and making a large gash in the liver. The lower rib was taken . . . through the incision on the right side."
"The body of the boy as follows—besides bullet wounds the scalp stripped off—a punctured wound in the right breast—the left hand gone being disarticulated at the wrist with a knife or other cutting instrument." Day and Winfrey, eds., *Texas Indian Papers,* 4: 347.

[25] Day and Winfrey, eds., *Texas Indian Papers,* 4: 343–344.

[26] Fort Richardson Post Returns, August-September 1873; Leckie, *Buffalo Soldiers,* 74.

[27] Fort Richardson Post Returns, October 1873.

[28] Ibid., October-November 1873; Battey, *Quaker Among the Indians,* 206.

[29] Tatum, *Our Red Brothers,* 187. Secretary Delano reported, "Since the release of Satanta and Big Tree, the Kiowas have once more joined the Comanches in expeditions for plunder and murder." CIA, *Annual Report,* 1874, 330.

[30] Forwood, "Monthly Sanitary Report, December 31, 1873," PMH, 2: 47.

[31] Edward Smith, Indian Commissioner, to Enoch Hoag, February

21, 1874, Kiowa Files, Depredations, OHS; Nye, *Carbine and Lance,* 182–184; Leckie, *Military Conquest,* 183; Battey, *Quaker Among the Indians,* 245. Nye reports that Lieutenant Hudson killed Tau-ankia with his pistol and that Hudson himself died inside of a month, when his roommate accidentally shot him while cleaning a gun.

[32] Nye, *Carbine and Lance,* 187.

[33] CIA, *Annual Report,* 1872, 529; Pratt, *Battlefield and Classroom,* 49–51.

[34] Tatum, *Our Red Brothers,* 190–191; Mooney, "Calendar History," 199–200.

[35] Carl Coke Rister, "The Significance of the Destruction of the Buffalo in the Southwest," *SHQ* 33 (1929): 48. Rister places the number of kills from 1872 to 1874 at 7.5 million. Richard Dodge, *Hunting Grounds of the Great American West* (1877), 133–134, states that 1,378,359 buffalo hides, 6,751,200 pounds of meat, and 32,380,650 pounds of bones were shipped to eastern markets from 1872–1874. Hornaday, "Extermination of the American Bison," 496–501; Martin S. Garretson, *The American Bison* (1938), 128; Leckie, *Military Conquest,* 186; Dee Brown, *Bury My Heart at Wounded Knee* (1970), 265.

[36] SW, *Annual Report,* 1874, 30; CIA, *Annual Report,* 1874, 528; Mooney, "Calendar History," 203; Nye, *Carbine and Lance,* 189–192.

[37] Nye's Indian informant, Hunting Horse, who participated in the battle, stated that several prominent Kiowas took part, including Satanta and Lone Wolf; Nye, *Carbine and Lance,* 191.

[38] Ibid., 188–189; Mooney, "Calendar History," 199, 338; Battey, *Quaker Among the Indians,* 307–308; Day and Winfrey, eds., *Texas Indian Papers,* 4: 386–387.

[39] Mooney, "Calendar History," 338.

[40] Nye, *Carbine and Lance,* 192–193.

[41] Paddock, ed., *Twentieth Century History of North and West Texas,* 1: 223.

[42] Nye, *Carbine and Lance,* 195. Loving wrote: "Today the Indians some forty in number run myself and three of my men a considerable distance, we barely escaping with our lives. This was about 11 1/2 o'clock a.m. and at a point about seven miles from the ranch, on or near the Overland road near the Cox Mountain." Loving to Commanding Officer, July 12, 1874, Miscellaneous Files, RFR.

[43] This account of the Lost Valley Fight of July 12, 1874, is taken from the following sources: Nye, *Carbine and Lance,* 192–200; Webb, *The Texas Rangers,* 312–313; Walter Robertson, "Reminiscences of Walter

Robertson, The Loss [sic] Valley Fight," *Frontier Times* 7 (December 1929): 100–104; Ed Carnal, "Reminiscences of a Texas Ranger," *Frontier Times* 1 (December 1923): 20–24; Horton, *History of Jack County,* 52–53; Loving to Commanding Officer, July 12, 1874, and Jones to Commanding Officer, July 12, 1874, Miscellaneous Files, RFR; Captain Theodore Baldwin, "Report of Scout, July 14, 1874," Reports of Scouts, RFR, 119 1/2. All of these accounts differ in minor details, but the major facts remain the same throughout.

[44] There is a discrepancy concerning the number of Rangers involved. Major Jones, in his brief dispatch to Fort Richardson, says that he had thirty-five men (not counting himself). Oliver Loving, in his letter of July 12 (see n. 42), said a Ranger who was cut off from the others during the battle came to his ranch and reported there were thirty-eight men in the command. Webb, in his classic account, states there were only twenty-four men present, while Walter Robertson, a member of Jones's escort, says there were twenty-five men in that group alone. Obviously, Webb made an error in stating that the total strength of the Rangers in the Lost Valley fight was twenty-four, when this really represented only the number of men in Jones's personal escort and did not include the men from Captain G. W. Stevens's company. Webb states that "[Jones] was very careful of records" (*The Texas Rangers,* 311), and therefore it must be assumed that he, if no one else, should have known the total number of men in his unit.

[45] Day and Winfrey, eds., *Texas Indian Papers,* 4: 383. According to T. W. Williams, Jack County Justice of the Peace, the Indians who killed cowboy Heath on July 10 also made off with two hundred horses and mules from the nearby ranches.

[46] Jones to Commanding Officer, July 12, 1874.

[47] Baldwin, "Report of Scout, July 14, 1874."

[48] The exact author of the strategy used in the Red River War is debatable. Utley, *Frontier Regulars,* 219, says that "Sheridan is generally credited with elaborating . . . the . . . master plan by which the Southern Plains tribes were conquered for all time," and the concept presented to Secretary of War Belknap certainly bears a close resemblance to Sheridan's campaign of 1868–1869 on the Southern Plains. However, Sherman's input and direction cannot be discounted. Indeed, as the campaign developed, it bore a marked similarity to that strategy known as "total war," which Sherman is generally credited with developing during the Civil War. See Maurice Matloff, gen. ed., *American Military History* (1963), 309–310.

[49] Belknap to War Department, July 20, 1874, in Joe F. Taylor, ed.,

The Indian Campaign on the Staked Plains, 1874–1875: Military Correspondence from War Department Adjutant General's Office, File 2815–1874, 11–12; Utley, *Frontier Regulars,* 214; Leckie, *Military Conquest,* 198–199.

[50] SW, *Annual Report,* 1874, 28, 40; Taylor, *Indian Campaign,* 14–16; Leckie, *Military Conquest,* 205.

[51] Fort Richardson Post Returns, August 1874.

[52] Carl Coke Rister, "Early Accounts of Indian Depredations," *WTHAYB* 2 (1926): 52.

[53] The following accounts taken from Nye, *Carbine and Lance,* 204–210; Leckie, *Buffalo Soldiers,* 120–123; SW, *Annual Report,* 1874, 41–42; CIA, *Annual Report,* 1874, 529, 546.

[54] Troubles such as these between the settled Indians and their more warlike brothers were not new. See the report of Jonathan Richards, CIA, *Annual Report,* 1873, 592, for previous incidents.

[55] SW, *Annual Report,* 1874, 42.

[56] Fort Richardson Post Returns, September 1874; Leckie, *Buffalo Soldiers,* 125–130.

[57] Ibid., 130–132; Davidson to AAGDM, October 10, 1874, in Ernest Wallace, ed., *Mackenzie's Correspondence, 1874–1879,* 134; Davidson to Augur, November 23, 1874, in Taylor, *Indian Campaign,* 109.

[58] Leckie, *Buffalo Soldiers,* 129, 135.

[59] Utley, *Frontier Regulars,* 223; Leckie, *Military Conquest,* 215–216; General Orders No. 14, September 17, 1874, in Taylor, *Indian Campaign,* 56–57.

[60] Wallace, *Mackenzie,* 128–146; Carter, *On the Border with Mackenzie,* 473–496; Strong, *Frontier Days,* 60; Nye, *Carbine and Lance,* 221–225; Charles Hatfield, "The Comanche, Kiowa, and Cheyenne Campaign in Northwest Texas and Mackenzie's Fight in Palo Duro Canyon, September 26, 1874," *WTHAYB* 5 (1929): 115–128; Mackenzie to AAGDT, October 1, 1874, Miscellaneous Files, RFR; "Mackenzie's Expedition Through the Battle of Palo Duro Canyon as Described by a Special Correspondent of the New York Herald," New York *Herald,* October 16, 1874.

[61] Leckie, *Military Conquest,* 230–231; Mooney, "Calendar History," 212–214. Quanah Parker was with the Kwahadis who came into Fort Sill in June; CIA, *Annual Report,* 1875, 774–775. Agent Haworth estimated that only ten Indians from his agency were killed in the Red River War but that the tribes "suffered severely in the loss of property." The Comanches were said to be "utterly impoverished and thoroughly humbled." CIA, *Annual Report,* 1874, 561; SW, *Annual Report,* 1875, 58.

[62] CIA, *Annual Report*, 1874, 272, 523, 542–544, and 1875, 774; Thomas Neill to AAGDM, October 1, 1874, and October 4, 1874, in Taylor, *Indian Campaign*, 64–68, 87–90; Mooney "Calendar History," 208; Leckie, *Military Conquest*, 218–219; Nye, *Carbine and Lance*, 219–220, 235; Jones, *Treaty of Medicine Lodge*, 114; Capps, *Warren Wagontrain Raid*, 242. General Sheridan explained that he did not return Big Tree to prison along with Satanta "because I never supposed him guilty. There is no doubt about Satanta's guilt." Sheridan to Belknap, November 17, 1874, in Taylor, *Indian Campaign*, 96. A recitation of Satanta's crimes leading up to the revoking of his parole can be found in the report of Captain B. J. Sanderson, Eleventh Infantry, which appears in Taylor, *Indian Campaign*, 97–98. The evidence against Satanta is highly circumstantial at best. In contrast, Big Tree was released, eventually joined the Baptist Church, became a deacon, and made several trips East, dressed in a Prince Albert suit, to illustrate the success of the Baptist Mission and to help raise money for it. See Corwin, *The Kiowa Indians*, 62–63, and Pratt, *Battlefield and Classroom*, 48.

[63] Sherman to Belknap, no date, and Belknap to Sheridan, October 6, 1874, in Taylor, *Indian Campaign*, 90–101, 183–184.

[64] CIA, *Annual Report*, 1875, 514, 567, 773–777; Mooney, "Calendar History," 215–216; Battey, *Quaker Among the Indians*, 294–297. The selection process made little sense. Enoch Hoag complained that the chiefs were convicted without trial, and many criminals were set free. CIA, *Annual Report*, 1875, 766. For short biographical sketches of the prisoners, as well as a listing of their alleged crimes, see Pratt, *Battlefield and Classroom*, 138–144.

[65] Nye, *Carbine and Lance*, 233.

[66] Ibid., 233–234; Maman-ti died on July 29, 1875, at Fort Marion, Florida. The army listed the cause of his death as consumption. Pratt, *Battlefield and Classroom*, 143; CIA, *Annual Report*, 1875, 567; Mooney, "Calendar History," 216. Agent Haworth wrote of Kicking Bird: "Though a wild, untutored savage, he was a man of fine native sense, and educated in the learning and history of his people. He abandoned the raiding habits, and determined to elevate his people and lead them from their bad road. His influence was exerted on the side of peace, and said he was dying holding on to the white man's hand." Believing it to be his wish, Haworth saw to it that Kicking Bird became the first Kiowa chief to receive a Christian burial. CIA, *Annual Report*, 1875, 776.

[67] Lt. Richard H. Pratt was placed in charge of the prisoners at Fort Marion and tells the story of their three year confinement in chapters 10

through 17 of his memoirs, *Battlefield and Classroom*; CIA, *Annual Report*, 1878, 555; Brown, *Bury My Heart at Wounded Knee*, 271.

Chapter Nine

[1] Fort Richardson Post Returns, December 1874–January 1875; Mackenzie to Augur, December 2, 1874, in Taylor, *Indian Campaign*, 117–119.

[2] SW, *Annual Report*, 1878, 33.

[3] Fort Richardson Post Returns, September-December 1874. During this four month period, Company I escorted thirty-two wagon trains full of supplies to Fort Griffin. Sheridan (who seemingly never tired of extolling the virtues of his troopers) wrote, "No other army in the world . . . has had such an amount of work put upon the same number of men." SW, *Annual Report*, 1878, 33.

[4] Fort Richardson Post Returns, January-March 1875; Leckie, *Buffalo Soldiers*, 141.

[5] Fort Richardson Post Returns, January 1875; Davis to Quartermaster General, War Department, June 23, 1875, Records of the Office of Quartermaster General, RG 92, NA.

[6] SW, *Annual Report*, 1875, 146–147; Fort Richardson Post Returns, March-May 1875; Wallace, *Mackenzie*, 165, 170; Paddock, ed., *Twentieth Century History of North and West Texas*, 1: 222. The post returns show that by May, only 144 officers and men were present for duty at the post.

[7] SW, *Annual Report*, 1869, 144.

[8] L. Tuffly Ellis, ed., "Lieutenant A. W. Greely's Report on the Installation of Military Telegraph Lines in Texas, 1875–1876," *SHQ* 69 (July 1965): 66–68.

[9] The Dennison to Jacksboro line was constructed of seventy-five miles of cedar poles, thirty-nine miles of post oak poles, Kenosha insulators, and Jackson no. 9 galvanized wire; it cost $66 per mile or $7500 in all. The Sill to Richardson line was "27 per cent post oak, 25 per cent red, or cedar, elm, 20 per cent red cedar, 14 per cent pecan, 6 per cent hackberry, and 1 per cent each walnut and chitten [sic]" and spanned the Red River with a compound wire one-third of a mile long; this section of the military telegraph system cost $72 per mile for a total of $7600. The Richardson to Griffin line, constructed of Johnson (English) no. 9 galvanized wire, Kenosha insulators, and cedar poles, averaged $75 per mile for a total of $5300. Ibid., 76–78.

[10] Friend, ed., *Kellogg's Texas Journal,* 89; Gen. William Wood to AAGDT, May 13, 1875, Letters Sent, RFR, 72; Special Order No. 83, August 8, 1876, Special Orders, RFR, 97.

[11] A Ranger company had been located near Jacksboro since 1874. McConnell states, "The Rangers were tolerable Indian fighters, but most of their time was occupied in terrorizing the citizens." Shooting incidents between Rangers, soldiers, and citizens became so frequent that the townspeople voted in 1874 to incorporate Jacksboro, name a marshal, and forbid the carrying of firearms within the city limits. McConnell, *Five Years a Cavalryman,* 296.

[12] Nye, *Carbine and Lance,* 235–236; Webb, *Texas Rangers,* 317; Horton, *History of Jack County,* 55–56.

[13] One of the duties of the medical officer at each post was to provide specimens for the Army Medical Museum in Washington, D.C.; see David Clary, "The Role of the Army Surgeon in the West: Daniel Weisel at Fort Davis, Texas, 1868–1872," *WHQ* 3 (January 1972): 53–66 (Dr. Weisel transferred to Fort Richardson in 1872). Henry Strong, the post guide, claims that he personally cut off the heads at the request of the assistant surgeon, W. H. Forwood, and later carried them to Fort Sill for identification. Strong, *Frontier Days,* 71. Special Order No. 94, dated May 12, 1875, directs Post Guide Henry Strong to proceed to Fort Sill in order to complete the history of "certain important ethnological specimens." Special Orders, RFR, 97. CIA, *Annual Report,* 1875, 561, reports that, "Five Quahadas Comanches were killed and beheaded by Jack County citizens." Moody, "Calendar History," 214. Oliver Loving, in a 1935 letter written to Wilbur Nye, said he was a witness to the decapitations. The heads were said to be bound for the Army Medical Museum, but their fate is unknown. This was not the first time Fort Richardson soldiers had committed such gruesome deeds upon their dead enemies. Lieutenant Carter relates that, in 1871 at Cañon Blanco, the two Comanche scouts that had been trapped and killed by Lieutenant Boehm and his Tonkawas (after one of the Comanches wounded Mackenzie in the leg) had suffered a similar fate. The army surgeon Rufus Choate decapitated the dead Comanches and left their bodies for the wolves and coyotes. Carter claims that he saw one of the Comanche skulls in 1912 in the Ethnological Bureau of the "New National Museum." Carter, *On the Border with Mackenzie,* 198–200.

[14] Fort Richardson Post Returns, August–November 1876; Special Order No. 86, August 12, 1876, Special Orders, RFR, 97; SW, *Annual Report,* 1876, 30–39, 66. Company B was ordered to the Standing Rock Agency, while Companies E and K and the headquarters went to the

Cheyenne Agency, Dakota Territory.

[15] *Frontier Echo* (Jacksboro, Texas), November 17, 1876.

[16] Fort Richardson Post Returns, August 1876.

[17] Ibid., December 1876; SW, *Annual Report*, 1876, 46–47, 61, and 1877, 20; Pratt, *Battlefield and Classroom*, 6; Lt. Samuel Woodward to Grierson, quoted in Frank Temple, "Colonel Grierson in the Southwest," *PHPHR* 30 (1957): 39. In July 1878, Capt. Baldwin finally could stand no more of Davidson's "tyrannical character" and officially complained to the adjutant general. When nothing came of this, Baldwin's wife wrote to President Hayes about the treatment her husband and men had received at the colonel's hands. The next year Davidson was promoted to full colonel of the Second Cavalry and retired. He died in 1881 as a result of a fall from his horse. Leckie, *Buffalo Soldiers*, 165, and Heitman, *Historical Register of the U.S. Army*, 20.

[18] Kiowa and Comanche Indian Agent Haworth reported in 1876 that "raids in Texas were almost nonexistant." CIA, *Annual Report*, 1876, 455. However, roving gangs of white bandits had become quite a problem in the area. See Strong, *Frontier Days*, 77–80; Charles Ramsdell, "Presidential Reconstruction in Texas," *SHQ* 11 (1908): 286; SW, *Annual Report*, 1876, 492.

[19] Fort Richardson Post Returns, February 1877; Davidson to AAGDT, February 21, 1877, Letters Sent, RFR, 73.

[20] Fort Richardson Post Returns, June 1877; Special Order No. 42, June 3, 1877, Special Orders, RFR, 97; *Frontier Echo* (Jacksboro, Texas), July 20, 1877; William Curry Holden, *Alkali Trails* (1930), 59. Two years later, in 1879, a travel guide would claim Jack County's population to be 10,000 people, with "8 or 10 cotton gins, grist and sawmills, brick yards, 17 churches, and numerous schools"; Paddock, ed., *Twentieth Century History of North and West Texas*, 1: 223. The Federal census of 1880, however, shows 3326 people in the county. Frances Walker, *Statistics of the Population of the United States at the Tenth Census* (1881), 345. General Sheridan, in his 1876 annual report, stated that, "The progress of the settlements and the increase of farming and grazing interests in Northwestern Texas has been very great"; SW, *Annual Report*, 1876, 34.

[21] Fort Richardson Post Returns, August-September 1877; Special Order No. 11, September 24, 1877, Special Orders, RFR, 97.

[22] Fort Richardson Post Returns, September-December 1877; Leckie, *Buffalo Soldiers*, 155–156, 167.

[23] *Frontier Echo* (Jacksboro, Texas), February 22, 1878.

[24] AAGDT to Lieutenant Robert P. Wilson, February 1, 1878, Miscellaneous Files, RFR.

[25] Fort Richardson Post Returns, January 1878; SW, *Annual Report,* 1878, 250.

[26] Ibid., March 1878; A. A. Yeomans, "Records for the Month of March, 1878," PMH, 2: 251; *Frontier Echo* (Jacksboro, Texas), March 26, 1878. The *Echo* reported that Doctors McClure and Gresham of Jacksboro assisted the army surgeon.

[27] Generally, the regular army at this time regarded chaplains as little better than nuisances. Colonel Benjamin Grierson wrote of his post chaplain, "He will be good to occupy quarters and eat commissary stores and to attend strictly to everybody's business but his own." Frank Temple, "Colonel Grierson in the Southwest," PHPHR 30 (1957): 44. Considering the prevailing attitude, it is small wonder that Richardson's chaplains could never find the money and labor necessary to build a chapel and had to be content to hold their little-attended meetings in tent shelters. General Sherman, when asked by a House Investigating Committee if he thought that chaplains were useful, replied, "I would not like to say anything against them, because the poor old gentlemen might be turned out, and you would have to support them in some other way. [However], we need praying for just as Congress needs praying for." House Report No. 384, 43d Cong., 1st sess., 1874, 283.

[28] Fort Richardson Post Returns, April 1878; Davidson to AAGDT, June 28, 1877, Letters Sent, RFR, 73. The editor of the *Frontier Echo* had long editorialized on the need for a flagpole at the post. On June 29, 1877, he announced that now, "as the traveller approaches Jacksboro from the South or East he can, when miles distant, observe the flag as the first object that attracts his attention."

[29] Fort Richardson Post Returns, May 1878; Yeomans, "Record for the Month of May, 1878," PMH, 2: 253.

BIBLIOGRAPHY

Government Documents and Publications

"Circular No. 4." *Surgeon General's Office Report: Barracks and Hospitals, with Descriptions of Military Posts.* Washington, D.C.: Government Printing Office, 1870.

Annual Reports of Commissioner of Indian Affairs, 1865–1878. In U.S. Serials as follows:

1865: House Ex. Doc. 1, 39th Cong., 1st sess. Serial 1248.

1866: House Ex. Doc. 1, 39th Cong., 2d sess. Serial 1284.

1867: House Ex. Doc. 1, 40th Cong., 2d sess. Serial 1326.

1868: House Ex. Doc. 1, 40th Cong., 3d sess. Serial 1366.

1869: House Ex. Doc. 1, 41st Cong., 2d sess. Serial 1414.

1870: House Ex. Doc. 1, 41st Cong., 3d sess. Serial 1449.

1871: House Ex. Doc. 1, 42d Cong., 2d sess. Serial 1505.

1872: House Ex. Doc. 1, 42d Cong., 3d sess. Serial 1560.

1873: House Ex. Doc. 1, 43d Cong., 1st sess. Serial 1601.

1874: House Ex. Doc. 1, 43d Cong., 2d sess. Serial 1639.

1875: House Ex. Doc. 1, 44th Cong., 1st sess. Serial 1680.

1876: House Ex. Doc. 1, 44th Cong., 2d sess. Serial 1749.

1877: House Ex. Doc. 1, 45th Cong., 2d sess. Serial 1800.

1878: House Ex. Doc. 1, 45th Cong., 3d sess. Serial 1850.

Annual Reports of the Secretary of War, 1865–1878. In U.S. Serials as follows:

1865: part 1, House Ex. Doc. 1, 39th Cong., 1st sess. Serial 1249.

part 2, House Ex. Doc. 1, 39th Cong., 1st sess. Serial 1250.

1866: House Ex. Doc. 1, 39th Cong., 2d sess. Serial 1285.

1867: House Ex. Doc. 1, 40th Cong., 2d sess. Serial 1324.

1868: House Ex. Doc. 1, 40th Cong., 3d sess. Serial 1367.

1869: House Ex. Doc. 1, 41st Cong., 2d sess. Serial 1412.

1870: House Ex. Doc. 1, 41st Cong., 3d sess. Serial 1446.

1871: House Ex. Doc. 1, 42d Cong., 2d sess. Serial 1503.

1872: House Ex. Doc. 1, 42d Cong., 3d sess. Serial 1558.

1873: House Ex. Doc. 1, 43d Cong., 1st sess. Serial 1597.

1874: House Ex. Doc. 1, 43d Cong., 2d sess. Serial 1635.

1875: House Ex. Doc. 1, 44th Cong., 1st sess. Serial 1674.

1876: House Ex. Doc. 1, 44th Cong., 2d sess. Serial 1742.

1877: House Ex. Doc. 1, 45th Cong., 2d sess. Serial 1794.

1878: House Ex. Doc. 1, 45th Cong., 3d sess. Serial 1843.

1882: House Ex. Doc. 1, 47th Cong., 2d sess. Serial 2091.

Bureau of American Ethnology. *Fourteenth Annual Report*, Vol. 2. Washington, D.C.: Government Printing Office, 1896.

Ferris, Robert S., ser. ed. *Prospector, Cowhand and Sodbuster: Historic Places Associated with the Mining, Ranching and Farming Frontiers in the Trans-Mississippi West*. National Survey of Historic Sites and Buildings, Vol. 11. Washington, D.C.: U.S. Department of the Interior, National Parks Service, 1967.

———, ser. ed. *Soldier and Brave*. National Survey of Historic Sites and Buildings, Vol. 12. Washington, D.C.: U.S. Department of the Interior, National Parks Service, 1971.

Heitman, Francis B. *Historical Register and Dictionary of the United States Army*. 2 vols. Washington: Government Printing Office, 1903.

Hodge, Frederick W. *Handbook of American Indians North of Mexico, Bureau of American Ethnology, Bulletin No. 30*. Vol. 1. Washington: Government Printing Office, 1912.

Hornaday, William T. "The Extermination of the American Bison," *Annual Report of the United States National Museum*. Washington: Smithsonian Institution, 1889.

Knox, Orion, et al. *Preservation Plan and Program for Fort Richardson State Historical Park*. Austin, Texas: Texas Parks and Wildlife Department, 1975.

Lorrain, Dessamae. *Archeological Investigations at Fort Richardson State Historic Site, Jack County, Texas*. Research Report No. 10. Austin, Texas: Texas Archeological Salvage Project, 1972.

———. *Fort Richardson Commissary and Quartermaster's Storehouse: Archeological Tests*. Austin, Texas: Texas Parks and Wildlife Department, 1973.

Matloff, Maurice, gen. ed. *American Military History*. Washington: Office of the Chief of Military History, U.S. Army, 1969.

The Medal of Honor of the United States Army. Washington: Government Printing Office, 1948.

Mooney, James. "Calendar History of the Kiowa," *Seventeenth Annual Report of the Bureau of Indian Ethnology, 1895–1896.* Washington: Government Printing Office, 1898.

Outline Descriptions of the Posts in the Military Division of the Missouri. Chicago: Headquarters Military Division of the Missouri, 1876.

Record of Engagements with Hostile Indians within the Military Division of the Missouri from 1868–1882. Washington: Government Printing Office, 1882.

Secretary of the Interior. *Population of the United States in 1860; the Eighth Census.* Superintendent of the Census Joseph C. G. Kennedy. Washington, D.C.: Government Printing Office, 1861.

———. *Statistics of the Population of the United States, 1870; the Ninth Census.* Superintendent of the Census Frances Walker. Washington, D.C.: Government Printing Office, 1871.

———. *Statistics of the Population of the United States at the Tenth Census.* Superintendent of the Census Frances Walker and Charles Seaton. Washington, D.C.: Government Printing Office, 1881.

Taniguchi, Alan Y., et al. *Texas Historic Forts, Volume V, Fort Richardson.* Austin, Texas: School of Architecture, University of Texas at Austin, 1968.

Westbury, William A. *Archeological Investigations at Fort Richardson State Park.* College Station, Texas: Texas A&M Press, 1976.

U.S. Congress, House of Representatives:

House Ex. Doc. 97, 40th Cong., 2d sess., 1867, Serial 1335. Investigation of the Battle of Sand Creek.

House Misc. Doc. 142, 41st Cong., 2d sess., 1870, Serial 1433. Indian Depredations in Texas: Memorial of Three Hundred and Fifty Citizens of the Northwestern Frontier of Texas.

House Ex. Doc. 228, 41st Cong., 2d sess., 1870, Serial 1418. Sites of Military Posts in Texas.

House Report No. 384, 43d Cong., 1st sess., 1874, Serial 1624. Report of the Committee on Military Affairs upon the Reduction of the Military Establishment.

House Report 395, 43d Cong., 1st sess., 1874, Serial 1624. Depredations on the Texas Frontier.

House Report 1084, 63d Cong., 2d sess., 1913, Serial 6560. Pensions for Indian War Veterans. Contains "Historical Resume of Certain Indian Campaigns," by S. J. Bayard Schindel, Captain, General Staff.

U.S. Congress, Senate:
Senate Report 555, 45th Cong., 3d sess., 1879, Serial 1837. Report of the Joint Committee on the Reorganization of the Army.

Manuscript Materials

National Archives

Record Group 75, Letters Received, Office of Indian Affairs, 1824–1880.

Record Group 92, Records of the Office of Quartermaster General.

Record Group 94, Records of the Office of the Adjutant General.

Fort Richardson Post Medical History, 1868–1878, 2 vols.

Fort Richardson Post Returns, 1866–1878.

Record Group 98, Letters Received, District of Texas.

Record Group 154, Records of the Office of the Judge Advocate General.

Record Group 159, Records of the Office of the Inspector General.

Record Group 393, Records of U.S. Army Continental Commands.

Letters Received, District of Texas.

Records of Fort Richardson, Texas.

vol. 57, Records of District of Brazos, 5/17/77–12/31/77

vol. 66, Letters Sent, 1867–1869

vol. 67, Letters Sent, 1869

vol. 67A, Letters Sent (Civil Affairs), 10/8/69–5/19/70

vol. 68, Letters Sent, 1/22/70–5/1/70

vol. 69, Letters Sent, 5/1/70–1/4/71

vol. 70, Letters Sent, 1/4/71–4/8/72

vol. 71, Letters Sent, 4/8/72–4/7/73

vol. 72, Letters Sent, 4/2/73–11/21/76

vol. 73, Letters Sent, 11/23/76–5/23/78

vol. 92, Special Orders, 4/20/67–4/21/69

General Orders &

Circulars, 4/20/67–
9/29/68
vol. 93, Special Orders,
4/22/69–5/10/70
vol. 94, Special Orders,
5/12/70–12/29/70
vol. 95, Special Orders,
1/1/71–11/3/71
vol. 96, Special Orders,
11/4/71–8/3/73
vol. 97, Special Orders,
8/3/73–5/23/78
vol. 98, General Orders
& Circulars, 10/2/
68–12/30/70
vol. 99, General Orders,
1/3/71–12/16/71
vol. 100, General Or-
ders, 12/19/71–6/
20/73
vol. 101, General Or-
ders, 6/21/73–5/
21/78
vol. 117A, Civil Affairs
vol. 119 1/2, Reports of
Scouts
vol. 129, Roster of Offi-
cers
vol. 131, Muster of Ani-
mals
Charges and Specifi-
cations
Unnumbered, Miscella-

neous Materials,
1868–1878
Unnumbered, Cemetery
Records, 2/10/69–
3/18/75
Unnumbered, Civilian
Employees
Unnumbered, Letters Re-
ceived, Civil Affairs

Oklahoma Historical Society
Indian Archives, Kiowa Files,
Depredations; Military
Relations; Trial of Sa-
tanta and Big Tree

*Texas Tech University, Rister Collec-
tion*
Minutes of the 43d Judicial
District Court of Texas,
Case No. 224, The State
of Texas vs. Satanta and
Big Tree

*University of Oklahoma, Phillips
Collection*
Extracts from Inspector General R. B. Marcy's Journal
of an Inspection Tour
during the Months of
April, May, and June
1871
The Sherman-Sheridan Papers

Newspapers

Army and Navy Journal
Austin *Daily Journal*
Dallas *Herald*

Fort Worth *Democrat*
Frontier Echo (Jacksboro, Texas)
Jack County *Herald*

Jacksboro *Gazette*
New York *Herald*
New York *Times*

New York *Tribune*
San Antonio *Daily Express*
San Antonio *Herald*

Primary Sources

Books

Anderson, Jack Van Gordon. *Recollections and Reflections of a Texian.* Waco, Texas: The Texian Press, 1966.

Bartlett, William Sylvester. *My Foot's in the Stirrup. . . .* Dallas, Texas: Dealy and Lowe, 1937.

Bates, Edward F. *History and Reminiscences of Denton County.* Denton, Texas: McNitzky Publishing Co., 1918.

Battey, Thomas C. *The Life and Adventures of a Quaker Among the Indians.* Norman, Oklahoma: University of Oklahoma Press, 1968.

Bedford, Hilary G. *Texas Indian Troubles.* Dallas, Texas: Hargreaves Printing Co., 1905.

Brown, John Henry. *Indian Wars and Pioneers of Texas.* Austin, Texas: L. E. Daniell, no date.

Carter, Robert G. *On the Border with Mackenzie, or Winning West Texas from the Comanches.* New York: Antiquarian Press, Ltd., 1961.

———. *The Old Sergeant's Story.* New York: Frederick H. Hitchcock Publishers, 1926.

Carter, W. H. *From Yorktown to Santiago with the Sixth U.S. Cavalry.* Baltimore: The Lord Baltimore Press, 1900.

Catlin, George. *Letters and Notes on the Manners, Customs, and Conditions of the North American Indians.* 2 vols. Philadelphia: Leary, Stuart and Company, 1913 (reprint of 1841 edition).

Corwin, Hugh A. *The Kiowa Indians: Their History and Life Stories.* Lawton, Oklahoma: Hugh D. Corwin, 1958.

Custer, George A. *My Life on the Plains, or Personal Experiences with Indians.* Norman, Oklahoma: University of Oklahoma Press, 1962.

Dale, Edward Evertt, ed. *Frontier Times: The Autobiography of Frank M. Canton.* Norman, Oklahoma: University of Oklahoma Press, 1966.

Day, James M., and Winfrey, Dorman, eds. *Texas Indian Papers, 1860–1916.* 4 vols. Austin, Texas: Texas State Library, 1961.

Deaton, E. L. *Indian Fights on the Texas Frontier.* Hamilton, Texas: C. M. Boynton, 1894.

Dodge, Richard Irving. *The Hunting Grounds of the Great American West.* London: Chatto & Windus, 1877.

————. *Our Wild Indians: Thirty-Three Years Personal Experience Among the Red Men of the Great West.* Hartford, Conn.: A. D. Worthington & Co., 1890.

Elkins, John M., written by Frank McCarty. *Indian Fighting on the Texas Frontier.* Amarillo, Texas: Russell & Cockrell, 1929.

Friend, Llerena, ed. *M. K. Kellogg's Texas Journal, 1872.* Austin, Texas: University of Texas Press, 1967.

Garner, Lucille Young. *Early Records of Jack County.* No publisher, no date.

Grant, Ulysses Simpson. *Personal Memoirs of U. S. Grant.* 2 vols. New York: C. L. Webster & Co., 1886–1887.

Greer, James K., ed. *A Texas Ranger and Frontiersman, Buck Barry.* Dallas, Texas: Southwest Press, 1932.

Grinnell, George Bird. *The Fighting Cheyennes.* New York: Charles Scribner's Sons, 1915.

Hodge, Frederick. *Handbook of American Indians North of Mexico, Bulletin No. 30, Bureau of American Ethnology.* Vol. 1. Washington: 1912.

Horton, Thomas F. *History of Jack County.* Jacksboro, Texas: Gazette Publishing Co., no date.

Huckabay, Ida Lasater. *Ninety-Four Years in Jack County, 1854–1948.* Jacksboro, Texas: Gazette Publishers, 1949.

Hunter, John Marvin. *The Bloody Trail: Sketches and Narratives of Indian Raids and Atrocities on Our Frontier.* Bandera, Texas: J. M. Hunter, 1931.

Jackson, Helen Hunt. *A Century of Dishonor.* New York: Harper & Row, 1881.

Marcy, Randolph Barnes. *Thirty Years of Army Life on the Border.* New York: Harper and Bros., 1886.

McConnell, H. H. *Five Years a Cavalryman; or Sketches of Regular Army Life on the Texas Frontier, Twenty Odd Years Ago.* Jacksboro, Texas: J. N. Rogers & Co., Printers, 1889.

Marshall, J. T. *The Miles Expedition of 1874–1875: An Eyewitness Account of the Red River War.* Edited by Lonnie White. Austin, Texas: The Encino Press, 1971.

Nye, Colonel W. S. *Carbine and Lance: The Story of Old Fort Sill.* Norman, Oklahoma: The University of Oklahoma Press, 1943.

Paddock, Captain B. B., ed. *A Twentieth Century History and Biographical Record of North and West Texas.* 2 vols. Chicago: Lewis Publishing Co., 1906.

Peters, Joseph P., comp. *Indian Battles and Skirmishes on the American Frontier.* New York: Argonaut Press, 1966.

Potter, Mrs. W. R. *History of Montague County.* Austin, Texas: E. L. Steck Co., no date.

Powell, Colonel William Henry. *List of Officers of the Army of the United States, 1779–1900.* New York: L. R. Hamersly & Co., 1900.

Pratt, Richard Henry. *Battlefield and Classroom: Four Decades with the American Indian, 1867–1904.* Edited by Robert M. Utley. New Haven: Yale University Press, 1964.

Rock, James L. and Smith, W. I. *Southern and Western Texas Guide, 1878.* St. Louis: A. H. Granger, Publisher, 1878.

Sherman, General William T. *Memoirs of General W. T. Sherman.* 2 vols. New York: Charles L. Webster and Co., 1892.

Smythe, H. *Historical Sketch of Parker County and Weatherford, Texas.* St. Louis: Louis C. Lavat, Printer, 1877.

Strong, Henry. *My Frontier Days and Indian Fights on the Plains of Texas.* No place: no publisher, 1924.

Tatum, Lawrie. *Our Red Brothers and the Peace Policy of President Ulysses S. Grant.* Philadelphia: John C. Winston & Co., 1899.

Taylor, Joe F., ed. *The Indian Campaign on the Staked Plains, 1874–1875: Military Correspondence from War Department Adjutant General's Office, File 2815–1874.* Canyon, Texas: Panhandle-Plains Historical Society, 1962.

Terrell, Captain J. C. *Reminiscences of the Early Days of Fort Worth.* Fort Worth, Texas: Texas Printing Co., 1906.

Thorndike, Rachel S., ed. *The Sherman Letters, Correspondence Between General and Senator Sherman from 1837 to 1891.* New York: Charles Scribner's Sons, 1894.

Wallace, Ernest, ed. *Ranald S. Mackenzie's Official Correspondence Relating to Texas, Vol. 1, 1871–1873. Vol. 2, 1873–1879.* Lubbock, Texas: West Texas Museum Association, 1967–1968.

Winkler, Ernest William, ed. *Journal of the Secession Convention of Texas, 1861.* Austin: Austin Publishing Company, 1912.

Primary Sources

Articles
Anderson, H. Allen, ed. "Indian Raids on the Texas Frontier: The Personal Memoirs of Hugh Allen Anderson." *West*

226

Texas Historical Association Yearbook 51 (1975): 85–91.

Archambeau, Ernest, ed. "Monthly Reports of the Fourth Cavalry, 1872–1874." *Panhandle-Plains Historical Review* 38 (1965): 95–154.

Carnal, Ed. "Reminiscences of a Texas Ranger." *Frontier Times* 1 (December 1923): 20–24.

Dorst, J. H. "Ranald Slidell Mackenzie." *Journal of the United States Cavalry Association* 10 (1897): 367–382.

Ellis, L. Tuffley, ed. "Lieutenant A. W. Greely's Report on the Installation of Military Telegraph Lines in Texas, 1875–1876." *Southwestern Historical Quarterly* 69 (July 1965): 66–88.

"List of Actions, etc., with Indians and other Marauders, Participated in by the Tenth U.S. Cavalry, Chronologically Arranged 1867–1897." *Journal of the United States Cavalry Association* 10 (1897): 742–750.

Merrill, James M. "General Sherman's Letter to His Son: A Visit to Fort Sill." *Chronicles of Oklahoma* 47 (Summer 1969):

126–131.

Remington, Frederic. "On the Indian Reservations." *The Century Magazine* 38 (July 1889): 394–405.

Rister, C. C., ed. "Early Accounts of Indian Depredations." *West Texas Historical Association Yearbook* 2 (1926): 18–63.

———. "Documents Relating to General Sherman's Southern Plains Indian Policy, 1871–1875." *Panhandle-Plains Historical Review* 9 & 10 (1936 & 1937): 7–28, 48–64.

Robertson, Walter. "Reminiscences of Walter Robertson, the Loss [sic] Valley Fight." *Frontier Times* 7 (December 1929): 100–104.

Sheffy, L. F., ed. "Letters and Reminiscences of General Theodore A. Baldwin: Scouting after Indians on the Plains of West Texas." *Panhandle-Plains Historical Review* 11 (1938): 7–31.

Thompson, W. A. "Scouting with Mackenzie." *Journal of the United States Cavalry Association* 10 (1897): 429–433.

Secondary Sources

Books

Athearn, Robert G. *William Tecumseh Sherman and the Settlement of the West.* Norman, Oklahoma: University of Oklahoma Press, 1956.

Barsness, Larry. *Heads, Hides and*

Horns: The Compleat Buffalo Book. Fort Worth: Texas Christian University Press, 1985.

Boatner, Major Mark Mayo. Military Customs and Traditions. New York: David McKay Co., Inc., no date.

Brill, Charles J. Conquest of the Southern Plains. Oklahoma City, Oklahoma: Golden Saga Publishers, 1938.

Brown, Dee. Bury My Heart at Wounded Knee. New York: Holt, Rinehart & Winston, 1970.

Buntin, Martha Leata. "History of the Kiowa, Comanche, and Wichita Indian Agency." Master's thesis, University of Oklahoma, 1931.

Capps, Benjamin. The Warren Wagontrain Raid. New York: The Dial Press, 1974.

Chandler, Melbourne. Of Garryowen in Glory: The History of the 7th U.S. Cavalry. Annandale, Virginia: Self-published, 1960.

Collinson, Frank. Life in the Saddle. Norman, Oklahoma: The University of Oklahoma Press, 1963.

Conner, Seymour V. The Peters Colony of Texas. Austin, Texas: Texas State Historical Association, 1959.

Debo, Angie. A History of the Indians of the United States. Norman, Oklahoma: The University

sity of Oklahoma Press, 1970.

Deetz, James J. F.; Fisher, Anthony D.; and Owen, Roger C. The North American Indians: A Sourcebook. New York: The Macmillan Co., 1967.

Dennis, W. W. Fort Richardson, Texas (1867–1878) and the Mackenzie Trail. Jacksboro, Texas: Compiled and published by W. W. Dennis, 1964.

Downey, Fairfax. Indian Fighting Army. New York: Charles Scribner's Sons, 1943.

———. Indian Wars of the U.S. Army, 1776–1865. Garden City, New York: Doubleday & Co., Inc., 1963.

Earle, J. P. History of Clay County and Northwest Texas. Austin, Texas: The Brick Row Book Shop, 1963.

Ensey, Joseph W. "Indian Hostilities of the Southwest, 1865 to 1875." Master's thesis, University of Oklahoma, 1931.

Farrow, Marion Humphreys. Troublesome Times in Texas. San Antonio, Texas: The Naylor Co., 1959.

Fehrenbach, T. R. Comanches, The Destruction of a People. New York: Alfred A. Knopf, 1983.

Fields, F. T. Texas Sketchbook. Houston, Texas: Humble Oil and Refining Company, 1958. Illustrated by E. M. Schiwetz.

Fowler, Arlen L. The Black Infantry in the West. Westport, Connecticut: Greenwood Publishing Corp., 1971.

Frazer, Robert W. *Forts of the West*. Norman, Oklahoma: University of Oklahoma Press, 1965.

Fulmore, Z. T. *The History and Geography of Texas*. Austin, Texas: R. S. Fulmore, Publisher, 1926.

Ganoe, William A. *History of the United States Army*. New York: D. Appleton and Co., 1924.

Gard, Wayne. *Rawhide Texas*. Norman, Oklahoma: University of Oklahoma Press, 1965.

Garretson, Martin S. *The American Bison*. New York: New York Zoological Society, 1938.

Gluckman, Arcadi. *United States Martial Pistols and Revolvers*. Buffalo, New York: Otto Ulbrich, 1939.

———. *United States Muskets, Rifles and Carbines*. Buffalo, New York: Otto Ulbrich, 1948.

Hagan, William T. *United States–Comanche Relations*. New Haven, Connecticut: Yale University Press, 1976.

Haines, Francis. *The Buffalo*. New York: Thomas Crowell & Co., 1970.

Haley, J. Evetts. *The XIT Ranch of Texas and the Early Days of the Llano Estacado*. Norman, Oklahoma: University of Oklahoma Press, 1929.

———. *Fort Concho and the Texas Frontier*. San Angelo, Texas: San Angelo Standard-Times, 1952.

Haley, James L. *The Buffalo War: The History of the Red River Indian Uprising of 1874*. Gardendale, New York: Doubleday & Co., Inc., 1976.

Hamner, Kenneth. *The Springfield Carbine on the Western Frontier*. Bellevue, Nebraska: The Custer Battlefield and Museum Association, 1970.

Harston, J. Emmor. *Comanche Land*. San Antonio, Texas: Naylor Publishing Co., 1963.

Hart, Herbert M. *Old Forts of the Southwest*. Seattle, Washington: Superior Publishing Co., 1967.

Hoebal, E. Adamson, and Wallace, Edward. *The Comanches*. Norman, Oklahoma: University of Oklahoma Press, 1952.

Hoig, Stan. *The Sand Creek Massacre*. Norman, Oklahoma: The University of Oklahoma Press, 1961.

Holden, William Curry. *Alkali Trails*. Dallas, Texas: The Southwest Press, 1930 .

———. *Rollie Burns, or An Account of the Ranching Industry on the South Plains*. Dallas, Texas: The Southwest Press, 1932.

Jackson, Clyde and Grace. *Quanah Parker*. San Antonio, Texas: The Naylor Publishing Co., 1959.

Jennison, Keith, and Tebbel, John. *The American Indian Wars*. New York: Bonanza Books,

1960.

Jones, Douglas C. *The Treaty of Medicine Lodge*. Norman, Oklahoma: The University of Oklahoma Press, 1966.

Jones, J. Lee. *Red Raiders Retaliate: The Story of Lone Wolf, The Elder (Guipagho), Famous Kiowa Indian Chief*. Colorado City, Texas: Pioneer Book Publishers, 1980.

Knight, Oliver. *Fort Worth, Outpost on the Trinity*. Norman, Oklahoma: The University of Oklahoma Press, 1953.

———. *Following the Indian Wars*. Norman, Oklahoma: The University of Oklahoma Press, 1960.

Laubin, Reginald and Gladys. *American Indian Archery*. Norman, Oklahoma: University of Oklahoma Press, 1980.

Leckie, William H. *The Military Conquest of the Southern Plains*. Norman, Oklahoma: The University of Oklahoma Press, 1963.

———. *The Buffalo Soldiers, A Narrative of the Negro Cavalry in the West*. Norman, Oklahoma: The University of Oklahoma Press, 1967.

Mardock, Robert Winston. *The Reformers and the American Indian*. Columbia, Missouri: University of Missouri Press, 1971.

Mayhall, Mildred P. *The Kiowas*. Norman, Oklahoma: The University of Oklahoma Press, 1962.

———. *Indian Wars of Texas*. Waco, Texas: The Texian Press, 1965.

McConnell, Joseph Carroll. *The West Texas Frontier*. Palo Pinto, Texas: Texas Legal Bank & Book Co., 1939.

Miller, Henry. *Pioneering North Texas*. San Antonio, Texas: The Naylor Co., 1953.

Mishkin, Bernard. *Rank and Warfare Among the Plains Indians*. New York: J. J. Augustin, 1940.

Morrison, William B. *Military Posts and Camps in Oklahoma*. Oklahoma City, Oklahoma: Harlow Publishing Corp., 1936.

Newcombe, W. W., Jr. *The Indians of Texas, from Prehistoric to Modern Times*. Austin: University of Texas Press, 1961.

Newton, Lewis W., and Gambrell, Herbert P. *A Social and Political History of Texas*. Dallas, Texas: Turner Co., 1935.

Nohl, Lessing H. "Bad Hand: The Military Career of Ranald Slidell Mackenzie, 1871–1889." Ph.D. dissertation, University of New Mexico, 1962.

Nunn, W. C. *Texas Under the Carpetbaggers*. Austin, Texas: University of Texas Press, 1962.

Nye, Wilbur S. *Bad Medicine and Good*. Norman, Oklahoma: University of Oklahoma Press, 1962.

———. *Plains Indian Raiders*. Norman, Oklahoma: University of Oklahoma Press, 1968.

Parker, Bruce L. "Indian Affairs and the Frontier of Texas, 1865–1880." Master's thesis, University of Texas, 1925.

Paschal, Lois. "The Frontier History of Jack County." Master's thesis, Midwestern State University, 1975.

Place, Marian T. *Rifles and War Bonnets*. New York: Ives Washington, Inc., 1968.

Priest, Loring Benson. *Uncle Sam's Stepchildren*. New York: Octagon Books, 1969.

Prucha, Francis Paul. *A Guide to the Military Posts of the United States*. Madison, Wisconsin: The State Historical Society of Wisconsin, 1964.

Richardson, Rupert Nouval. *The Comanche Barrier to South Plains Settlement*. Glendale, California: Arthur H. Clark Co., 1933.

———. *The Frontier of Northwest Texas, 1846 to 1876*. Glendale, California: Arthur H. Clark Co., 1963.

———. "The Comanches." In *Indian Tribes of Texas*. Waco, Texas: The Texian Press, 1971.

Rickey, Don, Jr. *Forty Miles a Day on Beans and Hay*. Norman, Oklahoma: University of Oklahoma Press, 1963.

Rister, Carl Coke. *The Southwestern Frontier, 1865–1881*. Cleveland, Ohio: The Arthur H. Clark Co., 1928.

———. *Border Captives: The Traffic in Prisoners by Southern Plains Indians*. Norman, Oklahoma: University of Oklahoma Press, 1940.

———. *Border Command: General Phil Sheridan in the West*. Norman, Oklahoma: University of Oklahoma Press, 1944.

———. *Fort Griffin and the Texas Frontier*. Norman, Oklahoma: University of Oklahoma Press, 1956.

Robertson, James I., Jr. *The Civil War*. Washington, D.C.: U.S. Civil War Centennial Commission, 1963.

Roe, Frank Gilbert. *The Indian and the Horse*. Norman, Oklahoma: University of Oklahoma Press, 1955.

Schmeckebier, Lawrence F. *The Office of Indian Affairs: Its History, Activities, and Organization*. Baltimore: Johns Hopkins Press, 1927.

Schmitt, Martin, and Brown, Dee. *Fighting Indians of the West*. New York: Charles Scribner's Sons, 1948.

Sears, Stephen W. *Landscape Turned Red: The Battle of Antietam*. New Haven: Ticknor & Fields, 1983.

Skinner, Francis. "The Trial and Release of Satanta and Big Tree: State-Federal Relations during the Reconstruction

Era." Master's thesis, University of Texas, 1937.

Stanley, F. *Satanta and the Kiowas.* Borger, Texas: No Publisher, 1968.

Steele, Aubrey Leroy. "Quaker Control of the Kiowa-Comanche Agency." Master's thesis, University of Oklahoma, 1938.

Tilghman, Zoe A. *Quanah: The Eagle of the Comanches.* Oklahoma City, Oklahoma: Harlow Publishing Corp., 1938.

Toole, K. Ross, ed. *Probing the American West: Papers from the Santa Fe Conference.* Santa Fe, New Mexico: Museum of New Mexico Press, 1962.

Utley, Robert M. *Frontiersmen in Blue.* New York: The Macmillan Co., 1967.

——. *Frontier Regulars.* New York: The Macmillan Co., 1973.

Vaughn, J. W. *The Reynolds Campaign on Powder River.* Norman, Oklahoma: University of Oklahoma Press, 1961.

Wallace, Ernest. *Ranald S. Mackenzie on the Texas Frontier.* Lubbock, Texas: West Texas Museum Association, 1964.

——. *Texas in Turmoil.* Austin, Texas: Steck-Vaughn Co., 1965.

Webb, Gilbert. *Four Score Years in Jack County.* Jacksboro, Texas: Gazette Publishing Co., 1940.

Webb, Walter Prescott. *The Great Plains.* Boston: Ginn and Co., 1931.

——. *The Texas Rangers: A Century of Frontier Defense.* New York: Houghton Mifflin Co., 1935.

Weigley, Russell Frank. *History of the United States Army.* New York: The Macmillan Co., 1967.

——. *The American Way of War: A History of United States Military Strategy and Policy.* New York: The Macmillan Co., 1973.

Wharton, Clarence R. *Texas Under Many Flags.* Chicago & New York: American Historical Society, Inc., 1930.

——. *Satanta, the Great Chief of the Kiowas and His People.* Dallas, Texas: B. Upshaw and Co., 1935.

Wilbarger, J. W. *Indian Depredations in Texas.* Austin, Texas: The Steck Co., 1935.

Wisenhunt, Donald. *Fort Richardson, Outpost on the Texas Frontier.* Vol. 4, Monograph No. 20, Southwestern Studies. El Paso, Texas: Texas Western Press, 1968.

Wright, Muriel. *A Guide to the Indian Tribes of Oklahoma.* Norman, Oklahoma: University of Oklahoma Press, 1951.

Articles and Periodicals

Armor Magazine 79 (November-

December 1970): 22–23.

Aston, B. W. "Federal Military Re-occupation of the Texas Southwestern Frontier, 1865–1871." *Texas Military History* 8 (Summer 1970): 123–134.

Baggett, James Alex. "The Constitutional Union Party in Texas." *Southwestern Historical Quarterly* 82 (January 1979): 233–264.

Breeden, James D. "Health of Early Texas: The Military Frontier." *Southwestern Historical Quarterly* 80 (April 1977): 357–398.

Bryan, Frank. "The Llano Estacado." *Panhandle-Plains Historical Review* 13 (1940): 21–37.

Buntin, Martha. "The Quaker Indian Agents of the Kiowa, Comanche, and Wichita Indian Reservations." *Chronicles of Oklahoma* 10 (Spring 1932): 204–218.

Clary, David A. "The Role of the Army Surgeon in the West; Daniel Weisel at Fort Davis, Texas, 1868–1872." *Western Historical Quarterly* 3 (January 1972): 53–66.

Crane, R. C. "Some Aspects of the History of West and Northwest Texas Since 1845." *Southwestern Historical Quarterly* 26 (July 1922): 30–43.

———. "Settlement of Indian Troubles in West Texas, 1874–1875." *West Texas Historical Association Yearbook* 1 (1925): 3–14.

Crimmins, Colonel M. L. "General Nelson A. Miles in Texas." *West Texas Historical Association Yearbook* 23 (1947): 36–45.

———. "General Randolph B. Marcy's Last Tour of Texas," *West Texas Historical Association Yearbook* 25 (1949): 74–86.

Crockett, Bernice. "Health Conditions in the Indian Territory from the Civil War to 1890." *Chronicles of Oklahoma* 36 (Spring 1958): 25–34.

Cutler, Lee. "Lawrie Tatum and the Kiowa Agency, 1869–1873." *Arizona and the West* 13 (Autumn 1971): 221–244.

Debo, Angie. "The Social and Economic Life of the Comanches." *Panhandle-Plains Historical Review* 3 (1930): 38–53.

———. "History and Customs of the Kiowas." *Panhandle-Plains Historical Review* 7 (1934): 42–53.

D'Elia, Donald J. "The Argument over Civilian or Military Control of the Indian Reservations, 1865–1884." *Historian* 24 (1961–1962): 207–225.

Essin, Emmett M., III. "Mules, Packs, and Packtrains." *Southwestern Historical Quarterly* 74 (July 1970): 52–80.

Ewers, John C. "When Red and

233

White Men Met." *Western Historical Quarterly* 2 (April 1971): 133–151.

Ewing, Floyd F., Jr. "Unionist Sentiment on the Northwest Texas Frontier." *West Texas Historical Association Yearbook* 33 (1957): 58–70.

Frantz, Joe B. "The Significance of Frontier Forts to Texas." *Southwestern Historical Quarterly* 74 (October 1970): 204–205.

Graham, Roy Eugene. "Federal Fort Architecture in Texas during the Nineteenth Century." *Southwestern Historical Quarterly* 74 (October 1970): 165–189.

Hagan, William T. "Kiowas, Comanches, and Cattlemen, 1867–1906." *Pacific Historical Review* 40 (August 1971): 333–355.

Haley, J. Evetts. "The Comanchero Trade." *Southwestern Historical Quarterly* 38 (January 1935): 157–176.

———. "The Great Comanche War Trail." *Panhandle-Plains Historical Review* 23 (1950): 11–21.

Hall, Martin Hardwick. "Planter vs. Frontiersman: Conflict in Confederate Indian Policy." *Essays on the American Civil War*, edited by William F. Holmes and Harold M. Hollingsworth, 40–58. Austin, Texas: University of Texas Press, 1968.

Harrison, Lowell. "Supplying Texas Military Posts in 1876." *Texas Military History* 4 (Spring 1964): 23–24.

———. "The Two Battles of Adobe Walls." *Texas Military History* 5 (Spring 1965): 1–11.

Hatfield, Charles. "The Comanche, Kiowa, and Cheyenne Campaign in Northwest Texas and Mackenzie's Fight in the Palo Duro Canyon, September 26, 1874." *West Texas Historical Association Yearbook* 5 (1929): 115–128.

Hill, Frank P. "Indian Raids on the South Plains." *Panhandle-Plains Historical Review* 7 (1934): 53–70.

Holden, W. C. "Frontier Defense in Texas during the Civil War." *West Texas Historical Association Yearbook* 4 (1928): 16–32.

———. "Frontier Defense, 1865–1889." *Panhandle-Plains Historical Review* 2 (1929): 43–65.

———. "Frontier Defense, 1846–1860." *West Texas Historical Association Yearbook* 6 (1930): 35–65.

Hunter, Marvin, ed. "The Battle of Palo Duro Canyon." *Frontier Times* 21 (January 1944): 177–181.

Jones, Russell. "Fort Richardson, Home Base of the 6th Cavalry." *Old West* 10 (Fall 1968): 58–61.

Kloster, Donald E. "Uniforms of

the Army Prior and Subsequent to 1872." *Military Collector and Historian* 14 (1962): 103–112.

Koch, Lean Clara. "Federal Indian Policy in Texas." *Southwestern Historical Quarterly* 28 (January 1925): 259–286, and 29 (July 1926): 19–35, 98–127.

Leach, John. "Search and Destroy: Counter-Insurgency on the American Plains." *Military History of Texas and the Southwest* 9, No. 1 (1971): 55–60.

Leckie, William H. "The Red River War of 1874–1875." *Panhandle-Plains Historical Review* 29 (1956): 78–100.

Leeper, Paul S. "Satanta and His Trial." *Frontier Times* 7 (April 1930): 300–305.

Loftin, Jack. "Kicking Bird's Face-Saving Battle." *West Texas Historical Association Yearbook* 51 (1975): 76–84.

———. "Oliver Loving's Little Lost Valley—Gertrudes." *West Texas Historical Association Yearbook* 53 (1977): 45–56.

Neighbours, Kenneth F. "Robert S. Neighbors and the Founding of the Texas Indian Reservations." *West Texas Historical Association Yearbook* 31 (1955): 65–74.

———. "Indian Exodus Out of Texas in 1859." *West Texas Historical Association Yearbook* 36 (1960): 80–89.

———. "Tonkawa Scouts and Guides." *West Texas Historical Association Yearbook* 49 (1973): 90–113.

Nye, Captain W. S. "An Indian Raid into Texas." *Chronicles of Oklahoma* 15 (Spring 1937): 50–56.

Perry, Dan. "The Kiowa's Defiance." *Chronicles of Oklahoma* 13 (Spring 1935): 35–36.

Ramsdell, Charles W. "Presidential Reconstruction in Texas." *Southwestern Historical Quarterly* 11 (April 1908): 277–317.

Richardson, Rupert N., ed. "Documents Relating to West Texas and Her Indian Troubles." *West Texas Historical Association Yearbook* 1 (1925): 30–95.

———. "The Comanche Indians at the Adobe Walls Fight." *Panhandle-Plains Historical Review* 4 (1931): 24–38.

Rister, Carl Coke. "Fort Griffin." *West Texas Historical Association Yearbook* 1 (1925): 15–25.

———. "Early Accounts of Indian Depredations." *West Texas Historical Association Yearbook* 2 (1926): 18–63.

———. "The Significance of the Jacksboro Indian Affair of 1871." *Southwestern Historical Quarterly* 29 (January 1926): 181–200.

———. "The Significance of the Destruction of the Buffalo in the Southwest." *Southwestern Historical Quarterly* 33 (July

1929): 34–49.
———. "Satanta, Orator of the Plains." *Southwestern Review* 17 (1931): 77–99.

Rogers, Jerry. "The Flint and Steel: Background to the Red River War of 1874–1875." *Texas Military History* 7 (Fall 1969): 153–175.

———. "To the Canyon of the Tule: Colonel Nelson A. Miles and the Indian Territory Expedition, 1874." *Texas Military History* 7 (Spring 1970): 267–294.

———. "The Indian Territory Expedition: Winter Campaigns, 1874–1875." *Texas Military History* 8 (Fall 1970): 233–250.

Russell, Don. "The Army of the Frontier, 1865–1891." *Westerner's Brand Book* (Chicago) 6 (July 1949): 33–35, 38–40.

Shook, Robert. "The Federal Military in Texas, 1865–1870." *Texas Military History* 6 (Spring 1967): 3–45.

Skaggs, Jimmy. "Military Operations on the Cattle Trails." *Texas Military History* 6 (Summer 1967): 137–148.

Snow, Richard. "Henry Ware Lawton." *American Heritage* 33 (April/May 1983): 40–42.

Steele, Aubrey Leroy. "Lawrie Tatum's Indian Policy." *Chronicles of Oklahoma* 22 (Spring 1944): 83–98.

Tate, Michael L. "The Frontier of Northwest Texas During the Civil War." *Chronicles of Oklahoma* 50 (Summer 1972): 177–189.

Temple, Frank. "Colonel Grierson in the Southwest." *Panhandle-Plains Historical Review* 30 (1957): 27–54.

Thoburn, J. B. "Horace P. Jones, Scout and Interpreter." *Chronicles of Oklahoma* 2 (Fall 1924): 380–385.

Thompson, Theronne. "Fort Buffalo Springs, Texas, Border Post." *West Texas Historical Association Yearbook* 36 (1960): 156–175.

Wallace, Edward S. "Ranald Slidell Mackenzie, Indian Fighting Cavalryman." *Southwestern Historical Quarterly* 59 (January 1953): 378–396.

———. "Prompt in the Saddle: The Military Career of Ranald Slidell Mackenzie." *Military History of Texas and the Southwest* 9, No. 3 (1971): 161–190.

West, G. Derek. "The Battle of Adobe Walls (1874)." *Panhandle-Plains Historical Review* 36 (1963): 1–36.

Whisenhunt, Donald. "Fort Richardson." *West Texas Historical Association Yearbook* 39 (1963): 19–27.

White, Lonnie. "The First Battle of the Palo Duro Canyon." *Texas Military History* 6 (Fall 1967): 222–235.

APPENDIX

Handwritten petition to General Sherman from the citizens of Jack County regarding Indian attacks.

Department of the Interior.

Received June 16th, 1871.

Dated " 14th, 18 "

From The Secretary of War

Subject.

Encloses abst. of letter from Gen. Sherman in regard to present depredations of Indians at Ft. Sill agency with suggestions from Gen S. Also Petition & Affidavits from persons near Ft. Richardson on same matters. Action.

Respectfully ref. to the Com'r of Indian Affairs

Clerk

June 16/71

Registered

Filed

Jacksboro Jack Co. Texas

May 187_

Gen'. W. T. Sherman.
    U. S. A

      Fort Richardson

          General

            We the Undersign

Citizens of Jack County, in consideration of a
just and present Sorrowful affliction in con-
-sequence of the many and increasing depreda
Committed upon us by the marauding savage
who are permitted to remain in our midst.

      We would respectfully present to you
the accompanying Synopsis, in brief of the
many and cruel Murders and outrages th
have been perpetrated against our peacef
citizens and neighbors. And respectfull
ask at your hands in _____ _____ ____
and investigation during your stay here
and give to it such an recomendation, As

238

our relief, as may in your opinion be applicable.

With a full knowledge and belief that our Government intends to aid us in protection and ~~have used through the efficient of~~ stationed here all the means at their disposal with their limited garrison. Yet we do most earnestly pray for some immediate relief, that we may feel a comparative safety in our lives and some protection and security in the possession of our property, thereby offering secure homes to those who may choose to come amongst us to aid in the development of a country, rich in all that pertains to man's comfort, and only needing adequate protection from the evils mentioned ~~to enable us to pursue our respective occupations~~ unmolested by the Savages. Eventually placing us upon that basis of safety so desirable to ourselves and due to us in the name of humanity.

Your very Obt Sots

Wm M. M. Turner

H. Horton

In behalf of the Citizens of Jack Co.

Statement of Murders and Outrages committed upon the Citizens of Jack County Texas by hostile Indians

Date	Names	Number Killed	Location of Outrage from Ft Richardson	Remarks
1859				
August	Families of Mason & Cameron	9	15 mile N.W.	Houses burnt
1860 Nov	Families of Gage & Landman	10	2½ M. N.	2 in Captivity
"	A. Buttoff	1	10 M. N.W	
"	T. Tasley	1	" " " "	
"	H. Chapman	1	" " " "	
"	M's Wife	1	" " " "	
Dec	Mrs Sherman	1	20 M. E.	
	John Brown	1	" " "	
1861 May	Mrs H. Wood	1	25 M. S.W	
	Miss Lemley	1	" " "	
1862 May	Alfred Lane	1	15 M. S.W	
"	W. D. Tackett	1	30 " S.E	
June	Rowlands family	2	11 " S	
Oct	Geo McQuerry	1	6 " S	body burned
	D. Nobles boy	1	20 " E	
	Heich Children	2	25 " S.E	
1863 March	Lewis family	4	10 M. N.	Houses burnt
	Mr Savage + 3 children	4	25 S. E	
"	Mr Magee + others	5	14 M. N	
Oct	W. Wynn + others	3	8 " W	Jno Wound
"	John Reasner	1	10 " S	

46

Name	Number	Distance/Direction	Remarks
James McKinney			
Wife & three Children	5	15 m . E .	House burned
Mrs Kemp & 2 of	1	12 m . S .	Wounded breast cut out.
White Children taken off			
.... family	5	20 m . W	
Widow Kilpatrick			
& family	6	30 M . W	House burned
W. Peneler	1	15 m . W	
S. Cox	1	15½ " "	
W. Weatherby	1	16 " N. E	
....on ...kins	1	25 " East	
Isaac Knight	1	18 m N. E	
....n Armstrong		1. " S. E	House robbed
Isaac Briscoe + wife	2	25 " E	two children carried off
2 Children			
S. Babbs Family	1	20 M E	
Mrs Roberts and two			in Captivity
of Babbs Children Carried off			
Mr Jones + others	11	12 m . E	
James Lauderdale	1	8 " S. E	
Young Blackwell	1	20 " S	
Unknown Teamster	1	5 " N	
Russell Family	3	20 m. E	
Brown		20 m E	House robbed
Alvin Clark	1	30 " E	
Thomas Sullivan			one Carried off and
Children	28	20 miles S. E	taken in Captivity

1869				
May	Ed. Rippy & wife	2	25 Miles South	
	H. Riley		8½ m. East	House 70 twice and the m...
1870	t. Dawson	1	33 Miles East	
March	...low Blackwell	1	22 Miles South	
April	...enley party	7	17 " West	
	...Green & 2 Col men	3	20 " N.E	
	Keegan family	4	30 " "	
	Lorenzo Young. Riley	1	10 " E	
	Frank Taylor	1	16 " W	Stage Driver
	Unknown (Col'd)	2	25 " N	
	Stevens' Boy		" "	Captured + nose cut
	Unknown Man		in Jacksboro	Arrow ...
	John Dosier & family	3	30 " North	
	Mr Lott	1	35 " S.E	
1871 March	Mr Crow	1	15 m. S.W	
Feb	Britt & 3 others (Colored)	4	16 m W	
	Mark Dalton & two others	3	20 m S	
	Jacob Myers	1	10 m. S.W	
	Geo. Hampton	1	18 m. E	Crazy m... tied to tree ... cruelly ...
April	Thos. Cranfield	1	28 m S.E	
	John H. Hoburn	1	30 m S.W	
		129		

Making a total of onehundred and twenty nine killed, beside the many taken into captivity

over

In addition to the above great sacrifice of life, hundreds have been driven from their homes through fear. Over more than Two thousand head of Horses stolen from the citizens of the County, [...] of Cattle, and destruction of out buildings [...] severely felt in their loss, have not been enumerated in this account.

Taking into consideration the smallness of our population (at no time exceeding Six hundred) our So fearful destruction of life and property is the only argument needed to show our want of protection. To which end we earnestly and respectfully ask your co-operation in our behalf.

Respectfully Submitted

INDEX

Tenth Cavalry, 136–39, 152, 161, 162, 167
Tenth Infantry, 152
Terry, General Alfred, 52, 166
Texas Rangers, 2, 5, 149–51, 166, 215n.11
Thomas, T. W., 16–17
Thompson, Lieutenant W. A., Fourth Cavalry, 118
Throckmorton, Texas Governor J. W., 6, 16
Thurman's Springs, 140, 142
Thurston, Lieutenant G. A., Fourth Cavalry, 67, 90–91
Tierra Blanca, 128
Tonkawas, 20–21, 105, 106, 108, 110, 133, 134, 157, 206n.38
Tourtellotte, Colonel J. E., 70
Treaty of the Little Arkansas, 49
Treaty of Medicine Lodge, 50, 71–76, 100
Tson-to-goodle, 80
Twenty-fourth Infantry, 52, 127, 129, 164

United States Army: equipment, 8–10, 180n.41, 181n.45; promotions in, 8; pastimes, 204n.9; pre-Civil War frontier, 2–3, 5; post-Civil War frontier, 6–11, 183n.62; routine, 46

Valentine, L. J., 142

Walker, Howell, 140–41, 209n.24

Ward, Lieutenant C. R., Tenth Cavalry, 142
Warren, Henry, 79, 201–2n.22
Warren Wagon Train Raid, xvii, 78–81, 197nn.46,51,61, 198nn.55; significance of, 96
Washington, Caddo George, 90
Weatherford, Texas, 3, 38, 51, 91, 138, 177n.1
Weburn, John W., 67
West Cache Creek, 102
West Fork of the Trinity River, 101
White Horse, 125, 159
Wichita Hotel and Saloon, 42–43
Wilcox, Captain J., Fourth Cavalry, 100, 101
Wiley, Moses, 141
Williams, James, 92
Wilson, Lieutenant R. P., Tenth Infantry, 169–70
Wilson, Sergeant W. H., Fourth Cavalry, 126, 207n.48
Wise County, Texas, 5, 18
Woman Heart, 159
Wood, Colonel W., Eleventh Infantry, 135, 164, 166
Wood, Assistant Adjutant General W. W., 96
Woodward, Lieutenant S., 167
Woolfolk, J. A., 92

Yellow Wolf, 79
Yeomans, Army Surgeon A. A., 170